THE SPORTS ENCYCLOPEDIA

THE SPORTS

ENCYCLOPEDIA

Ford Hovis, General Editor

Melanie James and Jeremy Friedlander,
Contributing Editors

A Rutledge Book
Praeger Publishers
New York

Library of Congress Cataloging in Publication Data
Main entry under title:
The Sports encyclopedia.
   1. Sports—Dictionaries. I. Hovis, Ford.
GV567.S643   796'.03   76-21340
ISBN 0-275-23400-2

Published in the United States of America in 1976
by Praeger Publishers, Inc.
111 Fourth Avenue, New York, N.Y. 10003

CONTENTS

Archery

In the days when Robin Hood let fly his arrows in Sherwood Forest, archery was more than just a sport; it was England's national defense. It is difficult for us, in an age of guided missiles and nuclear bombs, to imagine one nation conquering another with bow and arrow. But it did happen. In the England of the 1300s, archers were trained from childhood to use the longbow. After intense schooling and practice, medieval archers were capable of amazing feats: able to pull 100-pound bows, kill an enemy at 80 or 100 yards, shoot 12 arrows a minute. Such skillful archery defeated the French in the Hundred Years War, winning great English victories at Crécy, Poitiers, and Agincourt. But scarcely a century later, by 1600, the bow was replaced by the musket.

The first bow and arrow were used in prehistoric times. At first man used the bow for his survival—to hunt animals. Then, as men banded into tribes, bow and arrow were used against men.

Today, archery is primarily a sport. It is growing fast, in part because it can appeal to everyone. It doesn't take great strength or youth to shoot an arrow. Accurate shooting, whether at a target or at an animal, takes constant practice and great powers of concentration. Watch the face of any archer as he is about to "let fly" and you will see an expression of utmost concentration.

EQUIPMENT

Archery equipment has changed more since the end of World War II than in all the previous thirty thousand years of archery. Some say the new bows and arrows, though stronger and more accurate than ever before, destroy the purity of the sport.

Although simple wooden bows can still be bought today, the most common bow is one made of fiberglass and wood. The two most common types of bow are the recurved bow and the straight bow. The straight bow is a descendant of the old English longbow and is shaped in a simple arc. The recurved bow, fashioned after an ancient Turkish design, curves outward and away from the archer near its tips. Bows average five feet in length.

A lineup of target archers about to let fly brings to mind the time when the bow and arrow were a nation's most important weapon.

A bow is strung, or braced, only when it is to be used, and it should be used only by someone strong enough to string it. The bowstring is looped around either end of the bow in grooves called nocks. Most modern bowstrings are made of Dacron.

The power of a bow is expressed in pounds, or the amount of strength it takes to pull the string 28 inches—the length of an arrow—to full draw. The average man uses a bow of 40 to 50 pounds, the average woman one of 25 to 30 pounds. Men generally use 28-inch long arrows and women 25-inch arrows. Bows used for hunting require greater strength (from 60 to 100 pounds) because the arrow must be heavier and travel faster to kill an animal. Most state hunting laws specify a minimum power weight for hunting bows.

An arrow absorbs a terrific shock, traveling up to 150 miles per hour and then slamming suddenly into its target, so it must be stiff. The greater the bow power, the greater the stiffness, or spine, an arrow must have. The best arrows are made of aluminum or fiberglass. With modern factory processes, arrows can now be produced with little or no variation among them. This advance has been especially important in competition target archery because arrows that perform similarly allow an archer to shoot more consistently.

The material used to fletch, or feather, arrows is usually plastic. Other important archery gear includes the quiver, which holds the extra arrows; the armguard, a leather band worn on the bow-holding arm to keep it from being hurt by the snapping string and to give added support; and the tabs, which protect the fingers in drawing the string and allow the archer to release the string better.

TECHNIQUE

Bow in his left hand, the right-handed archer assumes a comfortable stance, his left shoulder facing the target. He then places the notched end of the arrow against the bowstring just above center. He moves the bow into a vertical position, extending his arm straight toward the target. He draws back the arrow with his right hand, gripping the string in the joints of the middle three fingers, the arrow between the first two. With his elbow high, he draws back steadily to full draw. The drawing fingers are now at anchor point, a point that varies among archers but is usually right under the chin for target archers. Then he releases, or looses, the arrow. This is one of the most difficult and most important skills to master in archery. A bad loose will usually result in a bad shot.

As it speeds to its target, the arrow doesn't move on a flat trajectory, as most people think. Rather, it inscribes a parabola, a sort of arc. Archers used to use a method of aiming called "point of aim" to compensate for this arc. They chose some fixed point and aimed at it rather than the center of the target to achieve a bull's-eye. Today's sophisticated sights, attached to the bow above the handle, have taken a lot of the guesswork out of archery.

Above: *At full draw, this target archer seems to be denting his nose with the bowstring. His drawing fingers are directly under his chin, anchor point. Opposite: In contrast, this archer's anchor point is at the side of his face.*

These sights are used in target archery and can be moved up and down the handle to suit the distance of the target and the strength of the bow. Hunters, who don't have time to make such fine calculations, rely on an instinctive method of aiming.

TARGET SHOOTING

In target archery the contestants stand in a line and shoot across a broad field at the targets. After all have shot from one distance, they move to the next.

The target is 48 inches in diameter and at least 6 inches thick. It is made of straw and covered with oilcloth or canvas. The exact center of the target is 48 inches from the ground with the center circle, or bull's-eye, 9.6 inches in diameter and colored gold. The gold circle is surrounded by four rings, each of which is 4.8 inches wide. The gold counts nine points when hit. The next ring is red (seven points), then blue (five points), and white (one point). Any arrow that bounces off the target or passes entirely through the facing of it is scored as five points.

After each archer shoots twice, three arrows to a turn, an "end" has been completed, and the archers retrieve their arrows. Usually, four archers are assigned to one target. An archer's score is counted after each end and is expressed by two numbers—the number of hits followed by the total score. For example, a score of 5–29 means that the archer has scored 29 points with his five arrows that landed on target.

There are a wide variety of rounds, ranging from the York round (twelve ends at 100 yards, eight ends at 80 yards, and four ends at 60 yards) to the Columbia round (four ends each at 50, 40, and 30 yards).

FIELD SHOOTING

Field shooting events are designed to simulate real hunting. Archers rove around the course in closely supervised groups and shoot at a variety of animal-like targets. Points are awarded on the basis of whether the shot would have killed the animal or merely wounded it.

DISTANCE EVENTS

Archers who like to shoot for both accuracy and distance can try clout shooting. The clout (Old English for cloth) is an exact replica of the standard target but has a diameter of 48 feet rather than 48 inches. The clout is laid flat on the ground, and archers shoot at it from distances of 120 to 240 yards.

Flight shooting is a type of competition in which distance is the sole objective. In freestyle flight shooting, no limitation is put on the strength of the bow or the means used to pull it. The archer lies on his back, braces the bow with his feet, and pulls back the bowstring with both hands. More than 200 pounds of force can be exerted this way. The freestyle flight shooting record is more than two thousand yards, considerably more than a mile.

ORGANIZATIONS

In 1878, two Confederate war veterans, Will and Maurice Thompson, wrote a book about their experiences shooting game, *The Witchery of Archery.* This book excited interest in the sport, and in 1879, the National Archery Association (NAA) was formed. The NAA holds a tournament each year to determine national champions and directs the Junior Olympic Development Program.

Another book that spurred the growth of archery was *Hunting with the Bow and Arrow,* by Dr. Saxton Pope. Pope thrilled sportsmen with tales of his hunting exploits. In one expedition to Africa he killed 11 lions with bow and arrows. (Of course, there was usually someone with a rifle nearby, just in case.) Bow hunting became more popular, and in 1939, the National Field Archery association was formed by bow-hunting members of the NAA.

Since 1931, the Federation Internationale de Tir a l'Arc (FITA) has held world championships in target archery. The United States, partly because of its superior equipment, has dominated these events. In 1972, target archery was reinstated as an Olympic event.

Automobile Racing

The automobile had hardly been invented when someone had the idea of racing it. The first recognized automobile race took place in France in 1894. By today's standards, it was hardly a race. The race, from Paris to Rouen, certainly wasn't fast—the winner, driving a steam-propelled car, averaged 11.9 miles per hour. It was not very exciting—the 21 cars struggled over rutted roads just to keep moving. And not many people were watching, except for some amazed French farmers, many of whom had never seen an automobile before. But some of the elements of modern racing were present. The winner, the Marquis de Dion, would never have finished without the aid of his able mechanic, who rode with him, constantly making repairs. Today, too, the race car driver relies heavily on his "pit crew," a team of super-fast mechanics, to keep his car in the race. And in 1894, as today, the race was organized by the automobile industry to help promote itself.

Auto racing is today on its way to becoming the most popular spectator sport in the United States. Approximately fifty million Americans each year pay to watch some form of auto race. It is easy to see why they go: no other sport offers such speed, excitement, and danger. But it is not so easy to understand what makes the drivers compete, since the chance of death, even for these skilled performers, is very great.

COMPETITION

Auto racing is popular wherever there are automobiles, but nowhere is there a greater variety of races than in the United States. American racing is regulated by a number of organizations, including the National Association for Stock Car Auto Racing (NASCAR), the Sports Car Club of America (SCCA), the United States Auto Club (USAC), and the National Hot Rod Association (NHRA). These groups sanction races—that is, the promoter of the race pays them to give their authorization to it. They also license drivers to compete in the races they sanction.

The international organization of racing, with a membership of about seventy countries, is the Fédération Internationale de l'Automobile (FIA). The FIA representative for the United States is the Automobile Competition Committee for the United States-FIA, Inc.

GRAND PRIX

The aristocracy of auto racing is Grand Prix competition. For these races the cars are open-wheeled, single-seat racers, known as Formula I vehicles. (Formulas are established by the FIA and are based on, among other things, engine size and overall

The most famous auto race in America is the Indianapolis 500, run every year on Memorial Day. Top right: *The cars and the speedway have changed radically since the race was first run, early in the century.* Bottom right: *The start of the 1976 race.* Top left: *The cars at Indy are similar but not identical to the Formula I vehicles that compete on the Grand Prix circuit, on such famous courses as Brands Hatch, England, bottom left.*

13

weight.) These fast, maneuverable machines are built for one purpose only—to race. They can attain speeds of more than 190 miles per hour on straight-aways and usually average more than 130 miles per hour over the dangerous, winding courses of the Grand Prix circuit. The drivers of these expensive machines are considered the best in the world. There are only about twenty-five men in the world who compete regularly on the Grand Prix circuit. Their number is limited not only by the heavy travel demands on them and the lucrative purses offered on other, less demanding circuits, but also by the extremely high level of skill that is necessary for Grand Prix racing. Each year these drivers compete in roughly a dozen road races for the Championnat du Monde des Conducteurs, or World Champion-ship of Drivers.

Each Grand Prix race is held in a different country and takes place on a closed-circuit road course, with three or four miles to the lap. The courses are about two hundred miles long and all challenge the abilities of man and machine to the utmost. The drivers must race over winding courses, up and down hills, as fast as they can without losing control. And their highly sensitive machines must be able to stand up to the strain of such diverse driving conditions. Because there are fewer cars in Grand Prix than in other types of auto racing, there are fewer accidents, but those that do occur are often fatal.

Although two Grand Prix events are held each year in the United States (one at Watkins Glen, New York, and the other at Long Beach, California), Grand Prix racing is a very small part of American racing. Road racing has never been as popular in America as it is in Europe. At one time the million-aire W. K. Vanderbilt tried to popularize road racing with his Vanderbilt Cup races, but he withdrew the

Cup after several years, perhaps because American cars weren't winning. To this day, the great majority of Grand Prix winners are non-American.

UNITED STATES CHAMPIONSHIPS OR CHAMPIONSHIP TRAIL

Each Memorial Day weekend, hundreds of thou-sands of Americans turn out to watch a 500-mile, 200-lap race held on an oval track in Indianapolis. The Indianapolis 500 is the biggest event in Ameri-can auto racing and the most important race in the USAC-sanctioned Championship Trail, or National Championship. It consists of about twelve races, ranging in length from 150 to 500 miles, all run on paved, oval tracks. The USAC drivers compete for the biggest purses in all of racing—around two and a half million dollars.

The first Indianapolis 500 was held in 1911 on a 2½-mile oval track that had just been resurfaced with brick (hence, the nickname, "the Brickyard"). It is the same track today, though it has since been repaved. The winner of that first race averaged 74.59 miles per hour. Today, the 33 cars that com-pete do close to two hundred miles per hour, often maneuvering within inches of each other.

SPORTS CAR RACING

Sports car racing in the United States gained great impetus when American soldiers returned home after World War II. The first races were among sports cars that had been manufactured for sale to the general public. Today, sports cars race in many categories, depending on their engine size and weight. Most sports cars are two-seaters and, unlike Grand Prix racers, are factory-produced and not intended solely for racing. The racing itself is usually done on road courses.

14

Two of the best and most popular stock car drivers are David Pearson (in car 21) and Richard Petty (in car 43), fighting it out at the finish of the 1974 Firecracker 490, opposite. They had another close race (and close call) at the 1976 Daytona 500, when they collided just before the finish, above.

The most famous sports car race today is the twenty-four-hour endurance race at Le Mans, France. It was at Le Mans that, in 1955, the worst disaster in racing occurred: a car ran out of control and 83 persons were killed. For a while there was a great public outcry against racing, but the sport continued, and today Le Mans is one of the most important races in the Championnat Internationale des Marques, or International Championship of Makes. This is a series of races after which awards are presented to manufacturers of the winning cars instead of to the drivers. These races are almost as glamorous as Grand Prix races. Indeed, many Grand Prix drivers compete in them. The races in the series are all endurance races of at least six hours. Manufacturers who win at Le Mans, Daytona Beach, Sebring, or Monza make much of these accomplishments in their advertising. Italy's Mille Miglia, a grueling 1,000-mile race, was considered by most drivers to be the most difficult in the world. It was discontinued in 1957 after several spectators and a driving team were killed.

STOCK CAR RACING

Stock car racing, so they say, began in the South where moonshiners (people who made illegal liquor) drove souped-up cars that could outrace the cars of government agents. This legend isn't completely true, but it is true that stock car racing is American through and through. It is the most popular form of auto racing in America, with more events, more prize money, and more spectators than any other form of racing. There are more than two hundred major stock car tracks in the United States and hundreds of smaller ones.

On the outside, the stock car looks like the family car. But there the resemblance ends. Top competition features automobiles traveling at speeds of up to two hundred miles per hour, as fast as the racers at Indianapolis. It takes lots of money to build and race cars like these, so most drivers and crews are backed by Detroit manufacturers.

Most stock car races take place on dirt or paved oval tracks with steeply banked turns. Racing is very rough, and the cars bump into each other at high speeds and tailgate in an alarming manner. Of all race car drivers, stock car drivers have the reputation of having the most raw courage. There is no gear changing on those banked tracks, so the man who is willing to take the turns fastest will be the most likely to win. Stock car racing is a blood-and-guts affair, and its fans love it that way.

DRAG RACING

Drag racing is racing reduced to its most basic element—pure speed. The purpose of a drag race is to see which of two cars is faster. Not much skill is involved—just the ability to keep the car aimed straight. Most drag races are on a straight course, usually paved. The dragsters begin from a standing start and end a quarter of a mile down the track.

On any Sunday, the chances are very good that about three million Americans will be watching drag races. The dragsters they watch will be of all kinds.

The NHRA, which sanctions most races, recognizes about one hundred categories of racers. The fastest cars are in the AA fuel dragster category. These are extremely long machines, light in the front, with powerful engines mounted in the rear. They can accelerate to speeds of up to two hundred fifty miles per hour and use parachutes to assist in braking.

Aside from the AA fuel dragsters, the fastest growing class in drag racing is the "funny car." Although funny cars may look simply like souped-up stocks, they are quite different. In fact it was while trying to improve stock cars that mechanics stumbled onto the funny car concept—a complete one-piece fiberglass body (no doors, no hood) and the rear seat location for the driver's seat. The cars were banned from stock competition, but interest in these weird machines became so great that a special class was created for them. Today's funny cars are only slightly slower than the giant fuel dragsters and much more difficult to handle. They run on highly specialized fuel blends.

DEMOLITION DERBY

Finally there is the low-comedy auto show known as the demolition derby. In this crazy event the winner is not the driver who can go fastest or farthest, but the driver who can simply keep going when all the other cars have expired. The sight of thirty to forty cars spinning across a racecourse purposely smashing into each other is one of the most bizarre in all of sports. The cars spend most of the time going backward because the drivers do not want to damage their engines when they smash.

In 1976, Janet Guthrie became the first woman to qualify as a driver for top-level Formula races.

Badminton

A badminton shuttle is potentially one of the slowest and one of the fastest objects in sports: tapped lightly, it drifts over the net; contacted solidly, it can leave the racquet at 110 miles per hour. The unusual qualities of this shuttle, or "bird," give the game its uniqueness. As most Americans play it, badminton is a rather sedate game, a pleasant way to spend a summer day in the backyard. But as played indoors by the experienced, badminton is extremely vigorous. Singles ranks among the top two or three most demanding sports. A top player must be tricky and very quick because deception and change of pace are keys to the game. And he must be strong—in one game he will do more running than an end does in a 60-minute football game. A singles player may run the court's long diagonal from net to base line as many as fifteen times a rally—and at the end, no point might be scored!

Badminton was certainly a more leisurely sport when it was first played—at the Duke of Beaufort's country estate, named Badminton, in Gloucestershire, England. One weekend in 1873, some of the Duke's houseguests, English officers on leave from India, began playing a game called Poona. The English aristocracy came to love the sport, and soon afterward everyone was talking about "that game from Badminton."

The game had been around in one form or another for a long time before that. The practice of trying to keep an object in the air may have come from a magic ritual: the longer one could keep an object in the air, it was believed, the longer one would live.

THE COURT AND EQUIPMENT

Very little is needed to play badminton:
1. A net, 30 inches by 20 feet, elevated with poles placed on the sidelines. The top edge of the net should be 5 feet above the ground at the center, 5 feet 1 inch at the sides.
2. A racquet, about 26 inches long, weighing between 3 and 8 ounces. The head of the racquet, about 8 inches by 6 inches, is oval and strung with gut or nylon at 12 to 16 pounds tension. A narrow shaft connects the head to the handle. The best "bats" are made of metal.
3. A shuttlecock, or "bird." The shuttle has a cork or plastic base in the shape of a half ball about 1 inch in diameter. From the flat side of the base, 14 to 16 real or plastic feathers extend out from $2\frac{1}{8}$ to $2\frac{1}{2}$ inches. At their ends, these form a circle with a diameter of about $2\frac{1}{2}$ inches. The weight of the shuttle will vary between 76 and 80 grams, depending on the volume of the playing room.
4. Some level ground, 44 by 20 feet, and lines to mark the playing area (see diagram).

5. A calm day. Even the slightest breeze makes the bird's flight erratic. All top-level competition is played indoors, usually with lighter birds than those used outside.

THE GAME

To begin play, the server drops the bird and, with an easy, forward underhand motion, strokes it diagonally across the net to the opposing service court. The bird must be returned on the fly because once it touches the ground, the rally is over.

Badminton began as a leisurely pastime, and it is still often played that way in parks and backyards. But in top-level competition it is a fierce indoor sport, with players bashing the shuttlecock at one another at speeds of more than 100 miles per hour.

Having the serve is very important because only the serving side can score points. In singles, because the service court is longer, a high, deep serve is best. In doubles a low service is almost mandatory because high serves are invariably smashed away. The server is given one attempt to serve legally. If he misses, the service goes to the other side of the net.

BADMINTON COURT

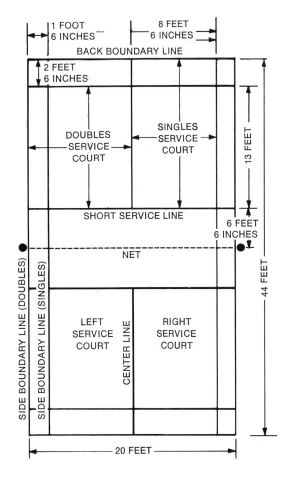

STROKES

Strokes are more similar to squash than to lawn tennis. Because the bird responds better to a quick, sharp blow than to a smooth stroke and because deception is paramount, a great deal of wrist is required to get enough "whip" into the stroke. Contacting the bird early and as high as possible after it crosses the net allows one to hit down, a great advantage: an opponent who is required to return the bird upward is always on the defensive and usually loses the rally.

The basic shots are the clear, the dropshot, the drive, and the smash. The clear, or lob, when used as an attacking shot, should be hit just over the opponent's racquet with the object of getting the bird behind him. The high clear can be either a defensive or a neutralizing shot, depending on its depth.

The dropshot is the most delicate shot in the game, intended to just clear the net and then drop steeply to the ground. If the opponent even gets it, he will have to "lift" the bird and go on the defensive. The dropshot requires more wrist and finger work than the other shots, but, most of all, deception. Because the flight of a dropshot is rather slow, a player cannot reveal his intention to use it. Otherwise an opponent will anticipate the shot, move to the net, and quickly end the rally with a smash.

The drive is a flat, hard stroke, hit in a direct line and low across the net. It is intended to go quickly past an opponent and drop to the floor.

The smash, or "kill" shot, is a hard, downward shot hit from the overhead position. It should be used sparingly, however, because it is a taxing shot and a player must try to conserve energy, especially in a long match. The smash, interspersed with dropshots, allows one to keep an opponent on the defensive and eventually forces a weak return that can be put away.

SCORING

The server scores a point whenever his opponent lets the bird drop to the floor inside the court, hits a shot out of the court or under the net, or lets the shuttlecock touch any part of his body. He also scores if his opponent touches the net with his racquet or body or steps under the net. For each point, the server alternates between the right and left service court.

Most games consist of 15 points, and all must be won by at least 2. Occasionally games are played to 21. When the score is tied at 13 in 15-point men's competition, the first side to have earned 13 may choose to "set" the game and play to 18. Similarly, at 14-all, the first side to have earned 14 can decide to play to 17. In women's competition the game is played to 11 and must be won by at least 2. There is a choice at 9-all of playing to 12, and at 10-all of playing to 12.

Baseball

Baseball is the sentimental favorite of sports fans. Football may be more violent and action packed; basketball may be faster; tennis may be more glamorous. But baseball resists and rises above all such comparisons, secure in a history more dramatic and colorful than all the other sports combined.

It seems as if Americans have always been playing baseball or watching each other play it. The game was well established by 1903 and has been played pretty much the same way ever since. While the changes of the twentieth century swirled around it, baseball remained the same lazy game, measuring time in innings and outs instead of minutes, defying an increasingly hurried age. Its star personalities have often meant more to Americans than their presidents. Its uncertainty has appealed to the American love for the underdog turned top dog. A weaker team can stage a miraculous ninth-inning rally to triumph over a stronger club. The act of an instant can raise one player to glory and cast down another.

In 1951, in the ninth inning of the final playoff game between the New York Giants and Brooklyn Dodgers, Giants' manager Leo Durocher called over his next batter, Bobby Thomson, and said, "If you ever hit one, hit one now." The Giants had won 37 of their last 44 games that year and had drawn abreast of a Dodgers' team that had had a 13½-game first-place lead in mid-August. Now with one out, two men on base, and the Giants down 4–2, Thomson stepped in to face fastballing relief pitcher Ralph Branca. The first pitch was high, but on the second Bobby Thomson hit the line-drive, pennant-winning homer that came to be known as "the shot heard 'round the world." That one feat granted Thomson immortal fame as patron saint of ninth-inning die-hards. It made Branca baseball's symbol of sudden death. And it demonstrated that the sometimes plodding game of baseball can produce drama that the rough-and-tumble sports can never surpass.

HISTORY

A certain proprietary feeling has accompanied America's love of the game. It wasn't enough to say that baseball was as American as apple pie; there was a felt need to show that the game had always been thoroughly ours. The British claimed that baseball had come from the old English game of rounders—a probable explanation. But some Americans thought this explanation diluted our claim to baseball as our national pastime. In 1907, major league baseball owners established a commission of some of baseball's finest citizens to determine the game's origins. Predictably, the commission concluded that baseball was indeed all-American and had been invented by a man

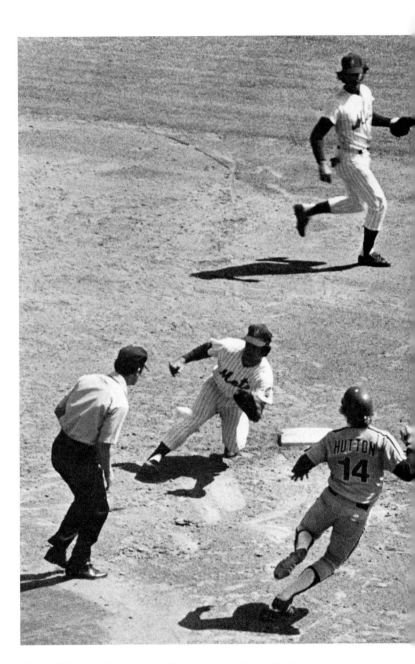

Baseball is an intricate game that many people call boring because they don't understand it. The action occurs in flashes, as with this attempted stolen base. The trick to enjoying baseball is appreciating some of the things that are going on when nothing seems to be.

named Abner Doubleday. In 1939, the National Baseball Hall of Fame was founded in Cooperstown, New York, home of Doubleday, and the legend that he was the game's inventor persists.

The man truly deserving the title of baseball's inventor may well be Alexander Cartwright, a well-born New Yorker who drew up rules and a playing field for a new game that was based on popular children's games such as rounders. One important change Cartwright made was eliminating "plugging," the practice of putting out baserunners by hitting them with throws. Cartwright limited physical contact to the more gentlemanly tag.

Cartwright's team of gentlemen, the New York Knickerbockers, was the first to play under these rules. On June 19, 1846, the Knickerbockers played the New York Nine (and lost 23–1). For a long time, who played whom was at least as important as how well the game was played. The early teams were careful not to play teams of inferior social standing. But baseball was too appealing a game to belong to any one group. Inevitably, men began to play for a living. In 1869, the first professional team, the Cincinnati Red Stockings, was formed. Luring the best players with its salaries, the Cincinnati team steamrolled the opposition, winning 92 games in a row during one stretch.

In 1871, the first professional league, the National Association of Professional Base Ball Players, was formed. The Association had many problems and was so badly managed that in 1876 the more efficient National League of Base Ball Clubs replaced it.

Today's other major league, the American League, was formed in 1900 by Ban Johnson. No other new league had had the muscle to force the National League to recognize it as an equal, but in Johnson the National League rulers met their match. When they denied Johnson's request that his new group be recognized, he enticed players away from the National League by offering them higher salaries. With its best players "jumping" week after week and American League teams waging ticket-price wars against them, the old guard was forced to recognize the upstarts. In 1903, the war ended and the terms of peace left baseball quite stable for years afterwards. Uniform rules were adopted, 16 permanent franchises for the two leagues were recognized, and baseball declared it was "answerable to no power outside its own." The United States government agreed to this manifesto and exempted the sport from the country's antitrust laws.

Another outcome of the 1903 settlement was the agreement that at the end of each season the league leaders would meet in a playoff, the World Series. The Series was a major event, even in 1903, though there were some differences from the modern spectacle. The fans for the first series between the National League Pittsburgh Pirates and the American League Boston Pilgrims (today the Red Sox), knew their teams so well that none of the players wore numbers on their uniforms. Today, the Series is a less intimate event. Tickets are expensive and hard to come by. Still, the best-of-seven series has always excited even the most complacent fans. Certainly, in this country no other sporting event, not even football's Super Bowl, attracts more attention. Almost everyone takes some notice, at least when he sees groups of people in the street clustered around transistor radios. Episodes of heroism always seem to shine brighter in the World Series than similar feats achieved during the regular season.

The year 1919 was a troubled one for baseball. The sport had always been subject to charges of corruption, but that year some players were caught red-handed. Members of the Chicago White Sox, bribed by gamblers, tried to throw the World Series. As a result of this "Black Sox" scandal, eight players, some of the best in the game, were barred from baseball, and Judge Kenesaw ("Mountain") Landis was appointed commissioner. A figure of great integrity, Landis restored some measure of public trust in the game during his tenure.

The biggest boost to baseball came, as it always has and always will, from one of its players. No matter how much scandal surrounds a sport, a new superstar will always draw the crowds. In the 1920s, this man was Babe Ruth of the New York Yankees. Ruth had been one of the game's finest pitchers and a part-time outfielder with the Boston Red Sox. When he came to New York, he quickly became a full-time star, though he scarcely looked the part. He was so portly from the waist up that pinstripes were incorporated into the Yankees' uniform to trim down Ruth's appearance. The Yankees made Ruth an everyday outfielder, and he responded to the switch by hitting home runs almost at will (54 in 1920, 59 in 1921, 60 in 1927, and a career total of 714). Fans packed the parks wherever he played. He was such a financial asset to the Yankees that their new Yankee Stadium was nicknamed "the house that Ruth built."

Ruth's home runs changed the style of the game. Previously, baseball had been played with a "dead" ball, which hitters tried to poke through the infield, relying on singles and tricky baserunning to score runs. After Ruth, many batters started aiming for the fences, and team owners, wise to the crowd appeal of the long-ball game, began substituting livelier, "jackrabbit" baseballs.

Perhaps the most famous team of the thirties was the 1934 St. Louis Cardinals, "the Gashouse Gang." Led by Dizzy Dean, his brother Paul ("Daffy"), and Pepper Martin, the Cards clinched the pennant on the last day of the season and then won the World Series, defeating the Detroit Tigers in seven games. The Dean brothers, both pitchers, won 49 games between them during the regular season and two each in the Series. Once, in a doubleheader, Dizzy pitched a one-hitter in the first game and Daffy followed with a no-hitter. "Why didn't you tell me you were going to pitch a no-hitter," Dizzy complained. "Then I would have pitched one, too."

In 1947, Jackie Robinson became the first black man to play in the major leagues. Branch Rickey, owner of the Brooklyn Dodgers and the man who signed Robinson, feared that without a black star to pave the way for other blacks, baseball would never integrate. He found a star in Robinson, but baseball mightly resisted the black man. From the first moment he stepped on the field, Robinson had to endure vicious abuse from fans and players alike. A less gifted and less courageous man would have cracked; Robinson just played aggressive, brilliant baseball and refused to be cowed. Gradu-

ally, other teams began to recruit black players, many from the Negro Leagues that for years had been the only outlet for black players. Today, a few of the black stars from the Negro Leagues have been inducted into the Hall of Fame, even though they never played in the majors.

On May 17, 1939, two colleges, Columbia and Princeton, were battling for fourth place in the Ivy League. A television camera witnessed this event, the first baseball game to be telecast. The camera couldn't focus on the pitcher and the batter simultaneously, so it settled on following the path of the ball. It presented a jerky telecast that must have given headaches to the four hundred or so viewers.

For better or worse, television more than any other factor has changed baseball. Certainly, it brings the game to more people. (By 1951, the World Series was being televised coast to coast.) The minor league teams that once flourished in small towns, where major league baseball wasn't accessible, have been practically eradicated because of television's long reach. Most of the rela-

Opposite: *A double play from a game in the late 1800s. For many years tight fielding, artful hitting, and fiery baserunning were the foremost skills in the game.* Right: *Then Babe Ruth, an awesome titan, made long-ball hitting the rage and almost single-handedly transformed the game.*

tively few minor league teams in existence today serve as farm clubs for the majors.

In the early sixties the New York Yankees completed the dynasty they had begun with Babe Ruth. They had become the winningest team in history, winning the American League pennant 29 times between 1921 and 1964, 10 times under manager Casey Stengel. Ruth passed the winning tradition through players such as Lou Gehrig, Joe DiMaggio, Mickey Mantle, and Roger Maris—great home run hitters all—and the Yankees became known as "the Bronx Bombers." Perhaps the two most famous individual feats of these lordly Yankees were DiMaggio's 56-game hitting streak, in 1941, and Maris's 61 home runs, in 1961—both records. But in a game that seems to love the underdog, the Yanks' record was unlovable. Too much success eventually made their fans blasé, even hostile, to the team's stars. First Mantle, then Maris, felt the wrath of fans so spoiled by success that they came to the ball park to bait the stars.

In the early 1960s, a newly formed New York team, one that may have been baseball's worst ever, easily outdrew the Yankees. They were the Amazin' Mets—amazing for their ingenious ways of losing ballgames and just as amazing for their rabid popularity. For their first seven seasons they finished no better than next to last, stimulating their first manager to write the book Can't Anyone Here Play This Game? The author was Casey Stengel, the same man who had been hailed as a wizard for managing the victorious Yankees. Stengel left the Yankees after the 1960 season, became the Mets' manager in 1962, and promptly learned how the

other half lived—ineptly but very profitably. Perhaps the essence of this team was best captured on those unlikely occasions when it won. In 1964, the Mets defeated the Chicago Cubs by the astounding score (even for a good team) of 19–1. Leading 13–1 after eight innings, the Mets scored six runs in the last inning of the rout. Afterward, the Mets' pitcher, Tracy Stallard, said confidently, "That's when I knew we had 'em."

In 1969, in an effort to stir up fan excitement with more playoff games, major league baseball reorganized itself. Each league was divided into an East and a West division. At the end of the 162-game regular season, the leaders of the two divisions in each league engaged in a best-of-five playoff for that league's pennant. The winners then moved to the World Series. The first year of the new system proved spectacularly successful, mostly because the once-hapless New York Mets rose from ninth place the year before and won the pennant and World Series.

After the 1972 season, in another effort to spark spectator interest, the American League introduced the "designated hitter." Designated hitters bat for pitchers (almost always notoriously weak hitters) but don't play in the field. In a close game in the late innings, a manager is no longer all but forced to remove his pitcher and send up a pinch hitter. Strong pitchers as well as aging hitters have profited from the new rule, but on balance the designated hitter rule has helped the offense, as its proponents hoped it would. The National League still requires the pitcher to come to bat or be removed.

Early in 1974, the aging black slugger of the Atlanta Braves, Henry Aaron, broke Babe Ruth's long-standing and admired record of 714 career home runs. When it became apparent in 1973 that he would surpass the Babe, Aaron encountered a milder version of the racist abuse that plagued baseball when Jackie Robinson broke the color barrier. But baseball drowned the bitterness in a torrent of ceremonies, celebrations, and other public relations "promos," and when the quiet star finally crashed number 715, hardly anyone begrudged him the new record.

THE ALL-STAR GAME

About halfway into the season, the best players from each league take part in a rite known as the All-Star Game. The first such match was the idea of Arch Ward, sports editor of the Chicago Tribune. (Babe Ruth won the first game for the American League with a home run.) Once picked by the various managers, the teams are now chosen by the fans through nationwide ballots. This method seems to work fairly well, though on several occasions a concerted newspaper campaign in one city has led to a stuffing of the ballot boxes with votes for home team players whose records may not have supported their selection. Such improprieties are rare, however, and on occasion the fans have

shown remarkable insight. In 1974, Steve Garvey of the Los Angeles Dodgers was chosen as the National League's All-Star first baseman, though his name did not appear on the ballot. Garvey's two timely hits and sharp defensive play earned him the All-Star Game's Most Valuable Player award. And at the end of the season, Garvey was selected as the most valuable player in the National League.

THE FIELD

Once all playing fields were made of natural grass. But in the late sixties, the Astrodome, baseball's first domed stadium, introduced a new playing surface called "AstroTurf," a carpetlike substance of bright green that is laid down in strips over a cushioned layer of padding. Although many ball parks now have some kind of artificial turf, not all ball players appreciate it. It is a more consistent surface than natural turf and it also seems to endure better in bad weather, but the ball seems to bounce so hard on it that many routine ground balls become base hits.

In 1881, the distance from the pitcher to the batter was 50 feet. That was long enough as long as the pitchers threw underhand, but it became a problem in 1884, when they were allowed to throw overhand. In 1893, the distance was lengthened to the present standard of 60 feet 6 inches. The distance between each of the bases is 90 feet in the major leagues. In 1969, the height of the pitcher's mound was reduced from 15 inches to 10 inches in an effort to boost the sagging batting averages throughout both leagues.

The distance from home plate to the fences differs in most ball parks, but as the older stadiums across the country have been torn down and replaced by new ones, the trend has been toward ball parks with symmetrical dimensions. In these new ball parks, there are no "cheap" home runs (a 250-foot pop-up down the right or left field line at the old Polo Grounds in New York reached the seats), but many fans long for the distinctive char-

acteristics of the more intimate, old-style stadiums.

One distinctive characteristic of the ball park that baseball has not yet forsaken is the dugout, the subground-level rectangular area that opens onto the field. There the players rest between fielding and batting stints, all but hidden from the spectators.

EQUIPMENT

The standard major league baseball is between 9 and 9¼ inches in circumference and weighs about 5 ounces. Since 1925, it has had a cushioned cork center, tightly wound with twine and covered by sewn horsehide. (A recent shortage in horsehide has lead to an influx of cowhide-covered balls imported from Haiti.) The cover is stitched around the ball, leaving a slightly raised seam.

The traditional bat is wooden—ash, hickory, or hackberry—though recently aluminum bats have become popular on the college and sandlot levels. Bats are no longer than 42 inches; those used in the majors usually weigh between 32 and 42 ounces.

Stars of the thirties and forties included Bob Feller, opposite, Joe DiMaggio, top, and the St. Louis Cardinals' Frankie Frisch (3) and Joe Medwick, above, debating with Commissioner Kenesaw ("Mountain") Landis during the tumultuous seventh game of the 1934 World Series, won by the Cardinals.

gloves as the prime reason for the lower batting averages over the last few decades.

In 1941, the Brooklyn Dodgers became the first team to wear batting helmets. Today's ball players all wear plastic helmets for batting, and most of them keep them on when running the bases. Many of the players use helmets with a protective extension that covers the side of the head facing the pitcher.

To protect them from injury to the top of the head, many catchers wear a plastic helmet instead of their normal cap when they are behind the plate. Catchers also wear a facemask (the first was worn in 1875 by Jim Tyng of Harvard), a padded chest protector (first used in 1885), and shin guards—two hard-plastic pads that are strapped around each leg between the ankle and knee.

Players wear low-cut leather shoes with metal spikes on the bottom, but on artificial turf they wear shoes with hard rubber cleats. Many players wear a glove, similar to a golf glove, on one or both hands while batting, and some wear sliding pads under their pants.

The most drastic changes in uniform style have probably taken place over the last several years. Twenty years ago it would have been unthinkable to field a major league team with yellow-tinted hats and yellow shoes. Yet Charles O. Finley did just that when he moved his Kansas City Athletics to Oakland, California, in 1969. Many teams still retain the traditional uniforms—for home games, white jerseys bearing the team nickname, for away games gray jerseys bearing the team city—but Finley's colorful concept has caught on in several cities.

For a long time the baseball uniform didn't have numbers. The Cleveland Indians introduced the concept in 1916, but it wasn't until 1931 that the American League officially adopted the policy. National League teams started wearing numbers two years later. Today, many teams include the player's name as well as a number on the back of the jersey.

THE GAME

"Wee Willie" Keeler, the two-time batting champion in the late 1890s, gave perhaps the most memorable advice on how to succeed as a baseball player. "Hit 'em where they ain't," he was reported to have said. Unfortunately, the game isn't quite that simple. The batter tries to hit the ball between the foul lines, which extend at right angles from home plate, and then to advance as many bases as possible before the fielders can retrieve the ball and put him out. Runs are scored by advancing players around the bases—from home to first to second to third and back home—and the team that scores the most runs in its nine times at bat wins the game. Each team is allowed three outs per time at bat. If the score is tied after each team has batted nine times—that is, after nine innings—extra innings are played until a winner is decided (or until a curfew is breached). Several games have lasted more than three times the regulation nine innings.

The style of bats has changed significantly over the years. The early ones were usually bottle-necked, with a very thick handle. They allowed for solid contact even if the pitch wasn't met squarely at the power part of the bat, near its end. As the emphasis on home run hitting increased over the years, the bats became much thinner at the handle and most of the weight became concentrated at the other end, in the "fat" part of the bat. (Stan Musial was the first to introduce this "tapered" model.)

Batters often warm up by swinging a lead-weighted bat or one with a heavy metal "doughnut" fitted around the end. They often apply fine tar or resin to the bat handle for a better grip.

The gloves worn by baseball's early fielders were little more than mittens. Their primary purpose was to protect the catching hand. The baseball glove has progressed greatly since then, what with giant first baseman's mitts, huge catcher's mitts (especially huge when a knuckleball pitcher is on the mound), and the long-fingered infielder's mitt. Many experts point to the improvement in fielders

Naturally, the best place for a hitter to hit the ball is over the fence for a home run (allowing him a complete circuit of all four bases), but singles (one-base hits), doubles (two-base hits), and triples (three-base hits) all contribute to the goal of scoring runs. Of course, the batter's first goal is simply to hit the pitcher's pitch, especially if the umpire will call it a strike. A strike is any pitched ball that crosses home plate (17 inches wide) between the batter's knees and armpits, any pitch that the batter swings at and misses, or, in most cases a ball he hits outside the foul lines, a foul ball. Three strikes make an out unless the third strike is a foul ball, in which case the batter is free to keep swinging until he takes a called third strike, swings and misses a third strike, makes an out some other way, or reaches base. Only if the batter deliberately taps at, or bunts, the ball instead of taking a full swing is he called out for a foul ball on the third strike.

Pitches that are not in the strike zone are called balls, and four balls result in the batter going to first base—a walk. The easiest way to reach base is on a walk because the batter need not even swing to get there. Hitters come in a variety of sizes, so the strike zone varies for each batter, but never to as absurd a degree as when Bill Veeck, the colorful one-time owner of the St. Louis Browns and, since, better teams, signed up a midget for a game, planning he would walk every time up. That incident if no other made a cliché of the baseball expression "He's just looking for a walk."

Once the batter has hit the ball in fair territory, it is up to the fielders to put him out or to prevent him from advancing. The fielder may put the batter out by catching the ball before it hits the ground (in either fair or foul territory) or by tagging the runner between bases, or on a grounder by getting the ball to the first baseman so that he can touch the base before the batter does. The first baseman need not tag the batter with the ball because the batter is obliged to run to first base on a batted ball, and whenever a runner must advance, or is "forced," the fielder need merely touch the bag while holding the ball in order to put out the runner. If a runner is on first base and his teammate hits a ground ball, the baserunner must run to second base because the batter is running to first and only one runner may occupy a base at a time. Thus, a force is created at second base, and to put out the runner the fielder need only touch the base while in possession of the ball. If the fielders are quick enough, they will make the force outs at second and at first—the traditional double play. With runners on first and second, there may be force plays at third and second as well as on the batter at first, and with runners on first, second, and third (with the bases "loaded"), there may be force plays at all four bases.

Once the batter is put out, the force on the baserunners as well as on him is erased. He is no longer advancing, so the runners don't have to either. Thus, after a caught fly ball or after a ground ball that is fielded and thrown to first ahead of the batter, none of the runners need advance. On fly balls, the runners are in great danger if they do try to advance because the rules require that they return to their bases if the ball is caught, and only afterward may they legally advance. If they stray from the base too soon, a fielder with the ball may put them out simply by touching the base they came from. If a runner advances on a fly ball by waiting until the ball is caught before running to the next base, he is "tagging up," and because the runner is advancing without being forced to, a tag is required to put him out. One of baseball's most exciting plays may occur when a runner tries to tag up from third base and score on a fly ball to the outfield. The plays are often close, with the issue

Opposite: *Jackie Robinson, the first black to play major league baseball, had to be great to make it. He was, and did.* Above left: *Willie Mays would be remembered for many great catches;* above right: *Sandy Amoros for one—this one against the New York Yankees in the seventh game of the 1955 World Series.*

being decided in a cloud of dust as the runner slides into home plate.

Another significant rule with regard to fly balls and force outs is the infield fly rule, which was instituted to protect baserunners from defensive shenanigans. At one time infielders used to drop pop flies deliberately when there were men on first and second or on first, second, and third. The runners naturally were forced to hold their bases on pop-ups lest they be caught off the base once the ball was caught. But the fielders soon learned that if they dropped the pop-ups, they could easily force out runners and thus kill many rallies with easy double plays. Then the infield fly rule was passed, stating that on any easy fly ball to the infield with less that two outs and men on first and second or on first, second, and third, the batter is automatically out. Thus the runners may remain at their bases without fear of being forced if the ball is dropped.

Baserunners have their tricks, too. The most notable, of course, is base stealing. The legendary Ty Cobb was the first of the great base stealers. In his 24 major league seasons, Cobb stole 892 bases, 96 of them in 1915—a single season record that lasted until 1962, when Maury Wills of the Los Angeles Dodgers stole 104. Twelve years later, Lou Brock of the St. Louis Cardinals broke the record again, but neither Wills nor Brock ever inspired quite as much terror as Cobb did. "The Georgia Peach" was no softy; indeed he intimidated his opponents. He would sit on the dugout steps before each game methodically sharpening his spikes, and opposing infielders would tremble.

On the steal, the runner sprints to the next base while the pitch is traveling to the plate, and he tries to beat the catcher's throw. Speed alone is hardly sufficient in mastering the art of base stealing. Maury Wills spent hour after hour studying films of opposing pitchers, so he knew exactly how big a lead to take and precisely when to take off for sec-

ond or third. Although the catcher is often the one blamed for a stolen base, most players agree that bases are stolen off the pitcher. If the pitcher fails to keep a close eye on the runner and prevent him from getting too big a lead, even the best throw from the catcher will be too late. One of baseball's most exciting—and rarest—plays is the steal of home. In this case the runner is starting from third base and coming home, so the catcher has no throw to make. It is simply a matter of the runner racing the pitch to home plate and trying to avoid the tag.

One weapon that pitchers use to keep baserunners close to the base is the pickoff throw. The pitcher simulates the start of his normal pitching motion, but then he suddenly whips the ball to the fielder covering the base. A good pickoff move can be very useful to a pitcher, not only in preventing stolen bases but also in keeping runners close enough to their bases so that they won't be able to take extra bases on hits. Most pickoff throws go to first base, though occasionally a pitcher will throw to second or third.

There are many restrictions on the pickoff move, however. Atop the pitching mound is a narrow rectangular plate called the rubber. Each pitch must be thrown with the pitcher's foot touching this rubber. Once the pitcher has placed his foot on the rubber and begun his pitching motion toward the plate, he cannot suddenly break his motion and whip the ball to first base. If he does, the umpire will call a "balk" and the baserunners will each advance one base. This rule gives the left-handed pitcher a distinct advantage over the right hander. His body is facing first base, and his front leg naturally kicks toward first during his pitching motion. Before beginning his motion toward the plate but after beginning his pitching motion, the left hander can easily throw the ball to first. To prevent a balk, the right hander usually must turn completely around for his throw to first base.

To keep the men on base from getting a running "jump" on the pitch, the pitcher tries to keep his motion toward the plate as brief as possible. Instead of using his full windup, he delivers the ball quickly after taking a "set" position—hands clasped near the waist, body facing first (for a left hander) or third (for a right hander). The rules require that once he assumes this position he must stop for an instant before beginning his pitching motion. And unless he steps off the rubber, he may not break his hands until he does so in the course of his pitching motion. Otherwise he is called for a balk.

With such detailed but not always clear restrictions on the pitcher, it is not uncommon during a baseball game to hear shouts of "Balk!" from an opposing dugout. But often these critics, or "bench jockeys," who make such suggestions don't take them seriously themselves. It is really just another attempt to rattle the pitcher rather than an attempt to influence the umpire.

THE UMPIRES

The umpires, those men in blue stationed behind the plate and at each base during the game, are patient men. A player or manager who disagrees with an umpire's call will often vent his feelings in no uncertain terms. Some of this protest is done to satisfy the fans' love of gesturing and shouting, and the umpire, like any good diplomat, understands this face saving. But he also endures many dirt-kicking, cap-throwing, face-to-face, tobacco-chaw-slobbering confrontations.

In baseball's early days, when fans used to stand on the field, the umpire's position was even less pleasant. Backed by managers who were quite willing to pay resulting fines, players would encourage fans to run riot after a bad call. In 1884, Baltimore had to install barbed wire around its field to restrain irate partisans. Today, of course, an umpire's decisions are somewhat more readily accepted. The shout "kill the umpire," when heard at all, is used metaphorically, and too strenuous an objection from a player or manager will prompt the ump to throw the protester out of the game. Yet even with the respect the umpire commands these days, his life is not easy. He stands for all nine (or more) innings without rest, unnoticed until someone wants to yell at him.

The plate umpire, who wears a facemask and chest protector similar to the catcher's, calls the balls and strikes as well as any plays at home plate. The first, second, and third base umpires call the plays at their respective bases. Balls hit down the first and third base foul lines are judged fair or foul by the first and third base umpires, respectively.

Each umpiring crew has a senior umpire to serve as the crew's chief. At home plate before each game, he explains to the two team managers or their representatives peculiar rules of the field—for example, how many bases a runner is entitled to if a ball lodges under the stands. Once he has received both teams' lineups and has explained these "ground rules," the senior umpire takes complete charge of the game. He can postpone it because of rain or other conditions that make the field unplayable. He can order the grounds crew to cover the field with the protective tarpaulin, or to remove the covering. And he has final jurisdiction on all calls of the other umpires.

STRATEGY

Baseball reveals its true mysteries only to the initiated. In most sports, strategy is easy to see. Baseball strategy is more subtle, and that subtlety is the very heart of the game's appeal to the knowledgeable fan. He can fantasize to his heart's content, second-guessing managers and players alike. The comic writer James Thurber once wrote that most adult American males put themselves to sleep by retiring the entire batting order of the New York Yankees.

The most obvious battle of wits is between the pitcher and the batter. The pitcher would seem to have all the advantages. First of all, he knows what kind of pitch he is going to throw—curve, fastball, slider, change-up, knuckler, or screwball. A good pitcher is master of many of these pitches. The batter can only react, and he has little time in which to do so—about three-fifths of a second. Most batters admit that at least unconsciously they usually try to guess what pitch is coming.

Almost every big league pitcher has a good fastball. Some, like Nolan Ryan, have almost invisible ones. The fastball is the basic pitch in the pitcher's repertoire and also the easiest one to control. A good fastball is not only fast but "alive"—that is, it will rise as it crosses the plate. A pitcher with

In the 1960s, Mickey Mantle hit a fair ball almost out of Yankee Stadium, above; *Sandy Koufax pitched four no-hitters,* opposite right; *and the New York Mets, once last-place laughables, became world champions,* opposite left.

good control of a live fastball will usually have an impressive strikeout record as long as his arm lasts.

A sharp, controlled curve ball is the perfect complement to the hopping fastball. Often, the curve ball breaks down as well as to the side. The faster or more sharply it breaks, the better. (Batters say that a good curve ball "rolls off a table.") A slow-breaking, particularly high, or "hanging," curve will usually be well hit.

The change-up, or change-of-pace, is a pitch delivered with the same motion as the fastball but with an invisible "let up" so that it travels much more slowly. The good change-up will cause the batter to be far off-stride and thus off-balance if he swings.

A slider is a very effective pitch and a relatively new one. It is basically a hard-thrown curve ball that doesn't break as much as the curve but just enough to make the batter realize (too late) that it wasn't the fastball it had so deceptively resembled.

The screwball is a curve in reverse, delivered with a rather awkward and difficult arm motion. Yet a good screwballer (Carl Hubbell of the Giants was perhaps the most famous) will almost always be one of the top pitchers on the team, especially if he has an effective curve ball to complement "the screwjie."

More pitchers have begun mastering the knuck-leball—a misnomer, actually, because the ball is gripped with the fingertips, not the knuckles. The knuckleball is delivered so that it spins as little as possible, causing it to break erratically and unpre-dictably. The knuckleball is especially popular among veteran pitchers because it is delivered with a very easy motion that puts little strain on the arm. Many pitchers whose careers seemed to have been over have revived or prolonged them by mastering this tricky pitch. (Hoyt Wilhelm was a top relief pitcher well into his forties.)

The spitball (also referred to as the greaseball, depending on the substance used) was outlawed as early as 1908, but it is nevertheless still used, often quite effectively. No pitcher admits to "loading up"

Roberto Clemente, below and bottom, *starred for the Pirates before he died in an airplane crash after the 1972 season. In 1974, Henry Aaron,* opposite, *knocked his seven hundred fifteenth career home run, eclipsing Babe Ruth's record of 714, which had stood for nearly forty years. In 1961, the Babe's mark of 60 homers in a season had been broken by the New York Yankees' Roger Maris, who hit 61.*

the ball until he has either stopped doing it or retired, and some not even then. Gaylord Perry of the Cleveland Indians, a self-confessed reformed spitballer, pitched better, ironically enough, after forsaking the pitch. Most spitballs come in like fastballs and then suddenly break straight down. The great Dodgers' pitcher, Preacher Roe, likened the effect of a wet ball being squeezed on delivery to shooting a watermelon seed from between the fingers. Clearly, the spitball is not easy to control.

Another pitch that is used to keep the batter off balance is the "brush back" pitch—usually a fastball thrown close enough to the batter to shave any stray whiskers that the razor missed. By using it, the pitcher hopes to intimidate the hitter and keep him from digging in for a good swing at the ball. The sane ball player will naturally try to avoid such a pitch, but then not all ball players are completely sane when a ball game is at stake. Ron Hunt of the Montreal Expos reached first base 50 times in 1971 by getting hit with pitched balls. Hunt stood so close to the plate that more than one pitcher accused him of stepping into the pitch intentionally. Such a tactic is not allowed, but umpires are reasonable men and not likely to accuse players of having suicidal tendencies.

No pitcher can strike every batter out, and the good ones don't try to. It's good enough to get the batter to hit the ball to one of the fielders. Depending on the batter, fielders will shift position, hoping to anticipate where the ball will be hit. In a close game such subtle defensive shadings may make a big difference. A good fielder must always be aware of such things as how many outs there are, where the baserunners are, what type of hitter is up, and so on.

THE FIELDERS

If there is a quarterback on a baseball team, it is the catcher. He must be a good strategist as well as a good defenseman. He signals the number of outs to his fielders before each batter, he calls the pitches, he cuts down baserunners trying to steal, and he is the last line of defense against a potential run. A good catcher must know how to control the pitcher, how to keep him calm in a tight spot, and how to pace him as he tires in the late innings. Catching is a grueling job, what with foul tips, balls bouncing in the dirt, and runners sliding into the plate. It is rare for a team to be a consistent winner without a good catcher.

Less important defensively is the first-base position, where many teams put their weakest-fielding slugger. One of the significant qualities a first baseman may have is good size. If he is big, he will not only give the infielders a better target but also be able to stretch for the throw on a close play. Of course, big first basemen are often clumsy, too, and indeed the best fielders are rangy, not just big.

The second baseman must be a quick, wide-ranging fielder who can not only cover his own position but also cover first base on bunts. Most

important is his ability to pivot and throw quickly on the double play.

The best infielder on the team should be the shortstop. Because 75 percent of the batters are right handed and right-handed batters naturally pull the ball to the left side of the diamond, the shortstop has to catch more sharp grounders than any other player. The true value of a shortstop to a team can be demonstrated by the 1973 New York Mets, who languished in last place for most of the season while their shortstop, Bud Harrelson, recovered from an injury. After he returned, the team made a late-season surge that took it to the division championship and eventually to the National League pennant.

The third baseman must be especially quick handed, because most balls that are hit to him are hit hard. Brooks Robinson of the Baltimore Orioles earned the nickname "the human vacuum cleaner"

by stealing many a sure base hit from American League batters. Robinson was exceptionally fine at foiling bunters, those bat-handling magicians who can transform a ninety-miles-per-hour fastball into a trickling hit that rolls tantalizingly just inside the foul line. Swooping in from third base, Robinson snatched the ball with his bare hand and in the same motion zipped the ball quickly to first base for the out. Clete Boyer spent many a year at third base with the New York Yankees despite a weak batting average simply because he could play the position so well.

Traditionally, the strongest hitters on the team play the outfield, but outfielders should be excellent fielders as well—fast, sure handed, and strong throwers. Some of the game's greatest hitting stars—Willie Mays, Henry Aaron, Roberto Clemente, Carl Yastrzemski—have often been even more effective in the field than at the plate. A fine catch or throw from an outfielder sometimes inspires a team even more than a home run.

THE OFFENSE

Ted Williams called batting the single most difficult skill in sports. Whether or not he was right, it is fairly clear that hitting has become even more difficult over the years. Williams was the last major leaguer to bat more than .400 (he hit .406 in 1941). Some new rules have been passed to help the hitter (the size of the strike zone has been reduced and the pitcher's mound has been lowered) but the sophistication of modern pitching and fielding coupled with frequent night games (when it is more difficult to see the pitch well) have made even .300 hitters a much rarer breed.

But there is a lot more to offense than merely hitting the ball well or far. Baseball teams use many strategic plays to advance a runner around the bases. These plays are usually relayed to the batter and baserunners via the third base coach with an elaborate system of hand signals.

The hit-and-run play is a play in which the runner on first will break for second base, as if he is trying to steal. His movement draws the shortstop or second baseman out of position—to second base to take the catcher's throw. But if the hit-and-run works, the catcher will never touch the ball—the batter tries to hit the pitch in the hole left by the moving infielder.

The suicide squeeze play is one of the most dramatic in baseball. It is used when a team desperately needs a run. It occurs when a runner on third base breaks for home with the pitch as if to steal home, and the batter then merely tries by bunting to keep the ball from reaching the catcher. Steals, double steals (two runners stealing simultaneously), and sacrifice plays (in which the batter's prime mission is to advance the runner rather than get on base himself) are just a few more strategems that managers use to win ball games.

Before the start of each game, the two teams must submit ·a lineup to the umpires and each other. Each manager naturally has his own ideas on who he wants to bat in each position, but there are some general rules that all managers follow. The leadoff spot is usually reserved for someone who can get on base· frequently. He is usually a singles hitter, a fast runner, and whenever possible, a switch hitter, a batter who can swing either lefty or righty. The man who bats second should be someone with good bat control, usually a hitter who doesn't strike out very much. He is the man that the manager will often call upon to execute the hit-and-run play. The first two batters are often called "the table setters" because it is their job to get on base for the heavy hitters—"the meat" of the order. The

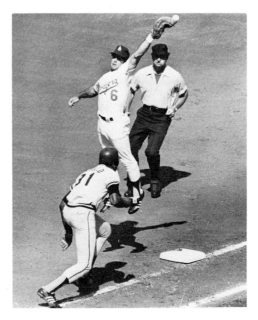

Opposite left: *For a pitcher, too high can be waist high, as Doc Ellis (17) found out, courtesy of Merv Rettenmund (14) in the 1971 World Series.* Opposite right: *Rounding third, a runner saves time by hitting only the inside corner of the bag.* Top left: *Managers like to make a scene.* Top right: *First baseman Steve Garvey needs every inch of his reach, and a bit more it seems, to nab an errant throw.* Above: *Catcher Manny Sanguillen blocks the plate.*

Bottom: *Three Rivers Stadium, Pittsburgh, Pennsylvania, during a night game. (Most major league games are at night.) The features of the modern stadium include AstroTurf or some other synthetic grass, symmetrical distances from home plate to the outfield walls, no pillars to obscure a fan's view, and a giant electronic scoreboard, whose function is not only to post the score.*

BASEBALL FIELD

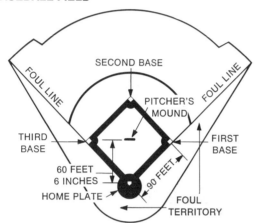

third batter is usually the best all-around hitter on the team. If one or both of the first two batters gets on base, it is the third man's job to bring them home. The fourth position, or "clean-up" spot, is reserved for the team's slugger, a power hitter who can drive in runs and hit the long ball. The remaining spots in the order are filled by the remainder of the team, usually in decreasing order of hitting ability, with the pitcher (at least in the National League, where there is no designated hitter) batting ninth.

Teams' styles vary greatly, of course. The 1963 world champion Dodgers relied primarily on superb pitching from Sandy Koufax and Don Drysdale. With the other team's score held down, the Dodgers eked out their own runs with bunts, singles, sacrifices, and steals. The Pittsburgh Pirates of the 1970s, notorious for their lack of pitching, boasted a batting order laden with sluggers down to the number seven position.

LUCK AND SUPERSTITION

A major league baseball team plays 162 games in a season that stretches from April to October. It seems fair that the season be so long, for baseball is a game of chance. Of course, players must be skillful; ball players need to be in good physical condition and must practice constantly to keep their reflexes finely tuned. One mistake can cost the team a game, and one game can cost the team a pennant. Yet all the skill in the world can't prevent the lucky bloop single over the shortstop's head or the bad-hop single that wins a ball game. A pitcher

can throw his best pitch and watch it sail out of the park. This element of chance is one of the game's attractions—the underdog always has a chance to beat the powerhouse, giving baseball the unpredictable quality that keeps fans dreaming impossible dreams.

Baseball players are known to be the most superstitious of athletes. Even the most reasonable of them may refuse to lend someone else his glove. Some players will always touch a base when running on or off the field; others never will. One player, in a particularly difficult batting slump, said he believed that he was hitting poorly because his bats were "tired," and he refused to let anyone else touch them while they were resting.

KEEPING SCORE

Baseball is probably the only sport in which many of the spectators reproduce the entire game on paper play by play. It is done by keeping a scorecard, a grid formed by lines from a side row listing players and a top column listing the inning numbers. Thus, there is a box to record what each player did each time at bat, though rarely does each player bat in each inning. The scorer assigns a number from one through nine to each player in the field in the following order: pitcher (1), catcher (2), first baseman (3), second baseman (4), third baseman (5), shortstop (6), left fielder (7), center fielder (8), and right fielder (9). A fly ball that the center fielder catches may be represented by the symbol F-8. An out on a ground ball to the shortstop would be recorded by the numbers 6-3 if the shortstop (6) threw the ball to the first baseman (3) for the out. Singles, doubles, and triples may be represented by "1B," "2B," and "3B," respectively. Home runs are registered as "HR," strikeouts with the letter "K." This scoring method or one like it is used by television broadcasters, who must recap the game at its conclusion, and by fans. Teams follow the game with even more sophistication. They keep pitching charts, on which a player in the dugout keeps track of every pitch in the game.

LITTLE LEAGUE

Each year millions of youngsters play baseball in organized leagues. The most important of these are the Little League, the Pony League (ages 13 and 14), the Babe Ruth League (ages 13 to 16), and the American Legion League (ages 17 and over). The most far-reaching junior baseball is the Little League, which has three divisions—8 to 12, 13 to 15, and 16 to 18. Today, more than two million children in 31 countries play Little League baseball. Teams in the 8 to 12 division from all over the world compete for the right to go to the annual Little League World Series each year in Williamsport, Pennsylvania, home of Little League headquarters.

With some exceptions, Little League rules are the same as those in the major leagues. The baseball diamond is smaller—60 feet between bases

and 46 feet from pitcher to home plate—but the main difference is in the style of play. In top Little League competition, the best fielding team almost always wins.

Little League has always been controversial. Many people feel that it is so intensely competitive for youngsters that it takes all the fun out of the game. In 1974, the biggest of all controversies raged. The organization, whose charter had included the terse statement, "Girls are not eligible," was ordered by the New Jersey Civil Rights Division to allow girls to play with boys in Little League games. The Little League lost its court battles and is now open to girls.

As the typical American male becomes older, slightly slower, and a little paunchy, he is likely to turn to an afternoon of softball for recreation on the weekend. After all, the ball is somewhat larger than that tiny pellet of a baseball, the bases are shorter (Little League dimensions), and the pitching (if one is in the right league) is usually lazy and inviting. However, at its highest levels (for both men and women), softball is hard work.

Softball

HISTORY

Softball is the result of a late nineteenth century attempt to adapt baseball to indoor play during the winter months. A Minneapolis firefighter, Lewis Rober, is credited with its invention, and it was in Minneapolis that the first softball league was formed, in 1900, five years after the game began.

Today, in parks and sandlots across the country, the game is played by church teams, college intramural teams, industrial teams, and teams sponsored by taverns and various civic organizations. The first national championships were held in 1933 and are now held for both men's and women's teams by the National Softball Congress and the American Softball Association.

For women, organized softball provides an outlet, however unpublicized, for some fine talent. One woman, Joan Joyce, pitcher of the champion Raybestos Brakettes of Stratford, Connecticut, has become a true star. Her impressive pitching record includes 330 wins, 70 no-hitters, and more than 4,800 strikeouts, in addition to a .316 batting average. A few years ago she pitched in an exhibition game against Ted Williams, one of baseball's greatest hitters. Williams never touched the ball.

Most championship softball games are seven innings long rather than nine, and many softball teams field ten players, the extra player being used as a fourth outfielder. He is known as the short fielder because his position is usually directly behind second base and closer to the infield than those of the other outfielders.

THE GAME

There are three basic kinds of softball: slow pitch, medium pitch, and fast pitch. In slow pitch the pitcher must loft the ball with an arc of 4 to 10 feet. Some leagues demand an arc of more than 10 feet, but in either case the ball is usually coming straight down as it crosses the plate. These slow pitches are more difficult to hit than they look.

In medium pitch the pitcher may throw as hard as he wants as long as he does not bring his pitching arm above his shoulder during the windup. Thus, "windmills" (spinning the arm in a 360-degree motion before throwing) and "slingshots" (bending the arm at the elbow and whipping the ball in) are prohibited.

In fast pitch no restrictions are placed on the pitcher's delivery, and most fast-pitch hurlers can deliver the ball at a surprisingly high speed. The fastest and best softball pitcher of all time is Eddie Feigner. He has crisscrossed the nation for years as the star of "the King and his Court," playing the best local teams with only a catcher, a first baseman, and a shortstop to back him up in the field. His fastball has been clocked at more than 100 miles per hour, and he has struck out batters pitching blindfolded, behind the back, and under the legs, among other ways. At last count, Feigner had chalked up more than 750 no-hitters, including more than 200 perfect games.

GLOSSARY

Around the horn: A maneuver that involves throwing the ball from third to second to first, or just generally to each infielder successively. It may describe a real play or it may be just an exercise for infielders after a put-out when there are no runners on base.

Bag: Any base other than home plate.

Balk: A kind of illegal motion by the pitcher when there are runners on base. There are many ways a pitcher can commit a balk, but it usually involves a feint; he makes a motion as though to pitch or throw to one of the bases but doesn't. When a pitcher is called for a balk, all baserunners advance one base.

Ball: A pitch that the batter does not swing at and that is not in the strike zone.

Baltimore chop: A batted ball that bounces high just in front of the plate. Also called a bounder or chopper.

Base coach: Each team has two base coaches while at bat. One stands in a box near first base, the other in a box near third base. They tell runners when to run, when to slide, and so on. The third base coach often gives signals to the batter to tell him whether to take the pitch, swing away, or bunt.

Base on balls: The accumulation of four balls by a batter, entitling him to reach first base. A base on balls, or walk, does not count as a time at bat in the box score or when a player's batting average is computed.

Batting average: A percentage figure that tells how often a batter is successful in getting a hit. It is computed by dividing the number of times at bat into the number of hits.

Batting cage: A portable wire-mesh screen that surrounds the home plate area on three sides. In the majors it is used only for batting practice.

Bobble: A momentary mistake while fielding the ball. It may or may not become an error.

Boot: To kick the ball while attempting to field it. Sometimes used to refer to any fielding miscue.

Box score: An abbreviated method of listing a game's statistics. There are different forms of box scores, but all list each player who entered the game, his at-bats, runs, and hits.

Bullpen: An area, often behind the outfield fences, where pitchers warm up before entering the game.

Bunt: To block the ball with the bat, rather than swinging away, thereby causing the ball to go only a very short distance. Used as a sacrifice or as a means of reaching base.

Bush league: A minor league.

Called strike: A pitch that the batter does not swing at and is in the strike zone.

Cellar: Last place in the league standings.

Choke up: To grip the ball several inches above the end of the handle. Choking up increases the accuracy of a swing but reduces its power.

Clothesline drive: A line drive.

Count: The record of balls and strikes on a batter.

Double: A two-base hit.

Doubleheader: Two games played on the same day.

Down the pipe: A waist-high strike across the center of the plate.

Dugout: The sheltered area next to the field, usually several feet below ground level, where players sit when not actively engaged in the game.

Duster: A pitch that causes the batter to fall to the ground to avoid being hit. Also called a brush-back pitch.

Earned run: A run that the batting team gains on its own, without help from fielding errors.

Earned run average (ERA): The average number of earned runs a pitcher has allowed per nine innings.

Error: A mistake made by a fielder that allows a batter or runner to reach a base he otherwise could not have reached.

Fair ball: A batted ball on which the batter may reach base. Although not all fair balls start or end in fair territory—that is, between the foul lines—all of them pass through it at some point.

Fielder's choice: A decision of a fielder to let one man reach base safely while attempting to put out another man.

Foul ball: A batted ball on which the batter may not reach base because it is hit outside the foul lines, in foul territory. If a foul ball is caught on the fly, it is an out. Otherwise, it is a strike, but a foul cannot be the third strike unless it is a foul tip caught by the catcher or a bunt.

Fungo: A batted ball that the batter throws into the air himself and then hits to fielders for practice.

Some players make it a common practice to
get hit by pitched balls. Ron Hunt managed
to do it fifty times one season, a record.

There are special fungo bats, longer than regular bats and with thinner handles.

Full count: Three balls and two strikes on the batter.

Gopher ball: A pitch that is hit for a home run.

Grand slam: A home run hit when the bases are loaded.

Grapefruit League: A nickname for preseason exhibition games played in Florida.

Ground-rule double: A two-base hit on which the ball is ruled dead before the play is completed. It usually occurs when a hit lands in fair territory and then bounces over the outfield fence. The batter is given an automatic two-base hit and all baserunners advance two bases.

Hit: A fair ball on which the batter reaches base without the help of an error by the fielders. Also used to refer to any batted ball, fair or foul.

Hit and run; run and hit: An offensive tactic in which all baserunners begin to run as soon as the ball is pitched and the batter tries to hit it through the spot vacated by an infielder who has moved to cover the base toward which the runner is moving.

Hit by a pitch: A batter being struck on any part of his body by a pitched ball. He advances to first.

Home run: A four-base hit. Most home runs are hit

Some people contend that hitting a baseball is the most difficult task in sports. Confronted with pitches traveling as fast as 100 miles per hour, a batter has less than a second to decide whether to swing.

into the stands or over the outfield fence, but it is possible to hit an inside-the-park home run.

Intentional walk: A defensive maneuver in which the batter is purposely given a base on balls. Intentional walks are most often given to good hitters when a weaker hitter is up next. They are also given when there are one or two baserunners but first base is vacant. Walking the batter makes a force play, and thus a double play, possible.

Junior circuit: The American League, so-called because it was founded later than the National League.

Knocked out of the box: An expression for a pitcher's removal from a game because the other team is hitting his pitching well.

Line drive: A fly ball that is hit hard and low.

Line score: A concise, inning-by-inning summary of scoring. At its end it lists the final score and each team's total of hits and errors.

Passed ball: A catcher's error that occurs when the catcher lets a catchable pitch get past him, allowing a baserunner to advance.

Pine-tar rag: A cloth with pine tar, a sticky substance, on it. A batter rubs his bat with the rag to help him grip the bat more firmly.

Pitchout: A defensive maneuver on which the pitcher throws the ball wide of the plate so that the catcher receives it in a better position to try to pick off a baserunner or to throw out a runner who is trying to steal a base.

Pop-up: A high but not very long fly ball. Also called a pop fly, or, if foul, a pop foul.

Rally: A scoring burst by the team that trails in the score.

Resin bag: A small pouch filled with resin. It is kept near the pitcher's mound. Pitchers pick it up to give their fingers a better grip on the ball.

Rhubarb: An argument, usually over an umpire's decision.

Round tripper: A home run.

Run batted in (RBI): Credit given to the batter whose batting causes a run to score. A batter is given credit for an RBI if he walks with the bases loaded but not for a run scored on his turn at bat because of an error or during a double play.

Sacrifice bunt: A bunt that the batter places so as to allow a baserunner to advance while the batter himself is thrown out at first. A sacrifice bunt does not count as a time at bat.

Sacrifice fly: A fly ball to the outfield on which the baserunner tags up and scores after the catch.

Senior Circuit: The National League, so called because it is the older major league.

Shift: The defensive alignment of the infielders when three of them are on one side of the infield, leaving only one on the other. Normally there are two infielders on each side.

Shoestring catch: A catch, often spectacular, made by a fielder who charges in and catches a fly ball just before it touches the ground, seemingly off his shoestrings.

Shutout: A game in which the losers score no runs.

Single: A one-base hit.

Southpaw: A player, usually a pitcher, who throws left handed.

Spitball: An illegally moistened pitched ball. The pitch breaks downward and occasionally to the side.

Squeeze play: An offensive maneuver in which the batter bunts, attempting to score a baserunner from third. On a "safety squeeze" the baserunner hesitates until the ball is bunted and he thinks it is safe to run. On the suicide squeeze, the baserunner begins to run with the pitch.

Stolen base: The base gained by a baserunner advancing on his own, without benefit of a batted ball, passed ball, or a wild pitch. When two baserunners steal bases simultaneously, the play is called a double steal.

Stretch: The position from which the pitcher delivers the ball when there are one or more baserunners.

Strike: A pitch that is swung at and missed, is hit into foul territory with less than two strikes already called, or is not swung at and is in the strike zone.

Strikeout: An out registered when the batter accumulates a third strike. He may do so by swinging and missing a pitch or by not taking a pitch that is in the strike zone. A foul ball is not a third strike unless it is a bunt. Striking out is often referred to as "fanning."

Strike zone: The area over home plate between the batter's knees and armpits.

Swinging away: Taking a full swing at a pitch.

Switch hitter: A player who can bat from either side of the plate.

Tagging up: A baserunner touching his base after a fly ball is caught.

Taking a pitch: Allowing a pitch to go by without swinging at it.

Texas leaguer: A short, looping fly ball that threatens to fall between the infielders and outfielders. Also called a "blooper."

Triple: A three-base hit.

Triple crown: The figurative award a batter wins when he leads the league for a season in batting average, home runs, and runs batted in.

Triple play: A play, very rare, on which three outs are made.

Utility player: A player who can play several positions but who is usually not a regular at any of them.

Walk: A base on balls.

Warning track: A dirt track next to the outfield wall. It allows an outfielder to judge his distance from the wall while he is tracking a fly ball without taking his eye off the ball.

Wild pitch: A pitching error, which results in the pitch going past the catcher and allows a baserunner to advance.

Windup: The motion used by the pitcher to add speed to his pitch. When there are baserunners, the pitcher usually takes no windup because he is not permitted to throw to the bases once the windup has begun.

Basketball

As fast, exciting, high-scoring, and American as the pinball machine, basketball is one of this country's most popular exports. A young sport, its rules still changing, it is already the second most popular team sport in the world. Many people argue that basketball tests as many skills as the decathlon and that basketball players, who must run, jump, shoot, think fast, and resist fatigue, may be the most gifted athletes in the world.

Basketball was an invented game. But it didn't spring full-blown from the head of its creator. After Dr. James Naismith hung up his famous peach baskets, basketball evolved a great deal, as most sports have. Rules changes and the on-court inventiveness of gifted players have transformed basketball over the years into a game scarcely similar to and far more beautiful than the plodding original version. Much of the credit must go to black play-

ers, bred largely in the schoolyards of America's urban ghettos. From the one-on-one and other pickup games there came new ideas, such as shooters hanging almost interminably in the air before finally releasing the ball—standard procedure in the game today.

HISTORY

During the winter of 1891, Dr. James Naismith, a YMCA instructor in Springfield, Massachusetts, tried to divert his bored calisthenics classes with a new game. Each team tried to score points by moving a soccer ball into a goal. The object of the game was certainly not original, but the goals themselves were—two peach baskets hung 10 feet above the ground at either end of the gymnasium. These elevated goals gave the game its character and its name.

America's big universities are the finishing schools for the best basketball players in the country—such as UCLA's Bill Walton, opposite, *and Indiana's Quinn Buckner,* above. *Years ago Madison Square Garden would have been their prime showcase. The Garden today,* above right, *is still glamorous but less prestigious.*

Any number could play the game, but to accommodate the 18 students in his class, Naismith decided on nine players per side. (By 1897, the number of players per side had been reduced to five.) Naismith's original 13 rules were quite practical, designed to prevent mayhem in the small enclosed area of the basketball court. Thus, running with the ball, cradling it under the arm football style, pushing, tripping, and striking were forbidden, and basketball gained a nonviolent tradition, which it has preserved, though greatly modified, through today.

The game spread more quickly perhaps than any other. The YMCA helped popularize the game, and in 1898, the first professional league, the National Basketball League, was formed. The pro game was fitful at best. Leagues came and went, though a few teams, such as the Original Celtics and the Troy, New York, Trojans, were quite successful. Those first pros played for meager salaries in trying circumstances. The game was rough because there was no limit to the number of fouls a player could commit, nor were substitutions allowed. Players threw their opponents against the wire-mesh cages surrounding the early courts and local "rooters" pestered the visiting players by hurling projectiles through the screens at them. In those days home court advantage was more real than psychological.

Early college basketball was more subdued and more popular than the pro game. A team's appeal was mostly regional, but a few teams toured. When Yale's Bulldogs went on tour in 1899, they billed their journey as "the longest trip ever taken by a United States college team."

Basketball really hit the big time in the thirties. In 1934, a sportswriter for the New York *World Telegram*, Ned Irish, had the profitable inspiration to promote college games in New York's Madison Square Garden. No less than 16,138 fans attended Irish's very first basketball doubleheader, in which St. John's played Westminster and New York University played Notre Dame. Such instant success bred two postseason college basketball tournaments that today are the brightest stars in a galaxy of tournaments: the National Invitation Tournament, also held in the Garden, and the nationwide National Collegiate Athletic Association (NCAA) Tournament, the winner of which is crowned the national champion.

Rules changes such as the elimination of the center jump after each goal quickened the game and widened its appeal, but popularity was not without its price. Basketball is a sport quite vulnerable to fixing, because one or two players on a team can easily and unnoticeably affect the outcome of a game or the margin of decision—"the point spread." The bettor's object is to "beat the spread," that is, correctly predict that one team will win more or less handily than the bookmaker predicts. Only when the bookmaker rates the game a toss-up is the bettor wagering solely on who will win. By the fifties, betting on the college contests had become quite heavy, and with so much money riding on easily manipulated point spreads, college players were drawn into "shaving" the point spreads in return for payments from certain bettors. In 1951 and again in 1961, such bribes for point shaving were uncovered, and the resulting scandals ruined the careers of some promising players.

In the sixties and early seventies, UCLA ruled college basketball, often without serious challenge. Coached by John Wooden and led by such nimble giants as Lew Alcindor and Bill Walton, the Bruins at one point amassed 88 consecutive victories, a feat so stunning that while it lasted many fans and writers all but conceded each year's national championship to the Bruins even before the season began. (They were right nine of eleven times from 1964 to 1974.) Even before UCLA finally ended its winning streak, in 1974 against Notre Dame, the same team that had last beaten the Bruins, sportswriters pronounced the Californians' winning streak the most impressive team achievement in sports history.

THE PROS

As exciting as the college game can be, the highest level of play has long been professional. The pro game has grown steadily since 1946, when the Basketball Association of America and the National Basketball League merged to form the National Basketball Association, better known as the NBA.

The league's first superstar was the giant George Mikan of the Minneapolis Lakers. At 6 feet 9 inches, he exacted frustration and admiration from the opposition. (One coach called him "a monster"; another team owner offered to trade his entire team for Mikan.) Mikan was the first of basketball's big men, the giants who can almost singlehandedly change a losing team into a winning one.

In 1954, the NBA took an important step to ensure that the pro game would be, if nothing else, fast. It instituted the 24-second rule, which stipulated that a team had to take a shot within 24 seconds after gaining possession of the ball. No longer would the professionals be permitted the stalling techniques that even today occasionally plague the college game.

The NBA's next star was a team, the Boston Celtics, led by Bill Russell, Bill Sharman, and Bob Cousy. Cousy was one of the finest, trickiest ball handlers ever, a master of the behind-the-back dribble and pass. The 6-foot 9-inch Russell joined the Celtics in 1957, swept an average of 20 rebounds off the boards that year, and led the team to 11 championships in 13 seasons. Playing center, he did what no one had done before him—he leaped high into the air to block shots before they descended. In an era of runaway scoring, he refocused the attention of basketball strategists on defense (particularly team defense, though at times he seemed to be a team himself). He so flustered other centers, even the taller, high-scoring Wilt

Chamberlain, that they became afraid to shoot with him nearby.

Chamberlain was in many respects the antithesis of Russell—clumsy where Russell was graceful, brutally direct where Russell was artful. At first the 7-foot 2-inch Chamberlain was simply a magnificent scoring machine. In 1962, while playing for the Philadelphia Warriors, he scored a phenomenal 100 points in one game, hitting 36 of 63 field goal attempts and 28 of 32 free throws. Chamberlain would not have reached 100 points had not his teammates kept feeding him the ball. Nonetheless, his performance was amazing and his record is not likely to fall soon.

Of course the Warriors won that game, but it soon became clear that seven-foot scoring machines did not, strange as it seemed, guarantee successful teams. Only when Chamberlain began to acquire the defensive tactics of Russell, his rival and friend, did his teams begin to win as consistently as Russell's Celtics.

Chamberlain, Russell, and most of today's pro basketball players are black, but basketball has not always been integrated. In 1927, when Abe Saperstein organized the Harlem Globetrotters, teams were all black or all white. Some of the best black players (including Chamberlain) toured with the Globetrotters, probably the most famous group of basketball players in the world. The Globetrotters don't play basketball so much as play with it. Their "games" are staged exhibitions of ballhandling and clowning loosely organized around the framework of a game and usually played against the same team of touring opponents. The Globetrotters perform such stunts as drop-kicking the ball into the basket, bouncing it through the legs and off the heads of their befuddled opponents, and sneakily substituting deflated or overinflated balls. The current master of the mischief is Meadowlark Lemon, an ageless basketball wizard and slapstick comedian.

The NBA lost its monopoly on professional basketball in 1967 when the American Basketball Association (ABA) was formed. The birth of a new league set the stage for the 1968 struggle for another black star, 7-foot Lew Alcindor, the finest college player in years and perhaps ever. Alcindor (who became a Muslim in 1971 and took the name Kareem Abdul-Jabbar) eventually signed with the NBA's Milwaukee Bucks for a reported $1.4 million to be paid over four years. Within three years Jabbar had reversed the team's fortune, leading the Bucks to the NBA championship in 1971.

The natural result of the formation of another league was predictable: players would "jump," enticed by the salary offers of a new league struggling to attract stars at whatever the price. And the older league would be forced at least to rival the salaries of the new circuit. Naturally, the players welcomed the pay raises the competition brought. Today, American basketball players are, as a group, the highest paid athletes in the world. The men who pay the salaries, the owners of the teams, looked wistfully to the possibility of merging the two leagues. In 1976, after long and hard negotiations, they finally achieved their objective. Four teams from the ABA, the New York Nets, the Denver Nuggets, the Indiana Pacers, and the San Antonio Spurs, joined the NBA, and the other ABA teams went out of existence.

In the NBA, the regular season runs for 82 games, beginning in October. The long regular season is followed by a series of playoffs. The winner of the playoffs is considered that year's champion, so postseason play has had the strange effect of making the entire regular season almost irrelevant. A team that finishes first during the regular season has no guarantee of even reaching the finals of the playoffs.

COURT AND EQUIPMENT

Basketball is one of the most accessible of sports. It can be played indoors or outdoors, on wood, cement, and sometimes dirt, on full-size courts or half-courts, with five-man teams or one against one. In addition, it is one of the few games that can be fun just to play alone. Many a champion has started out this way, perfecting his shots and his moves against an invisible crowd of opponents.

Collegiate and professional play is on a court 94 feet long by 50 feet wide. For grade school and high school players, who haven't as much stamina, the court is shortened by 10 feet.

By the sixties the great little men, such as Bob Cousy, driving above, had yielded much of their influence on the game to the great big men, the biggest of whom was Wilt Chamberlain, 13, left. His heir on the Los Angeles Lakers was Kareem Abdul-Jabbar, opposite.

BASKETBALL COURT

```
            BACKBOARD
            54 INCHES              4 FEET
                                   15 FEET

                     FREE-
                     THROW
                     LINE

                 RESTRAINING CIRCLE
                 6-FOOT RADIUS

                          CENTER
                          CIRCLE
                          2-FOOT
                          RADIUS

        CIRCLE
        6-FOOT
        RADIUS

                      6
                     FEET
        BASKET
        18 INCHES
```

84 FEET OR 94 FEET MAXIMUM

SIDELINE

76 FEET OR 86 FEET

END LINE
50 FEET MAXIMUM

Above right: Oscar Robertson makes dribbling a basketball seem easier than it is; the dribbler must control the ball without looking at it. Opposite left: Referee calls a foul on Dave DeBusschere by indicating his number. Opposite right: On a foul shot, players anticipate a rebound by moving into the foul lane as the ball leaves the shooter's hands.

In all cases the rim of the basket is 10 feet off the ground, the same as the height of the balconies to which Naismith first nailed his peach baskets. The basket itself consists of a metal ring, 18 inches in diameter, supporting a net basket. Narrower at the bottom than at the top, the net slows the ball slightly as it passes through and adds immeasurably to the pleasure of scoring a basket. (Anyone who has played with a net and without one will agree that a ball swishing through a net gives a much more satisfying effect than one silently passing through a naked hoop.) Of course, the net has a practical purpose as well: to make it apparent when a basket has been made.

The novice's boon, the backboard, was not always part of the game. Children dangling their legs from the balconies used to kick the ball away from the basket, so Naismith had to put up some backboards as a shield for the basket. The first "backboards" were sometimes constructed of flimsy, unreliable chicken wire or weak metal. Today, of course, it is essential that a backboard give a true bounce. The best backboards are glass or Plexiglas, but any rigid, flat material, such as wood or heavy metal, is suitable. For indoor play the board is usually rectangular, four feet high by six feet wide; outdoor backboards are often fan or kidney shaped.

The ball may be rubber, leather, or a "synthetic" leather with a grippable, pebbled surface. The leather-covered basketball is the best because it doesn't bounce as crazily off the rim as the rubber ball does, but it has a shorter life span on a cement surface. Balls are 9 inches in diameter, so there is much room for error as they approach the 18-inch hoop. They are inflated to weigh between 20 and 22 ounces.

THE GAME

Basketball is a taxing sport, so it is only natural that the stronger and older players play longer games. However, basketball players cannot usually maintain themselves at peak levels for long. Most pros retire in their early thirties. The professional game consists of four 12-minute quarters; the college and international game of two 20-minute halves; high school games of four 8-minute quarters. Games played between teams younger than high school age usually last for four 6-minute quarters.

Each team has a given number of timeouts. The clock is also stopped for violations, free throws, injuries, and whenever the officials think it will take an unusual amount of time to restart play after a whistle. Unlimited substitutions may be made whenever the clock isn't running. (The clock is restarted not when the ball is thrown in bounds, but when a player on the court touches it.)

If regulation play ends in a tie, the game goes into overtime. Professional and college teams play five-minute overtime periods. High school and younger teams play three-minute overtimes. If the game is tied at the end of an overtime period, as many more periods as necessary are completed until one team holds an advantage at the end of one.

Compared with today's game, the old-style basketball was fairly sluggish. First of all, there were all those center jumps—after every basket. Not only was this regimen tedious, but it gave an unfair advantage to a team with a tall man. So the center jump was drastically limited in 1937, and team scores soared. Today, the jump ball at center court is used to start only each half of the game. The guards line up next to their opposing forwards, the forwards next to the opposing guards, all outside the small restraining circle at center court. There, the referee tosses the ball straight into the air, and the two centers leap for it, each trying to tap it to one of his teammates.

The man who gains possession after the jump tries to advance the ball by dribbling—running downcourt while bouncing the ball with one hand—and passing to his teammates. The purpose is simple: to shoot the ball into the basket for what is officially termed a field goal, worth two points.

The defending team tries to frustrate these attempts by stealing the ball as it is dribbled, or by intercepting a pass, if possible, but most likely by

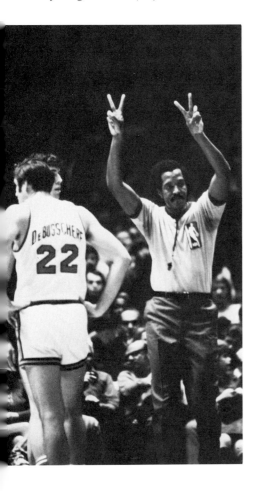

grabbing the rebound of a missed shot. After each field goal, or basket, the team that yielded it puts the ball in play from behind the end line beneath the basket where the points were scored, and the new offensive team tries to score at the other end of the court.

FOULS AND VIOLATIONS

The two men who officiate a basketball game, the referees, have one of the most difficult jobs of officiating in any sport. Before the end of the game, their judgments, of which there are many, will usually offend everyone—fans, players, and coaches. And in a sense, the critics will be right, for a perfectly officiated game is a perfect impossibility.

The refs do have some relatively easy calls such as traveling, goaltending, out-of-bounds, and double dribble. Traveling is running or walking with the ball without dribbling, and double dribbling is using both hands to dribble the ball or halting the dribble, then resuming it. Both these violations cost a team possession of the ball. Goaltending, interfering with a shot on its *downward* path to the basket, results in two points being awarded to the offended team. A ball knocked out of bounds is awarded to the team that did not last touch it. The team throwing the ball back in has to do so quickly—in five seconds. These common infractions are relatively easy for the refs to spot.

The referees' most difficult problems all involve body contact. Theoretically, basketball is not a body contact sport—which is not to say there is no contact. Sometimes the shoving is not only jarring and even vicious, but unprovoked. The more intense the competition, the rougher the sport and the more difficult to penalize each infraction. In the pros the action under the basket becomes rather brutal. Broken noses and knocked-out teeth are common. The action is so fast and close that it is hard for either referee to tell who did what to whom. And even if he can, he is restricted because he knows that if he calls every foul the game will become one long free-throw contest. He must call a substantial amount of fouls and, above all, call them consistently if he hopes to keep the game under control.

The referee has to establish a delicate balance between offense and defense. The player driving for the basket rightfully claims freedom from interference, to be able to score. But the defending team must not be penalized for merely standing its ground. The basic rule is that every player on the court has equal rights to any spot not already occupied by another player. However, once an offensive player has established a line of movement, a defender may not run into him, and once a defender has established a stationary position, an offensive player may not run into him.

Holding, pushing, pulling, striking, bumping into or tripping another player are all personal fouls. (The pros permit "hand guarding"—the defender's

44

method of keeping track of his opposite number by constantly touching him with the open hand. Some players complain that "hand guarding" often becomes "hand shoving.") If a player is fouled in the act of shooting, he receives two free throws from the free-throw line, 15 feet from the basket (see diagram). If he is not in the act of shooting, the fouled player may receive one shot or none at all.

A foul committed by a player in possession of the ball or by a teammate of that player is called an offensive foul and results in loss of the ball to the other team. Backcourt fouls, fouls a defensive player commits before the offense crosses the center line, result in two free throws for the offended player.

One can easily see that even with the referees calling fouls discreetly, the game could become a parade to the foul lines. Recently, the NBA adopted a new rule to make the game more lively. A loose-ball foul, a foul committed when neither team has clear possession of the ball, such as when two players are vying for a loose rebound, is now penalized simply by granting the victimized team possession of the ball. The ABA has only a very limited loose-ball rule: rebounding fouls committed by the team that shot the ball are not penalized by free throws.

All fouls (including the loose-ball foul) are registered both against the player guilty of the infraction (personal fouls) and against his team (team fouls). In the pros each player must leave the game after his sixth personal foul. College and high school players leave, or foul out, after their fifth. In pro ball each team is allowed four team fouls per quarter. The fifth puts the team into a penalty situation, in which the rules for awarding free throws change significantly. One-shot fouls become two-shot fouls. A player fouled either intentionally, in the act of shooting, or in the backcourt gets three chances to make two free throws. Loose-ball fouls and offensive fouls are penalized by giving two free throws to the offended team.

In college and high school play, the rule is a bit different. Teams are allowed six team fouls per half. When a team goes over the limit, two-shot fouls become three chances to make two free throws. One-shot fouls are increased to two only if the first free throw is made (the one-and-one situation).

For a free-throw attempt, three players from each team line up on opposite sides of the 12-foot-wide foul lane, a player from the defensive team closest to the basket on either side of the lane. Technically, the players may not enter the lane until the free throw touches the rim of the backboard. During normal play, no player from the offensive team may remain inside the foul lane for more than three seconds at a time (whether he has the ball or not) unless the ball is on the rim and he is fighting for the rebound. Without this three-second rule the offensive team could simply station its biggest man directly underneath the basket for an easy field goal or offensive rebound.

Elements of a good shot: Above: *Walt Frazier stops suddenly to shake his man.* Opposite left: *Pete Maravich has eyes only for his target.* Opposite right: *Oscar Robertson gets off the ground and flicks the wrist.*

45

Technical fouls are called for unsportsmanlike conduct, illegal delay of the game, illegal substitutions, or illegal timeouts (that is, calling a timeout when the allowed number has already been used). Technical fouls may also be called on anyone affiliated with the team, whether on the court or on the bench. Technicals are even called on overly partisan home-team fans. For a technical foul the referee awards one free throw, which any team member on the court may shoot. In college ball the team that shoots the free throw is also awarded possession afterward; in the pros the ball is kept by the team that had it when the foul was called. Technical fouls are not counted as team fouls or personal fouls.

SHOTS

The old style of basketball, which persisted well into the thirties, made heavy use of the backboard. Shots were banked into the basket much the way a pool ball is angled off a cushion into the pocket. Today, however, most players try to shoot the ball as cleanly as possible into the basket, avoiding bounces off hoop and backboard.

The two-handed set shot was basketball's first staple shot. Although today it is not used on higher levels, it is still a useful shot for young players who aren't strong enough to attempt one-handers. The ball is held in both hands as low as the chest or as high as the top of the head. The fingers are spread, the thumbs to the rear of the ball. The knees and elbows are bent slightly, and the body uncoils as the shot is taken, sometimes with a slight jump. Before Hank Luisetti, the great Stanford College player of the thirties, most shots were two-handed sets or lay-ups. Luisetti did something no one had done before—he shot the ball with one hand. Firing one-handed sets and one-handed shots taken on the run or in the air, Luisetti amazed fans and turned basketball upside down. His play for Stanford in 1936 in Madison Square Garden drew this comment from the *New York Times:* "It seemed Luisetti could do nothing wrong. Some of his shots would have been deemed foolhardy if attempted by anyone else, but with Luisetti shooting, these were accepted by the enchanted crowd."

The one-hand set, like the two-hand variety, is taken with the feet firmly planted, one foot slightly ahead. The elbow is pointed up, the wrist cocked, and the shooting hand right under the ball. The free hand is used to steady the ball till the shot begins. The knees bend slightly, and the ball is pushed up and forward, almost "rolling" off the fingertips, to produce backspin, the "soft touch" that allows an imperfectly aimed shot to balance on the rim and perhaps fall in the basket.

A tightly guarded player has no chance to take a set shot. To shake his defender, he jumps in the air and attempts one of the many versions of the jump shot. Because it is taken while the shooter is in motion, the jump shot is more difficult to sink, but the pros have perfected this maneuver. Almost all their shots today are taken from midair. The player jumps high and takes the shot while at the peak of his jump. The really skillful player also uses the jump shot to draw a foul. He fakes a shot, causing his defender to jump prematurely, and then as the defender comes down, the shooter jumps so that he is clipped on the way up—enough for a foul to be called but not enough to stop the shot. There are other ways, too, to draw a foul in the act of shooting. The most common is simply to prolong the act as much as possible, by hanging in midair and hoping that an overzealous defender will reach too quickly or inaccurately to block the shot.

Used only sparingly in professional play, the hook shot takes a while to learn and requires good coordination. It is taken with the hand farther from the basket and the shooter's back turned partly away from the hoop, his body between the ball and the defender. The shooter's arm makes a sweeping arc over the head, the ball being released when it is farthest from the body, the basket, and the defender. Taken by a big man, the shot is almost impossible to block. But because the shooter is not really looking at the basket, the hook shot is not one

Big men shooting—opposite top: *Kareem Abdul-Jabbar's sky hook;* opposite left: *Julius Erving driving for a lay-up; and* opposite right: *making one.* Big men rebounding—top: *Spencer Haywood;* bottom: *George McGinnis.*

of basketball's most consistent shots. Today's master of it is Kareem Abdul-Jabbar, who perfected it under John Wooden at UCLA. He has demoralized opponents with it ever since.

The lay-up is the player's bread and butter. The first to be learned, it is also the most reliable. Lay-ups are shots taken by a player driving for the basket. The right-handed shooter leaves the ground from his right foot as he approaches the basket and then may either bank the ball off the backboard into the hoop or simply "lay" it in over the rim. (Players should be able to make lay-ups with either hand and from either side.) A driving lay-up, particularly the hanging-in-midair sort, often forces a defender to foul.

In 1967, when the high-flying Lew Alcindor was slamming the ball down through the hoop, the "stuff," or "dunk," shot was made illegal in college basketball. (Repeal came in 1976, forced by fans who argued that the play was exciting and not harmful to the game. Dunking is quite permissible in the pros and in international play, and a sure-fire crowd pleaser.)

STRATEGY

One of the greatest compliments that can be paid a player is to call him "unselfish." The cliché "basketball is a team game" is so often repeated because many players, even professionals, forget it. An unselfish player is one who passes up a chance to shoot if he sees a teammate has a better chance. There's something about the feel of a basketball in the hands that sometimes inspires even the most lucid, game-hardened player to send it arching for the basket, even from thirty feet away. Such lack of discipline is particularly common in the game today, when many teams use the fast-break style of play, in which the offensive team tries to move downcourt as quickly as possible, often by means of long passes, as soon as it gains possession of the ball. "Shoot-and-run" basketball is sometimes more exhilarating than effective. A good coach restrains his players with the admonition, "Look for the open man, the *good* shot," and the successful team will find the percentage shot, though it means overcoming the instinct to shoot at less-opportune moments.

Once, the terms "forward," "guard," and "center," dictated the players' functions and skills. In today's game, a player must be skilled in all areas to take advantage of any opportunity. Nevertheless, some characteristics separate players.

Generally, the center is the team's tallest player or its best jumper. He usually plays close to the basket, where his height is the best asset for shooting and pulling down rebounds. The team that captures the most rebounds takes the most shots and usually wins. In fast-break basketball a team with a center who gets a lot of rebounds can send its speedier players racing downcourt in an attempt to sneak behind the other team for quick downcourt passes and easy lay-ups or open jump shots.

The forwards, or corner men, flanking the center, should be fairly tall and be good jumpers and accurate shooters from close range. On defense they must be rugged enough to withstand the body contact under the boards, where they will be helping the center rebound.

Guards needn't be quite as tall, though some pro guards today are as tall as 6 feet 6 inches. They do have to be good ball handlers, quick and tricky. One of the guards will bring the ball upcourt and begin to develop the play with a pass. Guards often shoot from farther away, so they should have an accurate outside shot, but the best guards are those who can penetrate close to the basket, challenging the big men to switch to them, then passing to their own big men for close-in shots. Basketball is often a game of creating and capitalizing on mismatches or shifting defenses, and an accomplished guard can cause both. Quite naturally, the fine-shooting guards have the advantage as playmakers, because the defense cannot lay back waiting for the pass but must guard against the quick jumper as well. The great Oscar Robertson had the infuriating talent of popping in jumpers consistently until the defense strayed for a moment from the other players. At this point Robertson would quickly whip a perfect pass to the open man, whose greatest task was enduring the embarrassment of scoring so easily.

THE STALL

The opposite of the fast break is the stall, sometimes used by badly outclassed teams. Because of the 24-second rule, the stall is impossible in professional play, but a college team that wants to win badly enough can freeze the ball by passing back and forth until it feels that its chances of scoring are excellent. Fans, of course, despise the stall, which is one of the reasons the pros outlawed it.

DEFENSE

There is no doubt that shooting is the most spectacular part of the game. Among most fans and even sportswriters, the high scorer excites more admiration than the tenacious defender. But the most winning type of basketball calls for grudging, hand-in-the-face defense in addition to proficient scoring. Teams such as the Boston Celtics in the Bill Russell years and the New York Knicks with Walt Frazier and Dave DeBusschere were probably stronger on defense than on offense, and they won championships as a result. Basketball is a team game, especially on defense.

The defender is always at a slight disadvantage because theoretically only the man with the ball knows what he will do with it. Dribbling on one side of his body or the other, passing, or shooting, he has the split-second advantage. A smart defender observes the other players until he can anticipate their reactions in many situations. He can even do some faking of his own to steal the ball. He can harry the opposition into "forcing" shots or bad passes. Most important, the good defensive team must "control the boards," that is, the rebounds. A

In a man-to-man defense, one person's breakdown can be critical. Opposite bottom: *The player at left seems to have beaten his man, and his teammate is willing to risk a cross-court pass to get the ball to him.* Opposite top: *Double-teaming the ball is exciting but risky.*

defense can rarely afford to allow the shooters a second chance or follow-up.

The two basic types of defensive systems are man-to-man and zone. In a man-to-man system, as the name implies, each man has responsibility for guarding one opponent. In a zone defense each player defends a certain area of the floor and is responsible for guarding any player who moves into that area. The basic idea of a zone is to keep players away from the basket by forming a kind of flexible wall to repulse invaders. There are many zone systems, and a coach will often use more than one in a game. The zone is defense with a vengeance, often used by weaker or less talented teams against stronger ones. A zone is less taxing on the players, who don't have to hustle as much as they would if they were each defending against one man.

In professional play zones are illegal. Zones take time to penetrate, so permitting them would transform the pro game into an outside-shooting barrage. Still, the pros make good use of one zone-like tactic: switching. A switch occurs when one defender is blocked out or otherwise loses his man in the fast action. He then yells to the teammate nearest the man he was just guarding to take his man while he picks up his teammate's man. In general the fewer switches the better. However, particularly quick players (Walt Frazier of the Knicks, for example) seem to make an asset of switching, recovering more quickly than the opponents calculate and stealing a dribble or intercepting a pass just when it seemed the offense had the defense helplessly out of position.

WOMEN'S BASKETBALL

"In a game of basketball played in public between the young ladies of Rowland Seminary and those of City High School, the play became so rough that two young ladies of the former institution fainted at the close of the first half, and during the second the captain of the Rowland Hall team, Miss Etta Wagner, was knocked unconscious."

It has taken women's basketball, like other women's sports, a long time to outlive its "unladylike" image. Senda Berenson, an instructor at Smith College in Massachusetts, modified the game to make it less rough. Since people thought girls lacked the stamina to run up and down the court, players were confined to one of three sections on the floor. Teams were made up of six players, and players were required to pass or shoot after a modest three-bounce dribble. Quite a few years later, in 1932, the court was divided in half; but each team still consisted of three forwards and three guards, the former restricted to the front court, the latter to the backcourt.

Rules continued to change as people recognized that women weren't so weak after all. For women playing in the sixties, each season brought a new refinement. "Which game are we playing this year?" became a common question-complaint. In 1962, the Division for Girls' and Women's Sports sanctioned the roving player (a player who could cover the full court) and in 1969 allowed the unlimited dribble. Finally, in 1971, a five-player game and a 30-second clock were adopted, making women's basketball the only amateur basketball with a time limit for shooting.

Despite all these changes, or perhaps because of them, basketball is the most popular girls' high school sport in the country. Some two hundred thousand players participate. In the state of Iowa, girls' high school basketball outdraws the boys' game, and the champions, unlike most girl ath-

Fast and action-packed, women's basketball has become similar to the men's game.

letes in school team sports, are virtual celebrities.

Despite official rules changes, women's basketball still lacks uniform rules. (In Iowa, for example, the six-player, halfcourt, three-dribble game is used.) Such confusing variations from region to region may disappear as more and more women participate. In 1976, women's basketball became an Olympic sport.

The female version of the Harlem Globetrotters is a professional team almost as old, the All-American Redheads, who started touring in 1936. Just as the Harlem Globetrotters weren't really from Harlem, all the redheads on the team weren't born that way. (Some tint their hair.) Unlike the Globetrotters, though, the Redheads really compete, playing male teams usually made up of former high school players. Usually, the Redheads win.

GLOSSARY

Assist: A pass to a teammate who then scores.

Baseline: The end line of the court.

Blocking: Illegally stepping into the path of an opposing player.

Bounce pass: A pass bounced off the floor between two players.

Buzzer: The horn that sounds at the end of each period.

Charging: An offensive foul committed when a player runs into a defender who is stationary.

Charity stripe: The foul line.

Clear the boards: Grab a rebound.

Control the boards: Dominate the rebounding game.

Cut: A quick change of direction used by an offensive player to get free of his defender.

Double dribble: A violation that occurs when an offensive player either bounces the ball with both hands or stops dribbling and then starts again.

Drive: A powerful move toward the basket.

Fast break: An attempt to move the ball quickly downcourt after a rebound and score before the opposing team can set its defense.

Foul trouble: The problem of being close to or, in the case of a team, over the limit of fouls.

Give-and-go: To hand or pass the ball to a teammate, then break toward the basket for a return pass.

Going backdoor: Eluding a defensive player and breaking along the baseline for a lay-up.

Gunner: A player who shoots very often.

Held ball: A situation that occurs when two opposing players grasp the ball at the same time and have equal possession. A jump ball then takes place in either of the free-throw circles or in the center circle, whichever is closest.

Home court advantage: Although it is still not fully understood why, teams always fare much better on their home courts than on the road. Travel, slight differences in physical conditions of a foreign court, and fan partisanship may make a slight difference, but the home court advantage is more than slight.

Some have suggested that the officials may subconsciously favor the team that all the fans are screaming for.

Jackknife: Position of a rebounder—arms and legs forward, backside and elbows out—that gives him more room as he comes down from a jump.

Key: The figure formed by the foul lane and the circle enclosing the foul line.

Keyhole: The free-throw circle.

Mismatch: A situation that occurs when the offense succeeds in having a tall man guarded by a short man or a fast man guarded by a slow man.

Outlet pass: The pass following a defensive rebound, often to start a fast break.

Palming: A violation that occurs when the dribbler brings his hand under the ball and allows it to rest momentarily in his palm.

Pick: The maneuver of an offensive player who hopes to free a teammate from the guard of a defensive man by setting himself in the path of the defensive man.

Pivot foot: The stationary foot when a player is holding the ball—he may move one foot as much as he likes as long as the other remains stationary.

Post position: Also called pivot position, the post position is one played by an offensive player, usually the center, around which the rest of the team deploys. A high post position is near the free-throw line; a low post position is near the basket but outside the free-throw lane. The post player faces away from the basket and remains relatively stationary. His teammates work to get the ball to him, then break past or around him. The post player may feed the ball to any teammate or he may shoot.

Press: Very close guarding by the defensive team, usually done over the whole court (full-court press). A very exhausting maneuver but often effective in the pros, where players have only 10 seconds to get the ball past midcourt and 24 seconds to shoot.

Pump: To fake a shot in order to force a defensive player to commit himself.

Rebound: Recovery of a shot that bounces off the backboard and/or the rim.

Screen: The position of an offensive player when he places himself between a defender and a teammate as a means of freeing the teammate.

Stuff: To forcibly block an attempted shot. Also to ram the ball through the hoop.

Tip-in: A basket scored by a player when instead of rebounding an errant shot, he lightly pushes it into the basket after the ball had begun to fall away. Also called a tap-in.

Traveling: A violation that occurs when the player in possession of the ball takes more than one step or moves his pivot foot without dribbling. Also called walking or steps.

Turnover: A team losing possession of the ball other than on a missed shot.

Two-on-one: Two offensive players moving to the basket with only one defensive player in front of them. The situation usually occurs because of an intercepted pass or an unusual rebound.

Bicycling

INDOOR BICYCLE TRACK

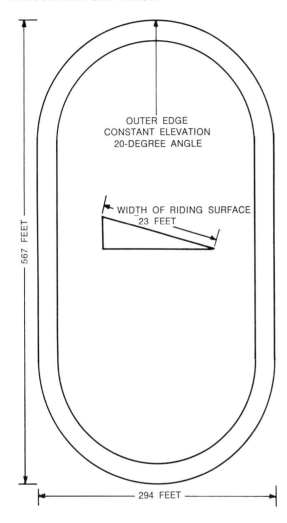

OUTER EDGE
CONSTANT ELEVATION
20-DEGREE ANGLE

WIDTH OF RIDING SURFACE
23 FEET

567 FEET

294 FEET

In the Gay Nineties a fad caught hold of America. People almost stopped buying and reading books; the watch and jewelry business was on the verge of collapse; piano sales were cut in half; and no one went to the theater anymore. The most popular song of the decade began "Daisy, Daisy, give me your answer do. . . ." Americans were riding bicycles and had little time or money for other entertainment. More than four hundred bicycle manufacturers were busy filling the demand for the new machines, which cost $100 each, a sum equivalent to several hundred dollars today. Professional racers toured the country. In 1895, there were more than six hundred professional cyclists in the United States, more than there are today.

The craze was short-lived. The automobile soon replaced the bicycle in America's affections. But the American love affair with the automobile has cooled since the price of gasoline has skyrocketed, and bicycles are again becoming popular, both as an almost unbeatable form of exercise and as a means of going places. Interest in competitive cycling is growing, too. In Europe, where the bicycle is still the best way of getting around for many people, racing is big sport. The Tour de France is followed with as much interest as the World Series is here, with no one very far from his television.

COMPETITION

Bicycle racing can be divided into two main types: road racing and track racing. Road races take place outdoors over long, often brutal courses. Strength and endurance of almost heroic proportions are necessary to win some of these races. Track races are usually much shorter, run on oval indoor or outdoor tracks. In track racing it is necessary not only to outlast your opponents but to outwit them.

ROAD RACING

Run over roads and highways, road races are very popular in Europe today. Races such as the Tour de France, the Tour of Belgium, the Giro d'Italia, the Giro di Lombardia, the Bordeaux to Paris race, the Milan to San Remo race, and the Paris to Brussels race, are followed avidly. The cyclists who win these events are rewarded with adulation and money. A professional European cyclist may earn from $50,-000 to $100,000 a year in prize money and advertising endorsements. In the United States alone there are now more than six hundred sanctioned races a year for twelve thousand registered riders.

The Tour de France, the most famous road race in the world, is a 22-day, 2,600-mile event. It starts in Lille, ends in Paris, and takes cyclists over a brutal course that includes the Pyrenees Moun-

Opposite: The Tour de France, one of the most famous road races, takes the contestants on a scenic tour of the country. Left: A cyclist competing in a 1,000-meter sprint time trial, a track race.

tains. The racers start together, followed by a caravan of radio and television crews in trucks and cars, and *domestiques* (servants) on bicycles. These domestiques, who are sort of apprentice cyclists, carry food for the contestants they serve and harass opposing cyclists. The cyclists follow each other closely to shield themselves as much as possible from the wind, and so crashes and injuries are common. More than one cyclist, rocketing down a mountain at sixty miles per hour, has run off the road and broken his neck.

Like all cyclists, tour racers must be in top condition. The average road racer in training cycles one hundred miles a day. His body becomes freakish under the strain. His heart grows much larger than the average man's, and as a result his body utilizes oxygen much more efficiently.

The bicycle used in road racing is lightweight but sturdy and is equipped with 10-speed *derailleur* gears. The seats are high and the handlebars turned down so that the racer's back is almost parallel to the ground—the most efficient, least tiring position.

The cyclists use toe clips to help them pedal faster and better.

TRACK RACING

Track bicycles are sturdier and more maneuverable than road bikes and are even capable of moving backward. They are fixed in one fairly high gear.

The different kinds of track racing (handicap, sprint, and pursuit), all use a similar track—a steeply banked, circular cement or hardwood surface from one-tenth to one-quarter mile around.

Handicap races are short, between one-quarter and one-half mile, and use the head start principle: lower-ranked cyclists are spaced ahead of higher-ranked cyclists.

Sprint races are usually 800 to 1,000 meters, two or three laps of the track. In a sprint race cyclists spend a lot of time looking at each other. Only the last lap counts, so during the first laps, competitors jockey for position, trying to hide their intentions from each other. Since all competitors are of about the same ability, the winner will be the cyclist who maneuvers best.

In pursuit racing two racers or teams of racers start on opposite sides of the track and try to overtake each other. They are usually evenly matched, so the rider who covers the specified distance first is the winner, even without overtaking an opponent.

A popular track race in Europe is "the madison," named after Madison Square Garden in New York City, where in the 1930s the most popular indoor races, the six-day bicycle races, took place. These were gruesome endurance events in which riders moved around the track for six days without rest, often falling over from lack of sleep. The winner was the man who made the most laps. The first six-day race in New York City was won by Charlie Miller, who covered 2,093 miles in six days. This type of race was later banned as too brutal, and the rules were changed to allow two-man teams, one man relieving the other. Today's madison races follow this principle. They may be as short as thirty minutes or as long as six days.

ORGANIZATIONS

The world governing body of bicycle racing is the Union Cycliste Internationale (UCI). In the United States the controlling organization for racing is the United States Cycling Federation.

Billiards

HISTORY

Like croquet, billiards probably comes from the game of *paille maille,* a game played outdoors. It seems likely that players of this game invented an indoor version of the game to play when the weather forced them inside. The game area had to be made smaller, and *paille maille* had to be changed to fit smaller quarters. So it was moved from the floor onto a table. Then guardrails were put around the table so that the balls wouldn't fall off. The mallet used in *paille maille* was turned around, and the smaller end was used to strike the ball. In seventeenth century England, the game consisted of players striking an ivory ball up and down the table, winning points by touching a peg, called the king, at the end of the table. Good placement of the ball was necessary. Pockets in the table were hazards—a player who pocketed a ball lost a point.

Other changes improved the game. The table was changed from wood, which sometimes warped and so was not the best surface, to slate. The guardrails were covered with rubber, making the shots that bounced (or banked) off the sides truer.

EQUIPMENT

The modern game of billiards, of which there are many versions, is played on a table that is twice as

54

long as it is wide. The playing surface is 30 to 31 inches from the floor, covered by felt, and surrounded by rubber-cushioned rails that are 1¾ inches high. Carom billiards tables have no pockets. Pocket billiards tables have six—one at each corner and one halfway down each long side. Corner pockets are from 4⅞ to 5⅛ inches large; side pockets are larger, from 5⅜ to 5⅝ inches. The balls in carom billiards are 2⅜ inches in diameter; those used in pocket billiards are 2¼ inches in diameter. Cues, the sticks with which players strike the balls, usually weigh from 14 to 22 ounces and are about 57 inches long.

THE GAME

There are two basic types of billiards: carom and pocket billiards, or pool.

CAROM BILLIARDS

Carom billiards is played with three balls—one red, one plain white, and one white with a small black spot. The red ball is always a target, or object, ball. The other two balls belong to the players, one ball to each. Each player shoots his ball, called his cue ball, and tries to make caroms—touching the other two balls on one shot. In this way he scores points. The basic strategy is to keep all three balls as close together as possible in order to make caroms. From one to eight people can play, though the game is best with two players.

To start the game, the red ball is placed on the foot spot of the table. This spot is midway between the longer sides of the table and close to one of the short sides. There is a head spot at the other end of the table. One white ball (whichever the starting player has chosen for his cue ball) is placed on the head spot, and the other white ball is placed six inches to the right or left of it. The first player must shoot his cue ball to contact the red ball first. After that, he can hit either ball first to make a carom.

There are several varieties of carom billiards. In straight rail billiards, the cue ball must contact one object ball, then the rail, then the other object ball. Or the cue ball may touch both object balls before touching the rail and either ball after it rebounds.

Balk-line billiards was invented to make caroms more difficult. Balk lines are drawn either 14 or 18 inches from the sides and ends of the table, making balk areas on the fringes of the playing surface. Only one carom may be made in a certain balk area at a time. In another sort of carom billiards, called cushion caroms, the cue ball must strike a cushion either before or after it hits the first object ball. Three-cushion caroms is a game for experts. To score, the cue ball must contact three cushions as well as both object balls at some time.

POCKET BILLIARDS

Pocket billiards, or pool, is much more popular than carom billiards in this country. There are fifteen colored object balls, numbered from 1 to 15, and one white cue ball. In basic pocket billiards, the

player must call which ball he intends to hit and the pocket into which he is going to hit it. This game may be played by scoring one point for each ball pocketed or by assigning to each ball the point value of its number. A player loses a point and his turn if he "scratches"—that is, misses the object ball, sends the cue ball off the table, or pockets the cue ball.

In rotation billiards, a type of pocket billiards, all fifteen balls are arranged in a triangle, or racked, with the number 1 ball at the front point of the triangle and the 2 and 3 balls at the other two points. The player who shoots first, or breaks, is allowed all the balls he pockets. Then he must pocket the lowest-numbered ball on the table and all the others in numerical order. The player (or team) with the highest score of pocketed balls wins.

The game of pocket billiards played in championships is called "continuous." It is usually played on a table measuring 4½ by 9 feet. The player tries to pocket fourteen balls in a row, calling both the ball and pocket and leaving only the number 15 ball on the table. The pocketed balls are then racked again, and the player tries to pocket the 15 ball. If he does, he then breaks the racked balls to continue scoring. Players receive one point for each ball pocketed, and the first player to reach the score agreed on wins.

Pocket billiards is the most popular form of billiards in America, which has produced such prodigies as Jean Balukas, opposite, a teenaged girl from Brooklyn. Above: The object of the game is to strike the unnumbered cue ball so that it knocks a target ball into a pocket.

55

Bobsledding

Surrounded by walls of rock-hard ice as they hurtle down mountains, bobsledders are protected from disaster only by some bulky clothing, helmets, goggles, and most of all their own skill. There is little room for error. A slight mistake by any member of the team can send the sled careening out of control and result in serious injury, sometimes even death, to the sledders. With such a fine line between success and disaster, bobsledding is thrilling to some, terrifying to others, and—everyone agrees—one of the world's most dangerous sports.

HISTORY

The first crude bobsled was rigged up around 1890. Two Americans vacationing in Switzerland, bored with the rather sedate pace of their toboggan, hit on the idea of putting runners on it. The idea became popular, and competition between bobsledders did, too. A toboggan run was too slow, so the world's first bobsled run was built at St. Moritz in 1904. Plenty of men were willing to risk life and limb for the thrills of high-speed sledding, and bobsledding became so popular that it was a part of the first Winter Olympic Games, in 1924.

EQUIPMENT

The bobsled itself has changed a lot since the first toboggan crudely fixed with runners. It is a large vehicle, with a sleek racing cowl in front, that rests on four runners. The two front runners are on a pivot and are used to steer. The back runners are

fixed. The brake, located in the rear, is a toothed piece of steel that the brakeman digs into the ice to slow the sled.

Weight is important in bobsledding. A two-man sled, 8 feet 9 inches long, may weigh 362.5 pounds. The four-man sled, 12 feet 9 inches long, may weigh 507 pounds, with 880 pounds allowed for the crew. Teams are allowed to load ballast-iron or lead weights on the sled to reach the weight limit, but dead weight can't hurl itself into curves as a hefty bobsledder can.

THE COURSE

A bobsled run is a fairly narrow, curving chute constructed of glare ice, with steeply banked turns. According to international rules, it must be at least 1500 meters long and have a minimum of 15 turns. Some bobsled turns are wicked, 180-degree hairpins. A bobsled team's key to success is the way it takes these curves. A sled must climb the banking as high as possible without turning over, then descend quickly into the chute for maximum speed in the straightaway. Practice runs before each event are vital because bobsledders have no time to learn the course during the 60 to 90 seconds of their run. Many captains spend time walking over the course, memorizing its details.

THE RACE

The race begins with a running start. The team pushes the sled and then jumps in as it begins to move. Like everything in bobsledding, the start

Above: Few teams in sport must be as close-knit as the members of a bobsled crew. One man's mistake may jeopardize not only the race but the lives of the entire team. Opposite: The competitor riding the luge rockets down a bobsled-type course virtually on his back.

must be well synchronized. A split second of clumsiness can cost the race. Events are usually made up of four runs. The team with the lowest total time wins. Even for all four runs, however, the difference between first and second place is often miniscule—as small as one-fifth of a second.

Bobsledding is not a particularly complex sport—in the end all that counts is speed. But to be fastest involves more than just jumping into the sled and hoping for the best. Each member of the team must work in harmony with his teammates. The captain, who steers the bob, is the most important. The crew must be alert to his every shift and must follow his lead without hesitation. During the run, there is no verbal communication among team members, for the roaring of the sled as it speeds across the ice drowns out the loudest shout.

Like auto racers, who also thrive on speed, bobsledders are daring men. Unlike auto racers, though, they race only for a medal of some sort, not for money. Bobsledders get all their satisfaction from the thrill and speed of the sport. Eugenio Monti, a great Italian bobsledder, was once caught shoveling snow from a run at night. Monti complained that the course was too slow. His team was fined four seconds and didn't bother racing.

Tobogganing

Toboggans have existed in one form or another for many centuries. The first ones were probably made of animal bone. American Indians used tree bark to make toboggans to carry dead game back to their villages in winter.

Toboggans are usually six to eight feet long and one and one-half to two feet wide. They are made from strips of wood, curved upward at the front end. A toboggan has no runners, but the bottom surface is highly polished.

Luge

Luge is the French word for sled, and the competition luge is a slightly more sophisticated version of the everyday sled used by millions of children every winter. Luge as a sport first surfaced in the Alps during World War I, but the first all-European championships were not held until 1951. By then specifications for the exact size and weight of the sleds had been developed.

The racers, either one or two per luge, sit in a reclining position. The luge is steered by pulling on a hand rope and by applying foot pressure to the outside runners of the vehicle's front end.

Races take place over an icy, 1,000-meter course that has 14 to 18 curves. There are usually two runs, and the winner, as in bobsledding, is the racer or team with the lowest total time. At full momentum, luges can travel as fast as seventy miles per hour.

Bowling

Bowling is a sport often scorned and neglected by sportswriters. Its professionals are not as well known as football, baseball, and basketball stars. But it thrives anyway, for bowling is more a participant than a spectator sport. More than thirty million Americans bowl each year, making it the most popular participant sport in the country.

HISTORY

It's no surprise that bowling is so popular. It has always been so. The urge to knock one object over with another is a basic one. Some sort of bowling was probably one of the first games ever played. Sir Flinders Petrie, a British Egyptologist, found pins and a ball in a child's tomb of about 5200 B.C.

Like many sports, bowling was once part of a religious ritual. Written records from 300 A.D. show that bowling was used in European churches to serve a moral purpose. In those days, German peasants carried exercise clubs with them all the time, even to church. Some priest must have thought of using these clubs for a game. Parishioners were instructed to think of the club as a *Heide*, or heathen, and then to roll a stone ball at it and knock it over. If a man succeeded, it meant he was leading a virtuous life; if he missed the pin, he was advised to take more care in spiritual matters and to practice his aim.

Although *Kegelspiel*, as it was known (even today, another term for bowlers is keglers), gradually moved out of the church, one of the most important figures in the history of bowling was the great religious reformer, Martin Luther. Luther was an avid bowler and is credited with giving bowling the form—nine pins set in a diamond shape—that lasted until the nineteenth century. He, too, could not resist using the game to make moral points, reminding the children of his household not to laugh when someone else missed or to become arrogant about their own skill.

Some form of the game flourished in other parts of Europe, too, sometimes to its disadvantage. Edward III of England issued an edict in 1365 prohibiting any games involving the "hurling of stones." He feared that his subjects were neglecting archery and thus weakening the defense of the nation. Other English kings forbade the game for various reasons. But none of the edicts or laws passed against it could destroy this enjoyable pastime. Sir Francis Drake was so fond of bowling that when a messenger one day interrupted his game with the news that the Spanish Armada had been sighted, Drake replied, "There's time to finish the game and beat the Spaniards afterwards."

The first version of the game to reach this country was lawn bowling, brought by Dutch settlers in the early 1600s. In the 1700s, a form of ninepins, first played on a clay path and later on a narrow board, came to America. By the nineteenth century, the game had moved indoors and was all the rage. In New York City there was a bowling alley on every block. Unfortunately the game attracted gamblers and was outlawed by some state legislatures. Legend has it that one clever entrepreneur, with typical American ingenuity, got around the prohibition of ninepins by adding one pin and changing the pin setup from a diamond to a triangle form. So tenpins was born. Since 1860, the game has been played that way.

One of the most important reasons for the growth of the sport was the invention of the automatic pinsetter. This machine, invented in the 1930s by Fred Schmidt of Pearl River, New York, swept pins away automatically and set up new ones in their place. It took the place of pin boys and greatly quickened the pace of the game. The automatic pin setter began to be manufactured on a mass scale in the 1950s.

In 1958, the top players of professional bowling organized the Professional Bowlers Association in order to develop tournaments. Today, a top professional bowler can earn more than one hundred thousand dollars a year.

ORGANIZATIONS

The American Bowling Congress (ABC) oversees the rules and sets equipment standards for male bowlers. Its annual tournament, with individual and team entries from all over the country, is one of the most important events in bowling. The first ABC tour was in 1901; 41 teams were entered, and the prize money amounted to $1,592. More than 1.2 million teams registered for a recent tournament. The ABC administers the Bowling Hall of Fame, set up in 1941 to honor the top men bowlers.

EQUIPMENT

Various materials have been used to make bowling balls in the past, including stone, wood, and iron. Today's regulation ball is made of solid composition rubber, and weighs from 10 to 16 pounds. The ball may not be more than 27 inches around. Before 1890 or so, bowlers held the ball in their palms before rolling it. Then holes were drilled in the ball, and the two-hole grip was introduced—one hole for the thumb and one for the middle finger—allowing the bowler to control his release better. Most modern bowlers use a ball with three holes—for the thumb, middle, and fourth finger.

Regulation pins are made of several layers of wood and are encased in plastic. Pins may weigh between 2 pounds 14 ounces and 3 pounds 10

Bowling is the most popular participant sport in America. The governing organization is the American Bowling Congress (ABC), which holds an annual tournament beginning with the simultaneous bowling of a first ball by each of the teams.

ounces, but are usually about 3 pounds 6 ounces. Some bowling alleys use very light pins so that customers will score higher. Pins are 15 inches high, 15 inches around at their widest point, and have a diameter of 2¼ inches at the base. The 10 pins used in a given set must not vary more than 4 ounces in weight.

THE ALLEY

The bowling alley is made of specially treated maple and pine wood. The two areas of the alley that get the most use—where the ball first hits and where it hits the pins—are made of maple. Across the lane at two points between the bowler and the pins are a set of arrows and a set of small circles. These sets are called markers and range finders. Bowlers use the marks as aiming guides to help them deliver the ball to the proper spot. On either side of the lane is a gutter, a groove into which poorly aimed balls drop and are diverted past the pins.

Alleys must be properly maintained. They are coated with oil so that the wood isn't destroyed. To the professional bowler, the amount of oil on any lane is quite important, and he must adjust his game accordingly. The televising of big tournaments has added an interesting element to these matches. High-intensity television lights tend to dry out the lanes and make the ball difficult to control. Since there are more right-handed than left-handed bowlers, most alleys are more worn on the right side. This gives left handers a slight advantage in competition.

THE GAME

Bowling is a simple game, and this is a big reason for its popularity. It is a sport that doesn't demand youth or a well-developed physique or any more strength than is necessary to lift and swing the ball. (Indeed, even blind people can bowl. In a tournament held in 1936, five blind boys, with the aid of a guide rail to help their approach, lost to a team of sighted boys by only 16 points, 654 to 670.) Accuracy, however, is important, and to develop it, the bowler must work on a good, consistent delivery.

THE DELIVERY

Most bowlers favor the four-step over the three- or five-step delivery, and this is the one recommended by experts. The bowler stands erect, about 12 to 15 feet from the foul line, with his shoulders squared toward the pins. A right-handed bowler holds the ball slightly above the waist in his right hand, supporting the weight of the ball with his left hand. This is the step-by-step process: A bowler takes his first step with his right foot, pushing the ball slightly away from his body and down. As the step is completed, he swings away the guiding left hand. As he steps with the left foot, the ball swings to the rear. The right foot takes the third step, and the ball reaches the height of its backswing, at about shoulder level. As the left foot comes forward, he begins the downswing, and he releases the ball as he slides to the foul line on his left foot. The follow-through should be smooth, and the shoulders should still be facing the pins after the ball has been delivered.

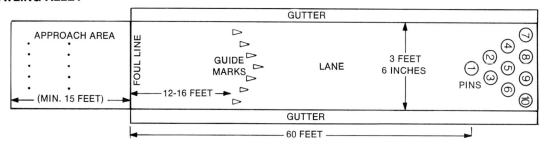

The ball must always be laid onto the alley, never thrown, or "lofted." Ball speed is important. Experts have even calculated the amount of time it should take the ball to travel the 60 feet from the foul line to the pins. A ball that covers this distance in less than $2\frac{1}{8}$ seconds, they have found, will not be able to "grip" the lane properly and will go out of control. Moreover, a ball thrown too fast will not give the pins enough time to "mix" and thus will not be as effective a shot.

To score a strike—that is, to knock down all 10 pins with one ball—the right-handed bowler aims at the 1-3 pocket, the space between the "1" and "3" pins. One may aim at the pins (pin bowling) and roll the ball, a method recommended for beginners; or one may make use of the range finders to lay the ball down (spot bowling). Spot bowling is favored by more advanced players because the margin for error is less.

There are three basic types of balls the bowler can throw: the straight ball, the hook, and the curve. The straight ball is a ball rolled in a straight path down the alley and is recommended for beginners. Starting from the right side of the alley, it moves diagonally across the alley to hit the 1-3 pocket. A hook ball, the ball used by most professionals because it yields a greater percentage of strikes, moves straight down the lane, then breaks and hooks toward the 1-3 pocket. The curve ball, which only the most experienced bowlers can master, starts from near the center of the lane, moves toward the gutter, then curves in to the pocket.

SCORING

One of the big attractions of bowling is the possibility of perfection. The aim of every bowler is a perfect game, a score of 300. This is achieved by rolling a strike in every frame, plus 2 extra strikes at the end, a total of 12 strikes. Not many bowlers manage this feat—only about five hundred per year—but every bowler dreams of it.

In this simplest of sports, scoring is the most complicated element. Even this part of the game is simple, though, once a few rules are understood.

1. Each game has 10 frames; a bowler gets a maximum of two balls per frame, or two chances to knock down all 10 pins.
2. If the bowler gets a strike, his turn is over. When he strikes, his score for that frame is 10 plus whatever he rolls on the next *two* balls. So the most points a bowler can score in any frame is 30 points. A strike in the last frame gets two extra balls.

3. If a player gets a spare, that is, knocks all the pins over with two balls, his score for that frame is 10 plus whatever he rolls with the next *one* ball. The most points that can be scored on a spare are 20. A spare in the last frame is awarded an extra ball.

The following symbols are used to score. "X" stands for a strike and "/" for a spare. The symbols "O," "—," and "Ø" have no meaning in the numerical score of a game; they merely help to keep a record of what happened in the game. The "O" signifies a split—that is, two or more pins, neither of which is the head, or number one, pin, left standing far apart after the first ball. The "—" means that the bowler failed to knock down any pins, or, sometimes only that the spare was missed. And the "Ø" is simply the split sign plus the spare sign, showing that the player picked up the spare after a split.

A few imaginary frames may clarify these principles:

In the first frame, the bowler gets a spare. The spare sign is indicated in the little box in the right corner, but no score is written in for the frame until the bowler takes his next turn. In the second frame he gets five pins on his first ball and three on the second, failing to make the spare. His score for the first frame is 15: the 10 points from the spare plus the 5 from his next ball. The total of eight pins that he knocked down in the entire second frame are added to his first frame total of 15, giving him a total of 23 at the end of the second frame.

In the third frame, he bowls a strike. The strike sign is indicated, and the frame box is left blank until he bowls two more balls. On the next time up, he bowls a spare, so 10 points are added to the 10 for his strike of the previous frame. His score for the third frame can now be added up—23 + 20, or 43.

In the fifth frame he knocks down seven pins on his first ball, and two on the next. The seven pins are added to the 10 from his spare in the fourth frame, giving him a score of 60 through that frame. The nine pins he knocked down in the fifth frame give him a total score of 69 through five frames.

Duckpins

Duckpins, so called because the pins fly up like startled ducks when struck by the ball, is popular in the Eastern United States. The governing body of the sport is the National Duckpin Bowling Congress, founded in 1928.

Duckpins are $9^{13}/_{32}$ inches high. The ball used

in regulation play is about 5 inches in diameter and has no finger holes.

The game is played in much the same way as tenpin bowling, except that each bowler is allowed three balls per frame. If the bowler knocks down all ten pins in three tries, he scores ten points, not a spare.

Canadian Five-pin Bowling

Five-pin bowling is one of Canada's more popular sports. It is played by 4 of every 10 Canadians.

The regulation ball is made from composition wood. It weighs from three to four pounds and varies from 4½ to 5 inches in diameter. It has no finger holes. The pins are 12⅜ inches in height; they are 1¾ inches in diameter at the base and 4³⁄₁₆ inches in diameter at the widest point. Each pin is encircled by a rubber buffer 2 inches from the base.

The five-pin lane is comparable to the tenpin lane.

The pins are arranged in a triangle:

2   2
 3   3
    5

Each pin has the value of its number in scoring. The two-pin on the left is known as the kingpin. The bowler must knock down the kingpin in order to gain credit for the frame. The two-pin on the right is the kingpin for left-handed bowlers.

There are 10 frames. A bowler may roll three balls per frame if necessary. A strike scores 15 points plus the total value of the pins knocked down on the next two balls. A spare scores 15 points plus the total of the next ball.

Lawn Bowling

Lawn bowling is a mixture of bowling, shuffleboard, and horseshoes. Played by the ancient Egyptians, Greeks, and Romans, lawn bowling is one of the oldest games in existence.

Lawn bowling is played on a rink, a flat, grassy area that is 20 feet wide, 120 feet long, and bounded by a shallow ditch. A bowling green is normally made up of six such rinks.

The balls used in lawn bowling are called bowls. They are made from a very hard and heavy tropical wood called lignum vitae and must weigh less than 3½ pounds. Bowls may not be more than 5½ inches or less than 4½ inches in diameter and are slightly lopsided. This irregularity, called a bias, causes the ball to roll with a looping trajectory.

The target in lawn bowling is called a jack. It is a white earthenware ball, measuring 2½ inches in diameter and weighing approximately 10 ounces.

Lawn bowling may take the form of singles or may be a team game. Teams are usually comprised of two, three, or four players. In singles competition each player rolls four bowls per round, or end. In team competition each player rolls two bowls per end. The first member of a team to bowl is called the lead; the last is called the skip, or captain. The skip will sometimes stand at the target end of the rink to direct his team.

To start the game, the lead rolls the jack, which must travel at least 75 feet. The lead then rolls the first bowl. The lead of the opposing team then rolls his first bowl. Play alternates until all the bowls have been played. One point is scored after each end for each bowl that is closer to the jack than any bowl belonging to the opposing team. The game is usually played to 21. Sometimes the winner is the team that is ahead after a predetermined number of ends, also called heads or innings.

Boccie

The Italian form of lawn bowling, boccie is played on a lane that is about 20 yards long and 3 yards wide. A trough, about 3 inches deep, runs across the alley at either end to stop balls that have been bowled too hard. In regulation play, a one-foot high barrier runs along either side of the alley.

The manner of play in boccie is very similar to lawn bowling, except that the standard game is 12 points.

One of the many varieties of bowling is lawn bowling, above, in which the bowler tries not to knock down pins but to place his ball as close as possible to a target ball, called a jack.

Boxing

Boxing in the form that most of us know it—prize fighting—is a story of men trying to fight their way to a better life. These fighters have been fighters in the ring, and they have also been the managers, trainers, matchmakers, promoters, mobsters, and assorted hangers-on who have fought to succeed by profiting (often immorally) from the boxer's quest for success. The boxer himself plays for the highest stakes. He tries to batter his opponent into senselessness and risks being battered senseless himself. If he succeeds, he wins fame and perhaps a modest fortune. If he fails, he is likely to have as bad a time in life as he had in the ring, because he usually knows little else but boxing with which to earn a living. More than other athletes, boxers have had to succeed at their sport in order to succeed at all.

Perhaps it is because so much is at stake that boxing has always attracted a devoted following, of critics as well as supporters. Some are appalled by the cruelty; others are enthralled by it. Still others are moved by the courage and stamina of the fighters. To them, boxing is a symbol of life: a struggle to prove oneself under great pressure; to knock down or be knocked down.

HISTORY

The earliest fist fighters of whom we know, the ancient Sumerians, Greeks, and Romans, were warriors for whom fists were weapons, not sporting equipment. When they had no wars to fight, the boxers, or pugilists, practiced their craft against their comrades, often as brutally as they did against the enemy. A Greek or Roman fighter who had pounded his opponent senseless often continued to batter the defenseless man to death. In Rome crowds of spectators encouraged such carnage. On each fist Roman fighters wore a cestus, leather thongs studded with devastating metal spikes, the quicker to pulverize each other and hold the spectators' interest.

Barbaric and sadistic as they were, the Romans did make some improvements in boxing. Unlike the Greeks, whose fighters battled each other head to head, the Romans permitted their boxers to maneuver and even to retreat within a limited area, the forerunner of today's ring. And the Romans gave us another boxing tradition: in 30 B.C., they outlawed the sport, the first of many times it would be banned.

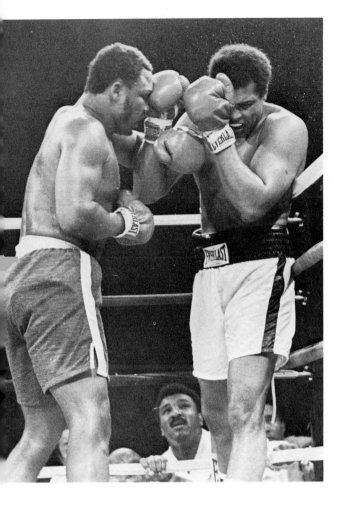

began the practice of dividing boxing matches into rounds.

In 1839, Broughton's rules were amended to prohibit kicking, eye gouging, butting with the head, biting, and blows below the waist. The amended rules also provided for a contrivance to separate the fighters from the often unruly fans—a ring, 24 feet square and bounded by ropes. Despite the new rules, boxing was not yet respectable, but it advanced anyway, for there was a major new, undeveloped yet lucrative market for the sport— America.

The first American boxers to win renown were black slaves who in late colonial times had impressed English army officers with their strength and were transported to England to perform. By the middle of the nineteenth century, America was supporting boxing on its own, and even attracting English fighters. Many of the immigrants who found jobs in America as laborers were men who brawled themselves and enjoyed wagering on other fighters. First the Irish and German immigrants, later the Poles, Italians, and Jews would provide America and the world with many of its finest fighters. At first they fought as much for the sport and glory as for the side bets, but when it became clear that boxing was a sport that vast numbers of people would pay to watch, many a poor immigrant's son tried to win his fortune as a fighter.

In 1867, John Sholto Douglas, eighth marquis of Queensberry, lent his name to the new set of boxing rules that John G. Chambers of the Amateur Athletic Club of London had devised. The new rules stipulated that the fighters would wear padded gloves, that each round would last three minutes, and that a fallen fighter would be allowed 10 seconds to recover before being declared the loser.

The Queensberry rules brought order to boxing (too much for the fans of bare knuckle, who denounced the rules as unmanly), but ironically, they made boxing more dangerous. Before fighters began using gloves, their hands were the most vulnerable parts of their body. The hands would easily break from a prolonged battering, so a fighter could inflict only limited damage even on a defenseless opponent. The winner's broken hands took longer to heal after the bout than the loser's broken nose and bloodied face. Now, with gloves to cushion his hands, a boxer could batter his opponent with as little restraint as the cesti-clad Roman. Moreover, with the three-minute round and the 10-second count, a weary fighter could no longer gain 30 seconds rest simply by dropping untouched to the floor, as many had under Broughton's Prize Ring Rules. The bare knuckle fights would not have lasted as many rounds as they had if a failing fighter had had to endure as much as three minutes before resting. Now many fighters would push themselves dangerously past their endurance limits in order to last three minutes.

The great English champion, James ("Jem") Mace immediately accepted the new Queensberry

Men did not stop fighting after the Romans banned boxing, least of all the Romans themselves, but it was not until the eighteenth century that a sport resembling fist fighting became popular again. An Englishman named James Figg used his fists, as well as the less sophisticated brawling tactics of the day, to conquer his country's strongmen, and by 1719, he was recognized (unofficially but effectively) as champion of England. Although Figg was popular wherever he fought, he earned little money from his exhibitions. The landed gentry did not care to attend these rowdy spectacles, and without their money for purses and side bets, Figg could win only the modest wagers of common people or the small prize put up by a promoter.

The next great champion of England, Jack Broughton, began the job of making boxing respectable. His greatest contribution was the London Prize Ring Rules of 1743, the official rules of boxing for more than a century. No longer were boxers permitted to grasp opponents below the waist or to attack them after they had fallen. Moreover, a fallen fighter was permitted the unprecedented luxury of 30 seconds to clear his senses before returning to the fray. These rest periods

Until you've witnessed a prizefight at close quarters, it is difficult to appreciate how violent it is. Opposite: Dick Tiger, left, lands a left against Emile Griffith. Above: Muhammad Ali fends off Joe Frazier in their famous confrontation in Manila, the Philippines, in October 1975.

At the turn of the century, when Jack Johnson, a black man, became heavyweight champion, white fight fans turned to any "Great White Hope" who might beat him. The search led to former champ Jim Jeffries, whom Johnson battered in 1910, top. The black champ ran afoul of the white man's law with more serious offenses than traffic violations (above) and eventually lost his title in a fight he later claimed he had thrown.

rules. His promotion of the new order made it respectable for the bare-knuckle fans to accept it as well, for everyone knew Jem Mace was no sissy. The American fight fans took somewhat longer to be persuaded. Not until 1892, by which time bare knuckle fighting had been banned in every state in the Union, did the king of the bare knucklers, John L. Sullivan, agree to defend his title with gloves on.

Sullivan was an immensely popular champion. He had toured the country with a theatrical troupe, offering $100 to any man who could last four rounds with him. He was boastful and almost always accurate in the high estimation he had of his boxing skill. But when he met Gentleman Jim Corbett in New Orleans in the first championship fight in America fought under Queensberry rules, he was 34 years old and well past his prime. Corbett won 20 rounds in a row, then knocked out Sullivan in the twenty-first, and America moaned. The era of bare knuckles had ended with the fall of the greatest bare knuckle champion.

At the end of the bare knuckle era, businessmen saw that there were handsome profits to be made from paying the costs of a championship bout in return for collecting the admission money people would pay. Of these early promoters, the most successful was George Lewis ("Tex") Rickard. He persuaded a dynamic young heavyweight, Jack Dempsey, to fight for him, and in 1920, shortly after boxing was legalized in New York, he leased Madison Square Garden for his prize fights. Rickard had hit on a formula for success that promoters would try to follow for the next thirty years: find a talented fighter, bind him with a contract, groom him for the championship, and reap the profits from promoting the championship fights.

In Jack Dempsey, Rickard had more than a champion. Dempsey was the boy from the tiny mining and lumbering towns of the West who would become the darling of the big city. He was handsome and he was a dynamic fighter—not the artful dodger nor the graceless brawler but a furiously fast and powerful puncher who gave the crowds what they most wanted to see: knockouts. He had gained the title in 1919 by battering huge Jess Willard so fearsomely in three rounds that many claim today, as Willard did then, that Dempsey's gloves had been tampered with before the fight. The critics accused Doc Kearns, Dempsey's shady manager, of having laced the inside of Dempsey's gloves with plaster of Paris that hardened for the fight and made Dempsey's blows almost lethal.

On July 2, 1921, Rickard matched his young champion against "Gorgeous Georges" Carpentier of France in what the promoter called "the Battle of the Century." Carpentier was closer to a middleweight than a heavyweight and Rickard knew he was no match for the powerful Dempsey, but Tex was not a man to spurn a certain box office success. Carpentier was a dapper dresser and a stylish boxer; Dempsey was the "Manassa Mauler." Carpentier was a World War I hero; Dempsey was said to have been a draft dodger. Eighty thousand fans flocked to Jersey City for the fight, and the result was the first million-dollar gate—the first of five for Rickard with Dempsey. The champion demolished Carpentier in the fourth round.

Two years later, after some wild escapades out West with Kearns, Dempsey returned to New York at Rickard's request to meet the imposing 6-foot 3-inch, 220-pound Argentinian, Luis Firpo, "the Wild Bull of the Pampas." It was another million-dollar gate and one of the most awesome fights in history. It lasted less than four minutes, but in that short time Firpo was knocked to the canvas *nine* times, often before he had a chance to recover from the last knockdown. Dempsey fell twice, once crashing through the ropes and demolishing the typewriter he landed on. He finally knocked out Firpo at 57 seconds of the second round.

Dempsey went on stage, married an actress, visited Europe, and generally lived the high life of the celebrity he had become. It was three years before he fought again, against underdog Gene Tunney in Philadelphia in 1926. For the first time, Dempsey's power and famed left hook could not overcome a skilled boxer. Tunney left Dempsey swollen, bleeding, and thoroughly beaten after 10 rounds. The boxing world was stunned, and no one more so than the dethroned champion himself. To earn another fight with Tunney, he met Jack Sharkey in July 1927, and knocked him out with a left hood when Sharkey turned to the referee to protest what he claimed were some low blows from Dempsey. Two months later, on September 22, Dempsey

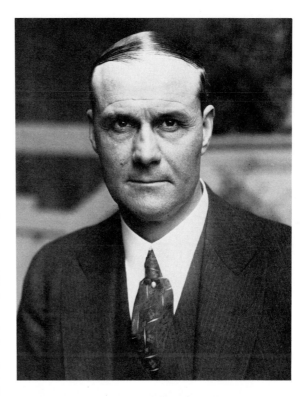

In the 1920s, promoter Tex Rickard, top, *began to rule the heavyweight class with his prize young prizefighter, Jack Dempsey,* above.

met Tunney again in boxing's perhaps most famous fight, "the Battle of the Long Count."

The beginning of the second Dempsey-Tunney fight was like the first. For six rounds Tunney punished Dempsey as he had the year before, but in the seventh Dempsey finally connected with his left. Before the staggered Tunney could fall to the canvas, Dempsey landed seven more solid blows until Tunney finally collapsed. The referee began to count, but then he noticed that Dempsey was standing over Tunney, waiting to attack him if he rose. Dempsey had done the same thing against Firpo, but for this fight a new rule was in effect. A fighter had to wait in a neutral corner while his opponent recovered from a knockdown. The referee stopped the count and ordered Dempsey to move to the farthest neutral corner. Only then did he begin the count again, but by "nine" Tunney was on his feet. Had Dempsey gone immediately to a neutral corner, Tunney might have been counted out. Now recovered, he controlled the rest of the fight and won by a unanimous decision.

Dempsey supporters screamed in protest but their cries could save neither their hero nor the great boxing era he had given them. Rickard, as well as the two fighters, profited enormously from the fight's record $2.65 million in gate receipts, but afterward Dempsey retired from the ring, Tunney soon followed, Rickard died, and the country plunged from the Roaring Twenties into the Great Depression. Boxing would languish for a decade, until a young dynamo would dominate the ring.

Joe Louis was not the first black champion and he may not have been the best, but he was a great fighter and an even greater symbol for people who believed that a man of any race or religion could succeed in America. In the early part of the century, the rise of a black champion, the great Jack Johnson, had sent white fight fans rushing to embrace any and every white challenger as the Great White Hope who would lick the black man and return the heavyweight championship to the white race. Less than 30 years later, American fight fans and many Americans who normally cared little for boxing were all cheering Joe Louis when he thrashed Max Schmeling, the German fighter who claimed to be the representative of the German master race. Louis brought to public attention the story of the black fighters, who had to overcome their skin color as well as their poverty and lack of education to succeed.

The forties and fifties were not without fine

66

In the first million-dollar gate, Dempsey knocked out Georges Carpentier in 1921, above. In 1923, Dempsey and Luis Firpo attracted another million-dollar gate (opposite top: crowds line up outside the Polo Grounds). Dempsey was knocked out of the ring in the first round, opposite bottom, but recovered and won.

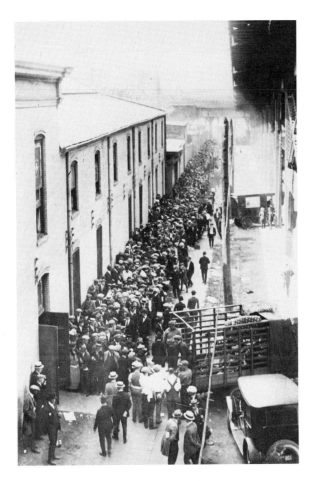

fights and fine fighters—Rocky Marciano, Archie Moore, Sugar Ray Robinson, and Floyd Patterson, for example—but it was not until the arrival of a talkative young Olympic champion from Louisville, Kentucky, that boxing, or at least heavyweight boxing, inspired something like the following it had enjoyed when Dempsey and Louis ruled the ring.

The newcomer was a gifted, graceful fighter who best described his style with the phrase, "Float like a butterfly; sting like a bee." Cassius Marcellus Clay floated and stung his way to the heavyweight championship on February 25, 1964, by conquering Sonny Liston, whom the experts had proclaimed a near-invincible 10–1 favorite. It was only the first of many times that Clay would upset boxing traditionalists.

After the fight, he announced he was a follower of Elijah Mohammad, the Black Muslim preacher who raged that whites had robbed and killed blacks and stolen from them their pride in being black. Clay changed his name to Cassius X and later to Muhammad Ali. "Cassius Clay is a slave name," he said, claiming that he and other black Americans had been named after the men who had owned their forefathers. When Ali espoused his new beliefs and demanded that he be called by his new name, the fans and sportswriters who had found him loud-mouthed and cocky in the past came to consider him unbearable. But to many other fans, particularly American ghetto blacks, Africans, and Asians, Ali became a hero.

No matter how controversial, Ali was still clearly the champion and, like Joe Louis, a fighting champion. He defended the title nine times in two

years. Then in 1967, he refused to be inducted into the United States Army, claiming to be a conscientious objector. Before he had been denounced as a pawn of a crazed, racist cult; after his refusal, Ali was branded a traitor. The various boxing commissions stripped him of his title and revoked his license to fight.

It was three years before Ali fought again. Still the hero to some, the villain to others, he returned to the ring because he wanted to, because the public demanded it, and as the ever-immodest Ali claimed, because boxing could not survive without him. His return to the ring set the stage for by far the biggest money-making boxing match in history. Via satellite and closed circuit television about three hundred million people watched the undefeated Ali battle the undefeated Joe Frazier in "the Fight of the Champions." As in all the great fights, the fighters seemed to be battling to decide more than just who was the better fighter. Ali taunted Frazier as a white man's Negro, a pawn of the white establishment, and Frazier replied by calling Ali a phony who needed someone to teach him humility. All fights have buildups (veteran boxing observers often don't take them seriously), but this one inflamed the boxing world.

Three and a half years since he had last fought for the heavyweight title, Ali was not his old self against "Smokin' Joe," who floored him in the fifteenth round and won a unanimous decision. Then, in 1973, newcomer George Foreman dethroned Frazier. When Ali bested Frazier in a rematch in 1974, much of the hysteria from their championship bout had subsided, but the decision over Frazier in the rematch gained Ali another shot at the title, this time against Foreman in October 1974 in the small African country of Zaire.

As always, Ali attacked his opponent with words as well as with his fists. It seemed to work. Foreman stumbled around the ring like a blind man, and Ali won by a knockout in the eighth round. Ali regained the championship that had been taken from him seven years before. It was a historic feat. Only once before had a heavyweight regained the title (Floyd Patterson in 1960), but never after a layoff.

Like most of the heavyweight championship fights in this century, the Ali-Foreman match pitted two Americans against each other. Yet the day when the United States will no longer dominate boxing is probably not long off. No longer do Americans worship the boxing champions or support the fight game as fervently as they once did. But this time-honored sport is not likely to die until man no longer values his fists as a way of proving himself, and that time, critics and supporters of boxing can agree, is a long way off.

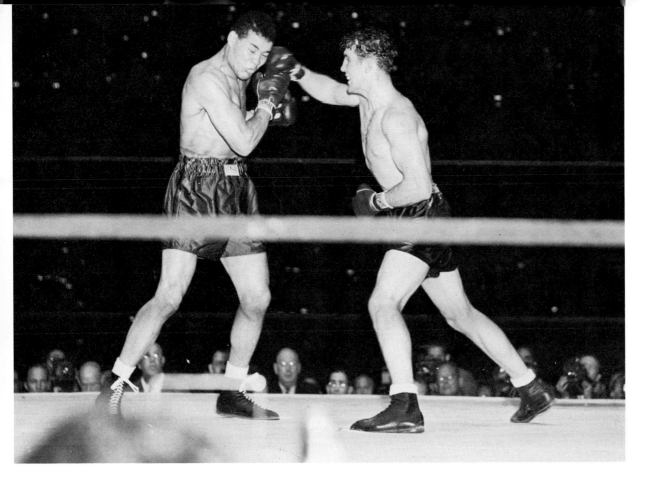

Opposite left: *In 1927, Dempsey lost a chance to beat his arch-rival, Gene Tunney, when he failed to retreat to a neutral corner after knocking Tunney down. The next superstar heavyweight was Joe Louis, battling Max Schmeling,* opposite right; *Billy Conn,* top; *and Jersey Joe Walcott,* bottom.

70

By the time Muhammad Ali successfully defended his
title with this first-round knockout of former champ
Sonny Liston, he had announced his conversion to
Islam and his membership in the Black Muslim sect.
Soon after he would refuse to be drafted and,
subsequently, be stripped of his title.

RULES OF THE FIGHT

In professional boxing each round lasts three minutes, and there is a one-minute rest period between rounds. In amateur boxing a round lasts either two or three minutes, and the rest period is one minute. Professional fights are normally scheduled to last between three and fifteen rounds; amateur fights usually have a three-round limit.

The rules of boxing are fairly simple. Fighters may strike blows only with their gloves. Hitting with the elbow, shoulder, heel of the hand, or head is a foul. Hitting below the belt and tripping are illegal. Hitting the opponent at the base of the neck—called a rabbit punch because it resembles a blow sometimes used to kill rabbits—is illegal. It is illegal to hit an opponent who is outside the ropes, down on one or both knees, or completely down. If a fighter remains down or outside the ropes for 10 counts (seconds) or more, the match is awarded to his opponent. When a boxer knocks his opponent down, he must move to a neutral corner—a corner that is not occupied by either fighter or the trainers during the rest periods—before the referee begins the count. If a fighter is knocked down and fails to regain his feet within 10 seconds, he is considered knocked out and loses the fight. Usually the 10-count must be completed before the end of the round. In some cases the count is continued even after the round ends, thus making it impossible to be "saved by the bell." If a fighter is unable to answer the bell at the beginning of a round, it is considered a technical knockout. A technical knockout also occurs when the referee, the ring physician, the fighter's trainers, or the fighter himself decides that he is unable to continue without risking serious injury.

SCORING

In the United States the referee and two ringside judges decide the winner if no knockout or technical knockout occurs. In Europe it is the referee alone. In the Olympics three ringside judges decide, the referee having no vote.

To score the match, the judges and/or referee use one of many different systems. In the round system, each scorer awards one point to the boxer whom he thinks won the round. At the end of the match, the rounds are totaled, and the fighter who won the most rounds is the winner.

In the 10-point-must system, the fighter who wins the round is given 10 points, his opponent between 9 and 0, depending on the closeness of the round. A 20-point-must system works on the same principle. In the 5-point system, the winner of the round is awarded between 1 and 5 points; the loser of the round always gets 0. If the round is even, each boxer is awarded the same number of points. In the 11-point system, 11 points are divided between the two fighters for each round. A very

close round would be scored 6 to 5, an even round 5½ to 5½. In all these point systems, the fighter with the higher total at the end of the event wins.

Fights decided by points or rounds are called decisions. For a fight with three judges, a decision may be either unanimous, if they all agree on the winner, or split, if one of them disagrees. A tie, called a draw, occurs when all scorers call a professional fight even, or when two scorers split and the third calls it even. There are no draws in amateur boxing—one of the boxers must be declared a winner.

TECHNIQUE

The right-handed fighter stands with his left foot, shoulder, and hand forward. He keeps his chin tucked in to protect it. His basic offensive weapon is the left jab, a straight, sharp blow that keeps his opponent off balance while it inflicts punishment. He stops his opponent's blows by blocking them with his gloves or forearms, or by slipping them—ducking under or around the blows.

When a boxer misses a blow, he usually leaves an opening in his defense. His opponent will try to take advantage of this opening with a counterpunch, which may be any of the basic punches. A combination is a series of blows thrown in a specific order.

WEIGHT CLASSES

Boxers usually fight only in their own weight class, though occasionally a fighter will box in a weight class heavier than his own.

HEAVIEST WEIGHT FOR EACH CLASS—PROFESSIONAL AND OLYMPIC

112 pounds—flyweight
118 pounds—bantamweight
126 pounds—featherweight
135 pounds—lightweight
147 pounds—welterweight
160 pounds—middleweight
175 pounds—light heavyweight
More than 175 pounds—heavyweight

HEAVIEST WEIGHT FOR EACH CLASS—AMATEUR

106 pounds—light flyweight
112 pounds—flyweight
119 pounds—bantamweight
125 pounds—featherweight
132 pounds—lightweight
139 pounds—light welterweight
147 pounds—welterweight
156 pounds—light middleweight
165 pounds—middleweight
178 pounds—light heavyweight
More than 178 pounds—heavyweight

Cricket

CRICKET FIELD

PITCH AREA

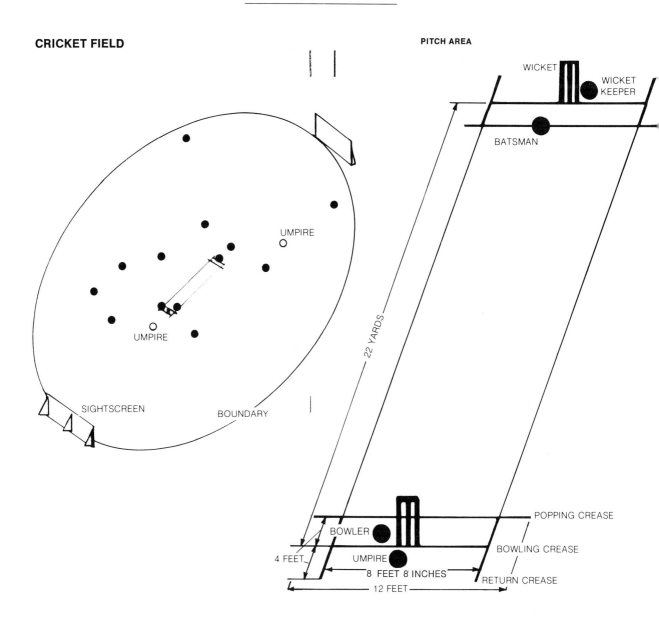

The essentials of cricket are the same as those of its American cousin, baseball. Cricket is a team sport, played with bat and ball, and involves pitching, hitting, fielding, and running between bases. The game is played in innings, one team batting while the other fields, and the winner is the team that scores the most runs. But cricket and baseball are more different than alike. Although both games may have descended from the same ancestor, each developed to suit the style of its own nation. Cricket is *the* game in England.

THE GAME

Cricket is played on a field about 450 to 550 feet long and from 400 to 500 feet wide. The central action of a cricket match takes place in the pitch area, the 66 feet between the two wickets. Each wicket is a little wooden structure consisting of three poles, or "stumps." Each stump is 28 inches high, and when three are placed together they form a 9-inch-wide wicket. Resting lengthwise in grooves atop these stumps are two long pieces of wood, the all-important bails. The batsman, standing at one end of the pitch, defends the wicket; the bowler, pitching from the other end, attacks.

A regulation cricket match consists of one or two innings—that is, one or two turns at bat for each team. During an innings (in cricket terminology the word *innings* is both singular and plural), each member of the 11-man team bats until his wicket is taken (in baseball terms, until he is out). In cricket it can sometimes take days to complete one match. In general a one-innings match is supposed to take one day, with intervals for lunch and tea. International, or "test," matches are always two innings long and usually last five days.

To start play, the defensive team places the bowler at one wicket and the wicketkeeper, the only member of the team permitted to wear gloves, at the other. The other members of the team are positioned in various parts of the field. There is no foul territory in cricket, so several fielders play behind the batsman. Two batsmen are always on the field—one at the wicketkeeper's end, batting, and the other at the bowler's end.

Cricket still retains the quaint custom of calling its pitcher a bowler. At one time, no doubt, the ball was rolled, but today a fast bowler, running up to the bowling crease and hurling the ball toward the batsman, is a human catapult. Not all bowlers rely on speed. Some bowl curves, or "swerves"; others bowl slow pitches, trying to deceive the batsmen. In all cases the bowler must deliver the ball with a straight elbow.

The bowler's purpose is to put out the batsman. The most dramatic way is for him to break the batsman's wicket—that is, to bowl the ball past the batsman and send the bails flying from their stumps. The ball he uses has a cork base and is covered with polished red leather. It is smaller than a baseball (about nine inches around) and slightly heavier.

The batsman stands near his wicket within a "popping crease," armored with a formidable amount of padding. His weapon is a triangular 38-inch long bat, or "blade," with a flat surface no more than 4½ inches wide. A cricket bat, unlike a baseball bat, is not designed for power; it is an instrument of more subtlety, intended to protect the wicket and to hit accurately and safely throught the weaknesses in the defense.

In cricket the baseball dictum, "Wait for your pitch," is often pushed to the limit. A batsman is not obliged to swing at any pitch he doesn't like, except to keep his wicket from being hit. And even when he does hit the ball, he doesn't have to run unless he thinks he and his partner can score—that is, exchange places without either of their wickets being broken. "Stonewalling," or extremely conservative offensive play, is common.

When the batsman does hit a ball to his satisfaction, he shouts to his partner (or if the ball is hit behind him, his partner signals to him), and they exchange positions, scoring one run each time they cross without being thrown out by a fielder. To throw out a man, the fielder must break the wicket before the runner reaches the safe area, marked by the crease. A ground ball hit beyond the boundary line scores four runs; a hit over the line on the fly scores six runs. Other runs, called "extras," are scored when the bowler bends his elbow (this is called "throwing" and is not at all cricket) or when he bowls out of the reach of the batsman.

In addition to being put out by having his wicket broken, whether by the bowler or a fielder, a batsman can be put out for hitting a fly ball that is caught by a fielder or by hitting the wicket with his bat or person. He is called out for touching the ball with his hands or purposely interfering with a fielder.

After the bowler has delivered six balls (eight balls in Australian play), the umpire calls "over," and play is directed toward the other wicket.

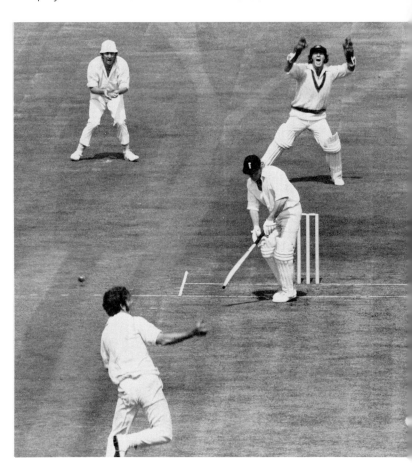

Unlike baseball, cricket doesn't require the batter to run when he hits the ball. His prime objective is to protect his wicket from being hit.

73

Croquet

HISTORY

The game of croquet is derived from the French *paille maille,* which is itself related to the Italian *pallemaglio.* The idea of this game was to drive the ball *(palla)* with a mallet *(maglio)* through iron hoops.

The game was played in France as early as the thirteenth century. It was introduced to England in the 1700s when Charles II returned from his exile in France. *Paille maille* was popular there for a while but died out. A similar game, again from France, called croquet after the word for hook *(croc),* came to England later, by way of Ireland.

In 1867, Walter Whitmore of England, an important man in the history of croquet, held a tournament, which he won. He provided systematic rules for the game and was instrumental in the formation of the All England Croquet Club.

EQUIPMENT

Croquet balls may be made of wood, hard rubber, or plastic and are usually 3⅝ inches in diameter. American wickets stand about 8 inches above the ground and measure 5 inches between the legs. Mallets have light shafts with relatively heavy heads affixed on the end. These heads are set perpendicular to the shaft.

THE GAME

The rules of American croquet differ from those of the English version. From one to eight people may play, either individually or in teams. The court should be level, and at least 60 feet long and 30 feet wide. A stake is placed at each end of the court; one stake, the home stake, is used for start and finish, the other stake to mark the midway point in the course. A typical court has nine hoops, or wickets, two in front of each stake, one to the right of each stake, two to the left of each stake, and one in the center of the court.

Players must hit their balls through all the hoops in some prescribed order and try to keep their opponents from doing so. A player gets one shot on every turn and one extra shot for every wicket he hits a ball through or for hitting a ball so that it touches the midway stake. If a player hits another player's ball, he may place his ball against his opponent's, put his foot on his own ball, and drive his opponent's away. This is called taking croquet. Afterward the player takes another stroke. Or, instead of driving his opponent's ball away, he may take two strokes.

Whoever completes the course first wins. In team play a player who completes the course becomes a rover and hinders the opposing team.

CROQUET COURT

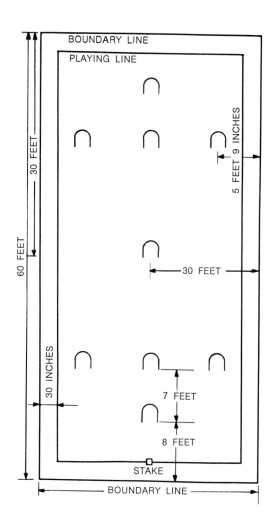

Curling

To most people, the sound of a curling stone as it roars across the ice is an unfamiliar one. But it is music to a Scotsman's ears. Curling has been called Scotland's own game, and it is played there with a passion. However, this ice game is also popular in other northern climates; it is one of Canada's most popular participant sports and is gaining popularity in the northern United States.

HISTORY

The origins of the game are unclear—historians from both Scotland and the Netherlands claim the honor for their countries. The Scotsmen produce the more solid evidence: ancient curling stones dredged up from the bottoms of ponds and lakes. One of these, the famous Stirling stone, is inscribed with the date 1511 and may be even older.

Whatever the sport's origin, the first curling match probably consisted of two men sliding rocks across the ice to see whose would go farther. Then a target was added—today called the "tee"—and curling became a contest of skill rather than strength.

THE GAME

Curling today, whether played outside on a frozen pond or lake or inside on a year-round ice rink, is still a simple game. It is played on a smooth ice surface, 138 by 14 feet, with a tee at each end. These tees are situated at the center of the "house," a target of concentric circles. Only stones placed within the house can score.

Curling is played by two teams, or "rinks," of four players each. In a manner somewhat like that of a bowler, each player delivers two stones, alternating with his opponent. Each rink scores one point for every stone it places nearer the tee than any of the other rink's. Each rink tries, therefore, both to get its stones as close to the tee as possible and to prevent the other team from doing so. In a way curling is a kind of shuffleboard on ice. A curler may help his rink and at the same time foil the opposition by placing stones to protect a rinkmate's stone, by bumping a rinkmate's stone closer to the tee, or by knocking away an opponent's stone.

The captain, or "skip," directs each team's strategy. He must be a master tactician because he directs each stone delivered by his teammates, and he must also be the best curler on the team because he curls last, when the ice is littered with stones. To start play, the skip stands at the target end of the ice, placing a broom on the ice for his rinkmate to aim at. His rinkmate, his eye on the skip's broom, tries to "curl" the stone where the skip has directed. Meanwhile, the other two members of the team stand on either side of the playing area, brooms at the ready. If the skip decides the stone is going to stop short of its target, he gives the command, "Sweep," and his rinkmates do just that. Originally a janitorial duty done to clear the ice of twigs and other debris blown there by the wind, sweeping is today an entrenched part of the game. It makes the ice slicker and helps the stone slide farther than it normally would.

When a rink has delivered all of its stones, it has completed an "end." After each rink has completed an end, both rinks play in the opposite direction. Most games today last for 10 ends, with extra ends added in case of a tie. The average game lasts about two and a half hours.

EQUIPMENT

Stones, called "granites," though they are no longer made of granite, weigh a maximum of 44 pounds and are no more than 36 inches around. Each stone has two sides, one for fast ice and one for slow ice, and a gooseneck handle that may be fitted to either side.

Curlers dress informally, without uniforms, and of course warmly. Some curlers have been known to play outdoors in temperatures of thirty degrees below zero.

CURLING RINK

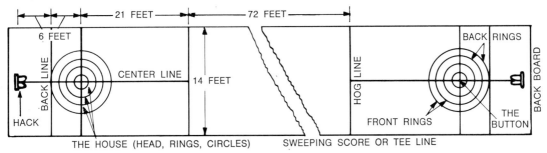

THE HOUSE (HEAD, RINGS, CIRCLES)   SWEEPING SCORE OR TEE LINE

Dog Racing

The greyhound is a phenomenally fast animal, capable of speeds up to forty miles per hour. A greyhound can match speed with a thoroughbred racehorse over a short distance and can cover up to twenty feet in a single stride. And unlike most dogs, it tracks by sight, not by smell. Speed and sight tracking are the two essential ingredients of modern dog racing, a sport in which real dogs chase a mechanical rabbit around an oval track. It is especially popular in the United States, Great Britain, and Australia.

Most of the spectators, like those who watch horseraces, come to the dog racing track to gamble. In Florida, where most of the dog racing in the United States is conducted, seventeen tracks operate each night and some afternoons at different times of the year. The four Miami-area tracks compete with jai alai and horseracing for vacationers' gambling dollars.

HISTORY

The rabbit in dog racing was not always mechanical. Coursing, the ancient ancestor of modern dog racing, was a sport in which two dogs chased one hare. Although the hare was given a head start, the dogs usually caught and killed it. The spectators would wager on which dog would reach the prize first. The original set of rules for this sport was established during the reign of Queen Elizabeth I, who greatly enjoyed coursing.

In this country humanitarians have always objected to what they consider the sickening cruelty of coursing. Yet the sport is still practiced, particularly in Kansas, where most American greyhounds are bred. (Most of the racing dogs in the United States are combinations of Irish and American bred greyhounds.) Ranchers contend that coursing serves a useful purpose in controlling the population of jackrabbits, which compete with herds of cattle for grazing land.

The cruelty to the rabbit in dog racing became a moot point with the invention of the mechanical

hare by an American, Owen Patrick Smith. Smith first demonstrated his patented device in 1919 at a race in Emeryville, California. He became quite a rich man as a result of his invention and organized the International Greyhound Racing Association. The chief governing body for the sport today is the American Greyhound Track Operators Association.

THE RACE

Races in the United States today are run on strips of sand and marl, and are five-sixteenths, three-eighths, or seven-sixteenths of a mile long. At the start of the race the dogs, wearing identifying numbers on their backs, are placed in starting boxes somewhat like those used in horseracing. As the mechanical rabbit passes the starting line, the barrier clangs open and the race begins. It ends a short time later as the dogs streak across the finish line.

Each dog's performance varies little from race to race; greyhounds are not only fast but also consistent in their performances. So to make the racing closer and more interesting, dogs are usually raced in classes with equally fast dogs. Anyone wanting to fix a race by tampering with a dog has to be pretty clever because if a dog runs much better or worse than usual, suspicions are apt to be aroused.

Two hours before each race, the dogs are turned over to the track officials. They check to see if the dogs have been given excessive food or drink, and they also take a close look at the dogs' feet, which in earlier days were sometimes tampered with. Every winner undergoes a urine test, and any dog that has run suspiciously badly may also be tested.

The world's most important races include the Hollywood World Classic, held in Hollywood, Florida; the International Classic and the Irish-American International Classic, both held in Miami, Florida; and Great Britain's Waterloo Cup, often called "the blue ribbon of the leash." All are annual events.

In dog racing, greyhounds specially bred for the track chase a mechanical rabbit around an oval track at speeds of as high as forty miles per hour.

Equestrian Sports

No other sport requires such harmony between the sensibilities of two such different creatures—man and horse. The horse is one of the most beautiful animals in the world but not one of the smartest. Left to its own devices, a horse would never jump fences, run races, or turn pirouettes on its hind legs. Yet it can be trained. Working well together, a horse and rider are one, with the man acting as the brain, and the horse the body.

Equestrian sports have always had an upper-class association. Unlike most stereotypes, this one was richly deserved. Members of the horsey set, a bit uneasy about this undemocratic image, point to statistics showing that the number of horses has doubled, from three to six million, in the past decade and that the number of entrants in competitions is also booming. Whether horseback riding is reaching down to the middle class or the middle class, with more time and money, is reaching up to it, equestrian sports are less elitist than they used to be.

Money alone won't make you a champion equestrian, however, nor will all the training money can buy. A champion horseman or horsewoman needs a certain innate sensitivity. This sensitivity, or "tact," is a quality of responsiveness and understanding of horses that cannot be taught. It may be the reason that women are often such fine equestrians. (In the Olympics the equestrian events are the only ones in which men and women compete on an equal basis.) Indeed, at least one noted authority, Captain Vladimir Littauer, considers girls more able riders than boys. He contends that girls are more sensitive to horses than boys and therefore more likely to use persuasion rather than force in getting a horse to accomplish something.

HISTORY

Men have been riding horses, scientifically or unscientifically, since at least 2000 B.C. But only in the last several centuries has man tried to systematize his knowledge. Various schools of riding, often engaging in fierce debates with one another, have contributed to the art.

One of the first to write about riding was Xenophon, a famous Greek general of the fourth century B.C. His theories were not very technical, but if they had been followed, countless horses would have been spared much pain. Among other things, Xenophon believed that whipping a horse to train it was no more useful than whipping an acrobat.

Frederiga Grisone, an Italian who wrote a book on riding in 1550, had other ideas about horse psychology. He belonged to the spare-the-rod-and-spoil-the-child school of horse training, believing that a horse that wouldn't obey did so out of willful

Olympic equestrian events include not only fancy dressage maneuvers but grueling endurance tests, the courses for which include a variety of obstacles.

obstinacy and should be punished. Many shared his belief and treated their horses with extreme cruelty.

Grisone may be considered the founder of dressage, a highly stylized type of riding that started in Italy during the Renaissance. To the aesthetically minded noblemen of the time, a prancing horse was a decided social asset. The science of dressage was advanced and greatly refined in the following centuries and flowered in the eighteenth century. Today, a more natural form of riding is favored, and dressage is mainly practiced in circuses and, in its most developed, *haute école* style, by the Spanish

Riding School of Vienna, where beautiful white Lipizzaner stallions perform movements that are learned and perfected over many years of training by both horses and riders.

In dressage movements a horse is considered "collected." That is, its head and neck are higher, and its center of gravity is more to the rear than normal, so that the hind legs carry more weight.

By the second half of the eighteenth century, military needs demanded simpler, more practical riding. Dressage teachers still insisted on the practical value of their method in battle, but such claims were dubious.

At the end of the nineteenth century, an Italian cavalry officer, Captain Frederico Caprilli, revolutionized riding. After mounting a dummy on his mare and observing the horse's movements, he formulated some new theories, the most important of which was the "forward seat." Before Caprilli, theories of where to keep one's weight while riding were based on the gaits of collected horses, and when a horse extended itself, as in a jump, horsemen sat back as they would on a collected horse. But Caprilli observed that the horse's center of gravity was toward the front, so such riding could only disturb it and produce some very awkward jumps (if the horse, anticipating discomfort, could be persuaded to jump at all). Caprilli's theories of placing the rider's weight over the withers, the ridge between the horse's shoulder bones and also its center of gravity, were spread by his pupils even after the master died (in a jumping accident).

TECHNIQUE

It is in the use of Caprilli's principles today that every trained rider earns the right to be considered a true athlete, even though ignorant observers are apt to conclude that the human atop the horse is just animate baggage.

SHOW JUMPING COURSE

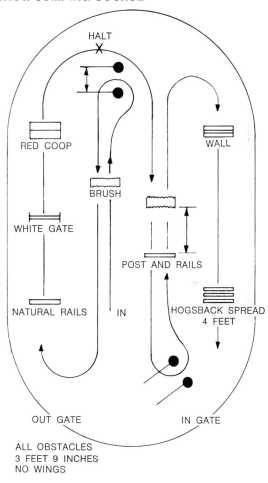

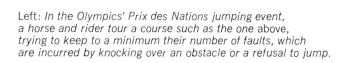

Left: *In the Olympics' Prix des Nations jumping event, a horse and rider tour a course such as the one above, trying to keep to a minimum their number of faults, which are incurred by knocking over an obstacle or a refusal to jump.*

The average rider adds weight equaling about one-fifth of the horse's to his mount. Shifted at random, this weight would be extremely uncomfortable to the horse, so the rider must maintain a good seat by adapting himself to the constantly shifting balance of the horse. When a horse is at rest, its center of gravity is the point where a vertical line drawn behind the withers would meet a horizontal line from shoulder to buttocks. As the horse moves, this center changes: a horse raising its neck shifts the center backward; lengthening its neck, it shifts it forward.

The rider's weight, voice, hands, legs, and heels are the rider's aids. The hands control the reins and the bit in the horse's mouth, which can be used to restrain the horse and, with the action of the rider's legs, change the horse's direction. The legs urge the horse forward or sideways. In addition the rider shifts his body weight to coax the horse to change gait or direction.

Artificial aids, such as whips and spurs, are also used when natural aids prove insufficient.

A horseman's form is judged directly only in horsemanship events, but good form is important because, as in all sports, good form generally does the best job. Nevertheless, horsemen have been known to carry their concern for good form to an extreme, complaining that a jump was successful but the form was bad.

HAUTE ECOLE DRESSAGE

The haute école movements in dressage are divided into two categories. First there are the "airs on the ground"—movements that the horse performs without leaving its feet. These include the *pirouettes,* either half or full turns done by the horse on its hind legs; the *piaffer,* a stylized trot done in place; its slow-motion counterpart, the *passage;* and finally the *levade,* in which the horse balances on its hind legs and draws its forelegs in.

Most dazzling is the second category, or "airs above the ground." The Lipizzaner stallions of the Spanish Riding School of Vienna are practically the only horses that still perform these movements, which are basically jumps from a stationary position. The *courbette,* for example, consists of a jump straight up from a *levade* position. The *ballotade* and the *capriole* are both jumps from a four-legged standing position. The difference is that the *capriole* involves a greater extension of the hind legs at the peak of the jump. All *haute école* movements, whether on the ground or above the ground, can be performed with a rider on board or not—with the horse either held by a rein ("in hand") or with the horse tied between two posts and untouched by the trainer ("between the pillars").

COMPETITION

Until this century, equestrian riding competitions were unheard of in America. Today, a wide variety of equestrian events take place, the most popular of which are the jumping events. The American Horse

Shows Association, founded in 1917, today regulates most of the events in this country.

Horse shows are an outgrowth of exhibitions held by breeders at country fairs. The most important horse show in the United States is the National Horse Show, held each year in New York City's Madison Square Garden. The first show, in 1883, was not quite as sophisticated as today's—besides horses it included mules, donkeys, and fire engines. At that time the horse was a creature of practical value, so there was even a mounted-police division event, in which the winner was the man who could jump on his horse and rescue a runaway the fastest.

The best known equestrian events take place every four years at the Olympic games. The competition consists of Grand Prix dressage, the Prix des Nations, and the three-day endurance event.

The Olympic Grand Prix dressage event is simpler than the dressage of the old Spanish schools because maneuvers such as airs above the ground are not part of the competition. Each nation enters three competitors, and each rider is given 12 minutes to complete the program. Both horse and rider are judged, earning as many as 10 points for a very good performance and as few as 1 for a poor one. Judging is often quite controversial, but controversy is probably unavoidable because there are no universally accepted standards. Dressage is, after all, an art form, and art critics rarely agree.

The Prix des Nations jumping event gets more difficult at each Olympics. In the 1912 Olympics, the highest obstacles were 4 feet 6 inches. In 1960, the highest were 5 feet 3 inches, with most between 4 feet 6 inches and 4 feet 10 inches. Half the teams were eliminated in the first round. The event is based on galloping cross-country, as one might when engaged in fox hunting or warfare. A knock-down of an obstacle scores four faults, and a first refusal to jump, three. The medal goes to the team or individual with the least faults. In case of a tie the team or rider completing the course in the least time wins.

The three-day event, or Complete Test of Equitation, is an object of some controversy. Consisting of three events on three successive days—dressage, then endurance, and finally a jumping event—the event makes it a triumph just to remain in competition until the last day. The aim of the event is to test the versatility of horse and rider (the same pair competes all three days), but it is more often a test of endurance. Quite a few teams are eliminated after the second day, which includes a grueling 22-mile course over swamps, roads, trails, and steeplechase obstacles. It is not uncommon for horses to die, and many equestrians complain that few horses are versatile enough for such a test. Almost invariably, the horses who do well in dressage do poorly in the cross-country section.

The Olympics and most international events are regulated by the Federation Equestre Internationale, founded in 1921.

Fencing

Modern fencing is a demanding skill, requiring the utmost coordination of mind and body. Good fencers must practice constantly to develop the necessary body control and lightning-fast reactions for this, perhaps the fastest of all sports. Even champion fencers, like ballet dancers, continue to practice under their masters far into their careers.

HISTORY

The art of fencing, or attack and defense with a sword, is an ancient one. A relief in an Egyptian temple of about 1190 B.C. clearly shows spectators enjoying a fencing match. The combatants, wearing masks and holding shields, are using swords with covered points. Says one of the fencers (his words shown in hieroglyphics), "On guard, and admire what my valiant hand shall do."

Fencing in Europe dates from the fourteenth century. The Marxbrüder (Fencing Guild) of Frankfort, Germany, existed in 1383, and by the fifteenth century, fencing was flourishing in Italy as well. The introduction of gunpowder made the sword less useful as a military weapon, but the gentleman called on to defend his honor in a duel or to defend his life from attack by brigands had to know how to use a sword. Fencing masters, many of whom had earned their living putting on exhibitions, began to do a lively business as instructors for the young men of the aristocracy.

By 1570, the major movements used in fencing today had evolved, and by 1680, a sleeker, more stylish sword had been introduced by Count Koenigsmarken of Poland. This weapon was to serve as the model for the three types of weapons used in modern fencing.

COMPETITION AND EQUIPMENT

Fencing competition is divided into three major categories, corresponding to the weapons used: foil, épée, and sabre.

The basic fencing weapon is the foil. Beginners are advised to learn with the foil because foil techniques can be applied to all kinds of fencing. It is the lightest of the three weapons, with a weight of no more than five hundred grams. The blade is quadrangular, and tapers from the handle so that it is quite thin and flexible near the point, or "button." The handguard is usually circular, with a maximum diameter of twelve centimeters. There are many forms of handles. The French handle, a straight shaft behind the handguard, is a popular one in the United States. In foil competition only hits by the point to the trunk are counted—hits to the head, arms, and legs are not.

Epée fencing, which developed in the seventeenth century, did not begin as a sport: its purpose was to train men for duels. Thus, when sporting

There are three forms of fencing competition, based on the three different weapons—foil, épée, and sabre. Epée, above, is a free form, stemming as it does from training for duels.

competition began, the matches were arranged to resemble as closely as possible the conditions of an actual duel. This is still true, and the relatively free form of épée fencing, one of the events in the Olympic pentathlon, makes it especially popular among spectators.

The triangular épée blade is stiffer and heavier than that of the foil. Hits, or touches, to all parts of the body count, so the handguard is larger (13.5 centimeters around) to protect against hits to the arm. The length of the épée is the same as that of the foil, 110 centimeters from pommel to tip; its weight may not exceed 770 grams.

The timing of a hit is all-important in épée competition. Two simultaneous hits count against both fencers, since in a real duel, both duelists would be wounded (or dead).

The sabre, based on the military weapon, was introduced to fencing as a practice weapon. Later, because of the efforts of some Hungarian fencing masters, it gained popularity in its own right. It has a flat, V-shaped blade, and its bottom, or "cutting," edge is blunted. The end of the sabre is folded over to make the button. The guard is half-circular and functions to protect the knuckles.

Sabre competition is particularly interesting because touches may be made with all of the front edge of the blade, the first third of the back edge, and the point. The targets are the head, arms, and trunk to just below the waist.

Around 1800, the introduction of the wire-mesh mask revolutionized fencing. Before then, rules were based very much on the idea of safety. Even so, many fencers lost their eyes—indeed, it was said that no good fencing master ever ended his life with both his eyes.

In addition to his mask, the fencer wears a padded bib, a sturdy glove, a jacket, a protective undergarment, trousers or knickers with long stockings, and flat-soled shoes. In competition fencers dress all in white.

Fencing competition takes place on a strip made of rubber, wood, linoleum, cork, metal, metallic mesh, or synthetic materials. The strip is at least 14 meters long and from 1.8 to 2 meters wide. Fencers are penalized one touch if after one warning they retreat off the rear of this strip during combat.

THE GAME

For many reasons fencing has been compared to chess. Both require an infinite and complex variety of movements; both stress deception and anticipation of the opponent's move far in advance; both are bound by strict rules. But the basis of fencing is and always has been simple: to hit and avoid being hit.

Foil and sabre competitions are ruled by certain conventions. According to these rules, or *phase d'armes*, the attacker has the right to attack until his attack is parried or defended. Then the right to counterattack, or riposte, passes to the other fencer, and the sequence is repeated. This back-and-forth character of the game explains why fencing is often called a "conversation with blades."

In most fencing bouts, five touches must be scored within six minutes to win. In épée events, since it is possible to score simultaneous touches, competitors will occasionally tie at five each. When they do, the bout continues until one competitor scores a clear-cut touch or time expires with the score still tied, in which case a double defeat is scored.

A bout begins in the *en garde* position, the basic position in fencing. In this position the body is well balanced, ready to advance or retreat. Basic fencing moves are the lunge, a rapid attacking move; the parry, or deflecting of the blade; the riposte, or counterattack after parry; the balestra, a short jump, usually followed by a lunge; and the flèche, or running attack.

Fencing bouts are judged by a director (or president) and four judges. Their task was never an easy one, as a journalist, writing in 1896, observed: ". . . it is necessary for the judge to possess the eye of a hawk and the agility of the tiger in order to keep the lightning-like movements of both points well under observation." Arguments were frequent. Today an electronic scoring apparatus has made judging easier. Used in foil and épée events, this device, attached by wires to the tip of the weapon, records valid hits. When it is used, the director alone, without the assistance of judges, presides.

FENCING PISTE

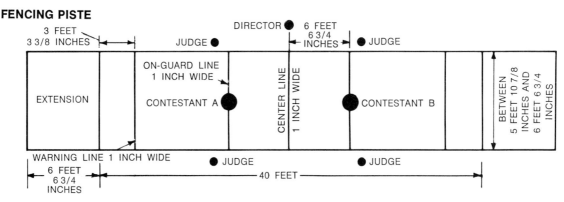

Foils, opposite bottom, *is the basic fencing competition. Only hits to the trunk are counted. In sabre competition,* opposite top, *hits are counted if they are made with the side or the point of the blade.*

Field Hockey

Neither as violent as ice hockey and lacrosse, nor as stagnant as soccer can sometimes be, field hockey may be the perfect compromise. The players run endlessly up and down a long field, testing not only their stamina but their speed, stickhandling skill, and teamwork. It's not the most spectacular sport, but it is one of the most accessible. Everyone can play—men and women—and enjoy the thrill of bashing home a goal without the fear of being bashed in retaliation.

HISTORY

The sport of field hockey started with the Persians, from whom the Greeks learned it. Perhaps the first representation of field hockey comes from a Greek bas-relief about twenty-five hundred years old. It shows several stick-carrying youths standing around a central pair engaged in a "bully," or faceoff.

Modern field hockey owes its development to the English, who took the game to heart, forming hockey clubs in the late 1800s and gradually developing rules. The British army spread the game to India, which today remains a field hockey power. The game caught on especially quickly among English women eager to emancipate themselves from the confining clothes and passive diversions of Victorian womanhood. In 1887, field hockey was proclaimed the national sport of British women. They shared the game with their American counter-parts, largely through the efforts of Miss Constance Applebee, a formidable Englishwoman. Field hockey, she believed, "develops strong nerves, will power, determination, discipline, and endurance."

FIELD AND EQUIPMENT

Field hockey certainly develops endurance. For two 35-minute halves, each team of players tries to maneuver a 5½- to 5¾-ounce leather-covered or plastic ball into a goal, placed at each end of the field, which is between 90 and 100 yards long and as wide as 65 or 70 yards. Substitutions are now allowed, but there are no timeouts.

Each team has eleven players—five forwards, who are offensive players, three halfbacks, two fullbacks, and a goalkeeper. Except for the goalie, who is well padded, field hockey players are equipped with nothing more than their J-shaped sticks. Shinguards, made of canvas with reed inserts, are available, but seasoned players shun their use in matches. The stick is about three feet long, with a curved blade rounded on the back side and flat on the front, striking side. Only right-handed sticks are allowed.

THE GAME

The object of the game is to score goals, worth one point each, by knocking the ball into the goal from within a semicircle, called "the striking circle," that surrounds the goal. Play starts at the beginning of

Right: *Dribbling a ball in field hockey is stickhandling under pressure.* Above: *Goals are scored on shots hit from within the striking circle, as on this penalty shot.*

each half and after each score with the bully. Two players, facing each other at the center of the field, quickly strike the ground, then each other's stick three times. Then they go for the ball, trying to gain control of it for their team.

A player with the ball attempts to advance it by dribbling—pushing it ahead of him with small taps of the stick as he runs. It takes a lot of coordination to develop the ideal dribble, in which the ball is only a few inches from the end of the stick. The dribble used, of course, depends on how closely the opposition is following; if all opponents are far away, the ball can be dribbled farther in front of the body. Passes to teammates are made by drive shots— strong strokes made with both hands held close together on the stick—or push shots, which are shorter strokes, made with the hands spread apart.

Opponents try to tackle the player in possession of the ball. This is not a tackle in the football sense, nor a crafty trip with the stick, but rather a simple play for the ball. Body contact is forbidden in field hockey.

Most fouls are called to discourage unsafe play. Raising the stick above shoulder level may be a good way of hitting the ball hard, but in field hockey it will only result in a call of "sticks," a foul. The obstruction rule forbids players from using their bodies to block others from getting the ball. Other infractions are hitting the ball with the foot or hand (either intentionally or unintentionally), and hitting the ball over one's own goal line. There is an offside rule in field hockey similar to the one used in soccer. Stated simply, the rule says that "no player may receive a pass in the offensive zone unless there are at least two defensive players between him and the

FIELD HOCKEY FIELD

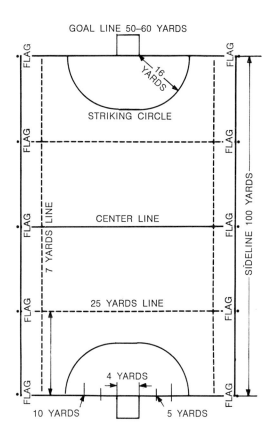

goal." The usual penalty for infractions such as offsides is to give the opposition a free hit from the point of the foul.

Penalty shots on the goal are awarded when infractions have obviously prevented a goal—for example, if a defender other than the goalie intentionally kicks the ball away from the goal.

COMPETITION

Field hockey is played everywhere as an amateur sport. In the United States even the most important matches are attended by only a handful of spectators. In countries such as Great Britain and India, however, important matches fill stadiums.

Field hockey, for men at least, has been an Olympic sport since 1908. It has been dominated by the Indians and the Pakistanis, who play an exuberant, highly skilled game, and lately the Dutch and Germans. International matches for women are organized by the International Federation of Women's Hockey Association and the Federacion Internationale de Hockey, the governing body of the sport.

85

Football

Some years ago certain movie houses in the United States began what to the nonfootball fan must have seemed a bizarre promotion. "Football Widows—Half Price," read the marquees. Football is a violent sport, but these football widows are not the former wives of deceased athletes. They are the millions of American wives whose husbands forsake them on autumn weekends and Monday nights for the weekly television broadcasts of the modern American mania—football. From September through January, football fever rages through the nation. Recent surveys show that it has replaced baseball as America's favorite spectator sport. Millions watch it, millions play it, and millions of dollars are bet on it.

In the major cities pro football teams, even those with lackluster records, play before crowds that overflow the huge stadiums. In rural towns and small cities, the local high school or college game is the high point of any fall weekend. College rivalries such as Army-Navy, Southern California-UCLA, Nebraska-Oklahoma, and Auburn-Alabama arouse the passions not only of undergraduates, alumni, and local supporters but of a nationwide audience for whom the schools would not exist but for their football teams. Shortly after his inauguration, President Gerald Ford received a telegram from Ohio State football coach Woody Hayes stating that Hayes would give Ford his fullest support "even though you're a Michigan man."

Football is a complicated game that is at its best when it boils down to a simple one, such as this: get the quarterback. Here, Roger Staubach bests Alan Page.

HISTORY

Football has become more and more scientific through the years. The modern football terminology—zig outs, checkoffs, automatics—could be confused by the uninitiated with an astronaut's checklist, and the playbooks used by football teams often look as complicated as electronic circuit diagrams.

Nevertheless, the game is still a battle for territory, not so different from the way it was in 1869, the date many recognize as the birthdate of American football. In that year, Rutgers and the College of New Jersey, now known as Princeton, met at Rutgers field in New Brunswick, New Jersey. The game the two teams played resembled British football, that is, soccer, much more than it did American football, and the final score resembled baseball more than either. Rutgers won 6–4. There were 25 men to a side, and running with the ball or touching it with the hands was for the most part illegal.

Five years later Harvard University played Montreal's McGill University in a game that bore a closer resemblance to our football. There were 15 men per team; running with the ball as well as tackling and blocking were permitted.

In 1876, Columbia, Harvard, and Yale banded together to form the Intercollegiate Football Association, which standardized rules for the first time in the United States. The association reduced the number of players per side to 11, divided the game into two 45-minute halves, reduced the size of the playing field to 110 by 53 yards, and designated a center to hike the ball and a signal caller to receive it.

The man behind most of these significant changes, the foundation of the modern game, was Walter Camp, the Yale coach and a member of the Intercollegiate Football Association's rules committee. But Camp soon realized that even with the changes the game remained nothing more than a battle to prevent the opposition from scoring. Players concentrated on keeping control of the ball, mostly by simply clutching it, and the style of offense was no more subtle than a herd of frontiersmen clearing a forest. The ball carrier's 10 teammates usually surrounded him in a flying-wedge formation and simply plowed their way through the opposition. If the runner was knocked down, he either crawled or was pulled along by his teammates.

Camp proposed the idea of halting play after the ball carrier was knocked down, allowing each team three sequences, or "downs," to advance the ball five yards. If the ball-carrying team succeeded, it would gain the chance to move another five yards in another three downs; if it failed, it would surrender the ball to the opponent.

These rules were adopted in 1882, but through the 1880s and past the turn of the century, the game remained a brutal defensive affair, with teams plowing downfield hoping to get close enough to the goalposts to kick a field goal—a kick that traveled over the crossbar and between the uprights. Serious injuries were common.

In 1905, President Theodore Roosevelt threatened to outlaw the game if it was not cleaned up. In response, representatives of the Intercollegiate Football Association (which had now grown to include 60 schools) met and outlawed many of the roughhouse tactics. Teammates were prohibited from locking arms with each other while they tried to clear a path for the ball carrier, and it was decreed that the offensive team must have seven men on the line of scrimmage at the beginning of each play. Even the ball changed. The old, nearly round ball had been ideal for a drop-kick (a kick in which the ball is bounced first), but it was unwieldy to carry and throw. It was replaced by a narrower ball that was the prototype of today's football. Each team was given four downs to advance the ball 10 yards and the scoring system was altered to put more emphasis on the touchdown rather than the field goal.

By the early 1900s, football had already reached many high schools and colleges, but—more important—independent teams were springing up in many villages and towns, especially in the Midwest. In 1905, the Massillon, Ohio, Tigers were formed and a short time later the Canton, Ohio, Bulldogs. The early rivalry between these two Ohio towns sowed the seeds of professional football. In 1915, the Canton Bulldogs acquired two stars, Pete Calac and a rugged-looking Indian, Jim Thorpe, both of whom had led their Carlisle Indian Institute team to the national collegiate championship. Thorpe would later be named president of the American Professional Football Association at a meeting of 11 team owners in Canton in 1921. The teams were mostly from small Midwestern towns, whose people still had simple tastes and a simple concept of football: Mow down the opposition by running right at it with as many and as strong blockers as possible. That philosophy would continue to rule football through the twenties.

Although the forward pass had been legalized in 1906, most early teams regarded it as a cheap, unmanly tactic. Pop Warner, one of the game's greatest coaches, felt that the forward pass should be made illegal. "I think a game of football should be decided strictly on merit," he explained.

In 1913, Gus Dorais combined with end Knute Rockne for a virtual exhibition of pass catching that led underdog Notre Dame to victory over a shocked Army team. Still, the dominating offense throughout the 1920s remained the run. The standard formation was the straightforward and uncomplicated single wing, in which one of the backfield men, the tailback, would take the snap from center and follow the other three backs through the hole, usually off tackle. Two blockers were assigned to the key defenders.

By 1923, there were 20 teams in the professional National Football League, including an entrant formed by Curly Lambeau from the Acme

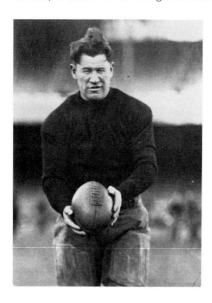

Packing Company in Green Bay, Wisconsin. Professional football was still a struggling enterprise. (The original $100 membership fee had been cut in half in 1922.) In 1925, professional football got the boost it needed when George Halas's Chicago Bears obtained football's most publicized college hero, Red Grange. His salary was generous— half the gate receipts—but the Bears and pro football were in no position to be stingy with a superstar. The investment proved to be sound; crowds in New York and Los Angeles reached seventy thousand when the Bears played a series of exhibitions there. In 1930, the Bears also signed Bronko Nagurski, the powerful running back from the University of Minnesota.

The economic depression of the thirties barely dampened the football boom. Beaver-coated crowds armed with "State" banners and whiskey flasks came by the thousands to see college games. A 1935 game between Notre Dame and Ohio State drew eighty-one thousand. In the pro game, meanwhile, George Halas and George Preston Marshall had pushed through several significant rules changes. The ball had been trimmed down even further, and the rule that a passer had to be at least five yards behind the line of scrimmage was abolished. Rules for a professional championship play-off were also formulated. The country was restless and looking for excitement. Football was about to accommodate it.

On his first play as a pro against the Chicago Bears, a wiry end from the University of Alabama, Don Hutson, raced upfield and caught a game-winning 83-yard bomb, the first of 99 passes Hutson was to catch before he retired. The pass was at long last to become an established, offensive weapon. In the first championship game, the Bears gained a last-quarter victory on a pass by, of all people, the great runner Bronko Nagurski. The acceptance of the pass would lead football through another major change, from single wing to T-formation.

During the thirties, the Bears were using a new formation designed by coach George Halas to add blocking power to their running attack. Three deep backs lined up tightly behind the fourth, the quarterback, who stood immediately in back of the center and received the ball from his hands rather than in a pass. Two imaginary lines—one from the center through the quarterback to the middle deep back, the other through the three deep backs—formed an inverted T, and thus the T-formation gained its name. The Bears were one of the lowest scoring teams in pro football (despite their fine record), but their new offense had very subtly shifted the strategy of offensive football from pure power to sly deception. Halas devised a man-in-motion play, in which a player would run laterally to one side during the count, before the ball was snapped, thus decoying opposing players away from the true area of attack.

In the late 1930s, Clark Shaughnessy, the football coach at the University of Chicago, began to see even greater offensive possibilities in Halas's T-formation. In 1939, when his school dropped the sport of football, Shaughnessy began visiting the Bears' practice sessions. Soon he had collaborated with Halas in revitalizing the offense with a series of quick openers and counter plays that suckered the defenders hopelessly out of position. That year, Halas had acquired an All-American tailback from Columbia, Sid Luckman, who led the Bears against the Washington Redskins in the championship game the following year. The Redskins had edged the Bears 7–3 three weeks before the big game, prompting the Bears to refine their counter plays. Now Luckman quarterbacked the quick-hitting attack to perfection, and the Bears mauled the Redskins 73–0, the most lopsided title victory ever.

By the mid-forties, most pro teams had changed to the T-formation. In 1943, Washington's great Sammy Baugh decided to try out the new system after years of success with his passes from the single wing. At first, the lanky Texan found the new system awkward, but after two years of study and practice, he was using it full-time.

The T-formation, with its emphasis on tricky ball handling and passing, changed football from a team game to a game marked more by individuals. A football offense was no longer composed of merely 11 cogs in a well-oiled blocking machine. No longer did one hear about the Four Horsemen, the Seven Blocks of Granite, or the Twin Engines of Destruction. In the 1950s, attention became riveted on the quarterback—Cleveland's Otto Graham, Los Angeles's Bob Waterfield and Norm Van Brocklin, Detroit's Bobby Layne, New York's Charley Conerley, and Baltimore's Johnny Unitas. The T-quarterback came to direct the game. Only he, it seemed, could rally a team after it had yielded a score and march it downfield with impeccable play calling and execution. He rarely had the ball when the play ended, but it seemed he never lost control of it.

Before long the defenses realized how vital the quarterback was. In the 1950s, the quarterback became the man to "get," and giant but nimble defensive linemen were acquired to do the job. Behind the defensive linemen was an even newer breed of defensive specialist, the three linebackers. The middle linebacker became the quarterback's opposite number, directing the defense against the quarterback-directed offense. He might call a "blitz" play and lead the charge on the quarterback, or he might "key" on a running back and rely on the back's movement to reveal the offensive strategy of a play.

The fifties will no doubt best be remembered as the era of the pass. Many offenses modified the T-formation to facilitate the passing game. One of the running backs was moved from behind the quarter-

The advent of the T-formation forced such accomplished single-wing operators as Sammy Baugh (running from the single-wing formation, above), to learn a new system. The first to master it was Chicago's Sid Luckman, left.

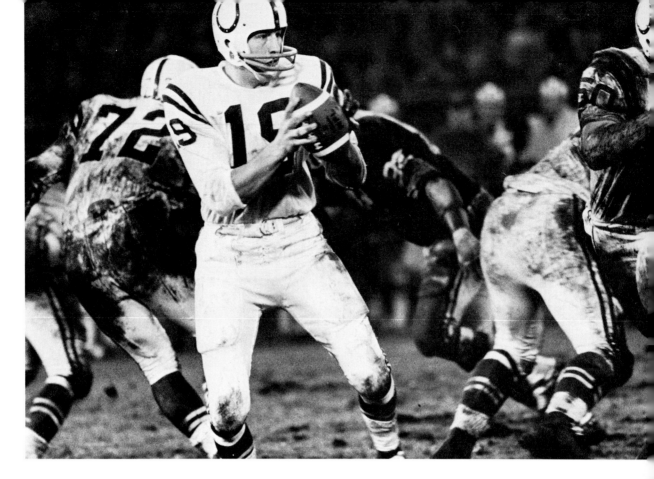

Top: *In the era of the quarterback, Johnny Unitas showed just how fully a quarterback could control a football game.* Above: *Jim Brown was one of few running backs who could run around tackles or through them.* Right: *Baltimore's Gino Marchetti rushing New York's Charley Conerly in the 1958 NFL championship game, which many people regard as the best football game ever.*

back to a position close to the line of scrimmage just beyond the linemen. Sometimes the end was split from the line, too. Thus, the wing-T and split-T were derived, formations that allowed a fleet receiver to move downfield for passes without having to negotiate the tumultuous line play. The Los Angeles Rams took a great running back, Elroy ("Crazylegs") Hirsch, and moved him well clear of their line formation to the "flank," from which position he would race downfield and haul in long passes for quick, killing touchdowns. "The bomb" had come to football.

In December 1958, the American public learned more dramatically than ever before of the brilliant struggle pro football had become. The high-powered offensive machine of the Baltimore Colts, led by quarterback Johnny Unitas, running backs Alan ("the Horse") Ameche and Lenny Moore, and split end Raymond Berry confronted the steadfast defense of the New York Giants in the NFL's championship game. When Unitas hit Lenny Moore for a 60-yard touchdown pass early in the game, it looked as if the offense that had averaged more than 30 points per game during the regular season might trample the Giants too. At halftime Baltimore led 14–3. But led by their sterling front four of Andy Robustelli, Rosey Grier, Dick Modzelewski, and Jim Katcavage and middle linebacker Sam Huff, the Giants stymied the Colts in the second half. In the third period the defense stopped the Colts for minus one yard on four tries from the Giants' 3-yard line. Inspired by this stand, the Giants' offense finally exploded, first for a bizarre, 89-yard pass-fumble-and-run play that set up the New Yorkers' first touchdown, then on a more common touchdown pass, from Charley Conerly to Frank Gifford. That score gave the Giants a 17–14 lead in the final quarter. The clock seemed to be counting out the Colts, but with two minutes to play they regained the ball, and the masterful Unitas began moving his team inexorably downfield. He hit Raymond Berry with three remarkable passes for 62 yards, and with 15 seconds left in regulation play, Steve Myhra kicked a 20-yard field goal that tied the score and sent the championship game into a sudden death playoff, the first in NFL history.

The overtime period was almost anticlimactic. Unitas once again overcame the Giants' stubborn defense, and at 8:15 of the extension sent Ameche tumbling into the Giants' end zone for the winning score. The triumph was all of pro football's, not only the Colts'. The game had been viewed by millions on national television, and their interest sold the television executives on the sport. Bolstered by a national television contract, pro football began its meteoric rise to the very top of American sports.

Other businessmen soon realized the potentials of this nationwide audience. In 1959, the American Football League was formed and announced that it would begin play the next year with an eight-team league. NFL owners first scoffed at the thought, but the AFL quickly gained television

backing, and its success was assured. The new league gave its fans wide-open, high-scoring football, partly because it lacked the talented defensive players of the NFL.

Determined and often rich enough to buy the talent they wanted, the AFL owners embarked on a bitter legal and financial battle to lure the top college players with huge money offers. Player salaries and bonuses soared. Suddenly, football was big business. Farm boys from Nebraska and ghetto youths from Watts suddenly saw the opportunity for fame and fortune in a football career. Colleges, too, were feeling the pressure for success in the world of big-time football. The big money from television coverage and postseason bowl games set off recruiting wars for high school talent. Promising prospects were offered cash, automobiles, and no-study courses as a lure to attend the big football schools. The system persists today at many of the football factories, where star athletes live generally isolated from the student body and many of the usual aspects of college life.

Perhaps the best of this new generation of carefully bred football players was Joe Namath, a country boy from Beaver Falls, Pennsylvania, who became a star quarterback at the University of Alabama under the legendary coach, Bear Bryant. When Namath graduated in 1964, he inspired the highest bidding yet between the two leagues. The AFL's New York Jets finally won him for $400,000, and a small-town boy almost overnight became "Broadway Joe." He would soon prove to be worth every bit of his salary.

In 1966, the two leagues finally agreed to merge, a decision aided by court rulings favorable to the AFL. The terms of the settlement provided for the eventual formation of two conferences, the American and the National. The two 13-team conferences were to be further divided into three divisions each. In both conferences the Eastern Division would include five teams and the Central and Western divisions four teams each. (Expansion in 1976 filled out each division to five teams.)

Under the rules of the merger, the division winners of each conference were to compete in playoff games at the end of each season to determine the conference champion. The two winners would then meet in a final title game for the world championship. This "Super Bowl" was a fan's dream and a promoter's gold mine. The tremendous publicity buildup before the first Super Bowl was unmatched in the sports world, but the game itself hardly lived up to its billing. Before sixty-one thousand fans in the Los Angeles Coliseum, Super Bowl I, between the Kansas City Chiefs and the Green Bay Packers, only proved what everyone already knew: the young AFL was no match for the established league. Under their martinet of a coach, Vince Lombardi, the Packers had combined a methodical ground attack and conservative but precise passing with a defense so grudging as to compare favorably with Fordham's old Seven

very capable offense but, more important, a defensive system that would dominate pro football during the late sixties and into the seventies—the zone pass defense.

To stop the pass, coaches had begun to reprogram for the defensive backfield players who had starred on offense in college. But the Colts went beyond matching great pass catchers with great defenders. In their system each defender covered an area rather than a particular receiver. Using a version of the zone defense that conceded the 5- to 10-yard pass but closed viselike on anything longer, the Colts had allowed just 144 points during the regular season—half as many as the Jets.

Jets' quarterback Joe Namath, who, with a flamboyant style and a great passing arm, had already begun to pay handsome dividends on his huge salary, openly scoffed at the odds-makers and "guaranteed" a Jets' victory. Joe's prediction proved to be more than idle boasting. His pinpoint passing was sharp enough to penetrate the Colts' zone; his quick drop and release frustrated the Colts' rushers. Namath guided the Jets on an 80-yard touchdown march in the second period and then completely controlled the game in the second half with brilliant play selection. Not even the dramatic reappearance of the aging John Unitas at the Colts' helm could save Baltimore and the old guard NFC from a first Super Bowl defeat, 16–7.

The game was very significant in many ways. First, it proved that at long last the former AFL teams had finally achieved competitive parity with the longer-established teams. Perhaps even more important was Namath's sudden rise to superstardom; he set the style for the modern professional athlete. Like many others of his generation, Namath was outspoken, flamboyant, and honest. His rebelliousness often aroused bitter criticism, but eventually he was accepted and in many quarters idolized.

It soon came to be commonly accepted that at least some pros were men of learning. Some football players pursued graduate degrees in the off-season. Others became involved in politics and charity work. The stereotype of the grunting, semiliterate football animal whose only goal in life was to knock people down began to crumble.

The American public has not always easily adjusted to the fact that football sometimes shares the problems of the society around it. Much of the public reacted with disbelief to the news of widespread drug use on both college and pro teams. The 1974 players' strike (in which players sought freedom to bargain with different clubs) brought much criticism from fans who had had more than enough labor-management troubles elsewhere. The mammoth salaries paid to the stars irked some ticket holders, unaware or uninterested in the fact that for every six-figure-salaried star, 10 players have left the game with little money, scarred bodies, and empty futures.

Despite its many problems, both college and pro football have grown bigger than ever. College

Blocks of Granite, of which Lombardi had been one. In Super Bowl I, the Packers humbled the Chiefs and the new league 35–10.

The story was much the same in Super Bowl II. The Packers had won their third straight conference championship by narrowly defeating the Dallas Cowboys in 13-below temperatures in Green Bay. The weather and the opposition were less rigorous in Miami, where the Packers whipped the Oakland Raiders 33–14.

Super Bowl III seemed as if it would be another embarrassing affair for the American Conference. The NFC Baltimore Colts had breezed through the season with a 13–1 record and then soundly defeated the Cleveland Browns for the NFC championship, 34–0. To no one's surprise, they were established as 21-point favorites over the AFC champion New York Jets. The Colts had not only a

campuses are witnessing a new boom in interest and attendance following the Vietnam war protest years of the sixties.

Although it lasted only two years, a new professional league, the World Football League (WFL), opened in the summer of 1974 with teams in 12 cities. A new money war began and many players were quickly lured to the new league. Once again pro football was accommodating even more teams, names, numbers, and demand for talent.

FIELD AND EQUIPMENT

Football is played on a a field 120 yards long and 53½ yards wide. The goal lines are 100 yards apart with 10 yards of end zone on each end of the field. There are yard lines running from sideline to sideline every five yards; these yard lines are numbered at 10-yard intervals from zero at each goal line to 50 at the midfield stripe, or the 50-yard line.

Between the yard-line stripes that cross the field are hashmarks marking every yard. Hashmarks run along the sidelines and in two columns down the field. In high school and college football, each column is 53 feet 4 inches from the sidelines. In professional football the hashmarks are 70 feet 9 inches from the respective sidelines. When a play ends outside the hashmarks or out of bounds, the ball is marked on the nearest hashmark column for the beginning of the next play. If the ball is whistled dead on a spot between the two columns of hashmarks, the next play begins from that spot.

The goalposts in high school and college football have always been located at the back line of the end zone, but it was not until the 1974 season that the pros decided to move them back from the goal line to that position. The purpose was to make it more difficult for the field goal kickers, who had begun to dictate the offensive strategy of many teams. The goalposts themselves rise 20 feet from a crossbar that is 10 feet above the ground and is eight yards wide. This structure is supported by a single curved post that is usually padded to prevent serious injury to the player who runs into it.

Today's football is an oblate spheroid that weighs between 14 and 15 ounces. It is about 11 inches long and 7 inches in diameter at its center. Once made chiefly from pigskin—hence its nickname—most footballs are now made from cowhide, though a few are made from synthetic materials, such as plastic or rubber.

The modern football player wears equipment and padding that makes his counterpart of the 1920s seem almost nude by comparison. He certainly wasn't as well protected. For example, in those early days helmets were made of leather and offered minimal protection, if they were worn at all. Today's helmets are made of sturdy plastic and usually come equipped with facemasks for added protection. Shoulder pads, knee pads, thigh pads, and forearm pads are also used to prevent injury. The fully suited football player weighs 30 pounds more than he does in his street clothes.

During a game, a measuring crew on the sidelines uses chains and a downs marker to keep track of the position of the ball, the down, and the distance the offensive team must move in order to gain

When football fans began to realize the importance of defense, they acclaimed such huge defensive linemen as Alex Karras, opposite. *Vince Lombardi,* above right, *founded a dynasty in Green Bay on such meticulous execution as that of Jim Taylor (31), Jerry Kramer (64), and Forrest Gregg (75), above left.*

93

Below: *The life of an offensive lineman is not a glamorous one.* Right: *Because they handle the ball, quarterbacks attract more attention (and higher salaries).* Opposite: *A common Sunday afternoon scene in the fall—a stadium packed for a pro football game.*

a first down. The chain is 10 yards long with a pole attached to each end. When a team gains possession of the ball, a crewman marks the spot by planting one of the poles on a spot on the sideline that is even with the position of the ball on the field. Another crewman stretches the chain taut in the direction of the defensive team's goal and plants the second pole. The chains remain in place until the offensive team either makes a first down or yields possession of the ball to the defense. A third crewman operates the downs marker, a pole with a stack of four numbered plates attached to it. The crewman in charge of the marker indicates the down by showing the appropriate plate. This crewman also has the responsibility of marking on the sideline the position of the ball for each down. In the event of an incomplete forward pass, or a play nullified by a penalty, the officials can refer to the marker in order to reposition the ball.

THE GAME

Before the game begins, the referee flips a coin and the winner of the toss may choose whether to kick off or receive or, if he prefers, which goal his team will defend for the first and third periods. (On windy days, this decision could play a significant part in the game.)

In high school and college football, the kicker sets the ball on the ground (usually supporting it with a kicking tee) at his own 40-yard line. He then retreats 5 or 10 yards, moves forward on the run, and kicks off. In pro ball a 1974 rule calls for the

kicker to kick off from his 35-yard line. (This rule was designed to ensure more runbacks of kickoffs.) The opposing team must remain 10 yards away from the ball until after it has been kicked.

Once the kickoff has traveled 10 yards, the ball is free and may be recovered by any member of either team. (Teams behind late in a game often try an "onside kick." The kicker taps the ball so that it bounces just the minimum 10 yards, and the kicking team tries to reach the squibbler first.) If the ball goes out of bounds without being touched, the kicking team must kick again, this time from 5 yards farther back. If the kickoff should hit the goalposts, go through the end zone, or be downed by a receiver (that is, held by him with his knee on the ground) in the end zone, a touchback is called and the ball is marked for play at the receiving team's 20-yard line.

If the kickoff falls short of the end zone or if a receiver elects to run it out of the end zone, the receiving team begins its first series of downs from the spot at which the ball carrier is tackled on his runback. A ball carrier is considered to be tackled when any part of his body (other than one hand and his feet) touches the ground. In pro games a runner who slips down may get up and continue to run if he has not been touched by an opponent while on the ground. A ball carrier may be considered tackled while still on his feet if the officials judge that the tacklers have stopped his forward progress and that there is no way he can escape from them. The ball is then placed for the next play at the most advanced position the runner reached. This rule discourages the defensive team from carrying a runner backward.

Once the ball has been marked ready for play, the offensive team has four plays, or downs, to move the ball 10 yards, and 30 seconds (25 in college play) between plays before it must hike, or snap, the ball for the next play. In this brief time the offense clusters together in a huddle some 10 yards behind the ball, receives from the quarterback the brief coded instructions that call the play, breaks the huddle, and trots in unison to the line of scrimmage for the snap of the ball. The line of scrimmage is simply an imaginary line drawn across the field through the front tip of the ball before each play. Within a yard of their own side of this line, the offensive team must place seven men: a center (who snaps the ball), at his sides two guards, at their sides two tackles, and two ends, who may be either at the sides of or split away from the tackles. The other four players on the offense comprise the backfield, usually a quarterback, who receives the center's snap, two running backs, set in various positions behind the quarterback, and a flanker, set to the side, near one of the ends.

Just before the snap, the quarterback begins to shout certain numbers or other signals, some of which are directions to his team, others of which are thrown in merely to confuse the defense. One genuine direction is the "set" signal, at which the offensive players assume the stance they will maintain until the ball is snapped. Most often it is a three-point stance, in which the player rests his weight about equally on the balls of his feet and on one hand placed on the ground in front of him. Other than one man in motion, who may run parallel to the line while the quarterback calls signals and the ball is snapped, each offensive player must be in some sort of set position for at least the one second immediately before the ball is snapped. The defensive players, on the other hand, are free to move about, shifting places on the line ("stunting"), making fake charges, even crossing the line (if they can do so without touching an offensive player and if they can return to their side before the ball is snapped). These defensive maneuvers are all part of an attempt to confuse the offense and perhaps to make one of the players break his set position just before the ball is snapped—a five-yard penalty. Of course all the jumping about can be costly. The quarterback may immediately call the number on which the ball is to be snapped, and the defense may be caught badly out of position.

After the snap, the game changes from cat and mouse to block and tackle. Football has grown sophisticated since its post-rugby days, but the basic way of moving the ball is still by blasting defenders out of the way (blocking) so that the ball carrier has a free path or the passer has time to throw. And the basic way of stopping the ball carrier is still by bringing him to the ground (tackling). Both blocks and tackles may be done singly or in combi-

FOOTBALL FIELD

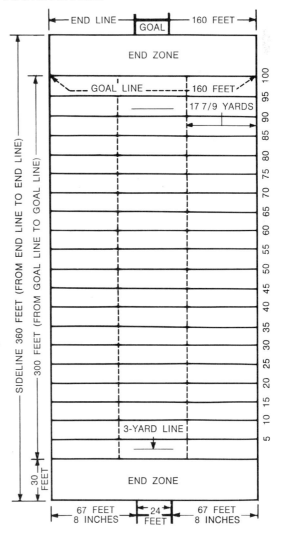

nation, lightly or violently. It depends on their purpose. With the ball on the 1-yard line of the defense, first down and goal to go for the offense (that is, first down with no possibility of gaining another first down because the goal line is less than 10 yards away), the quarterback is likely to call a straight-ahead, power running play. The blockers will "fire out" at the defensive linemen with no other purpose than to clear a sliver of space through which the runner can squirm into the end zone.

For a more sophisticated running play, one of the offensive linemen, usually a guard, may "pull," moving back from the line at the snap and heading for the flank. With this move he may be trying to help convoy a runner around the end in a sweep, or he may be trying to lure the defensive lineman across the line, where he can be neatly blocked aside by an offensive lineman coming from an adjacent position. The defensive lineman is thus "trapped," and the runner breezes past him up the middle. Whatever the situation, the blocker must tailor his block to the position of the man to be blocked. If the defender is crouched with his weight close to the ground, the blocker may choose to topple him with a charge to the shoulder. If the defender is upright, a knifing slice to the knees will be more effective. In all cases the blocker must remember not to turn his head aside and rely solely on the shoulders; if he does, the defender will easily brush him aside.

Tackling is often more spectacular. Blocking merely sets the stage for a successful play; tackling is stage center. Like the blocker, the tackler changes his technique as conditions warrant but usually must lead with the head rather than the shoulders. Some players (usually lighter ones who have no other choice) acquire such skill at tackling that they can bring down men fifty pounds heavier than themselves. A really crushing tackle may force a fumble—a ball carrier losing the ball—which the defense may recover (and in the pros, run with).

The offense may advance the ball in two basic ways: passing and running. Only rarely does it combine the two methods. On running plays the quarterback usually hands or pitches the ball to one of the three backs. Members of the modern backfield often specialize (a lesson learned from Blanchard and Davis), one back having the power and bulk to bull through the middle of the line and another having the speed and agility to enable him to run wide around the ends. An example of such a duo is fullback Larry Csonka and halfback Mercury Morris of the 1973 and 1974 champion Miami Dolphins. Of course, the finest backs are those who are equally dangerous up the middle or around the end. The Chicago Bears' Gale Sayers was one such superstar.

On a pass the quarterback (or occasionally another player) throws the ball forward from behind the line of scrimmage. (It is illegal to throw a forward pass from ahead of the line or more than once during a play.) If the ball touches the ground before

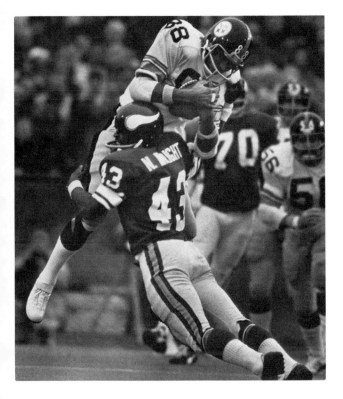

it is caught, or if it is caught out of bounds, the pass is incomplete and the ball is returned to the original line of scrimmage for the next play. In the NFL the pass receiver must touch the ground inbounds with both feet after catching the ball for the pass to be complete. In high school and college, one foot suffices.

The fans love the pass play, not only because it is a greater gamble than a run, but because they can watch it develop. First the offensive linemen drop back to prevent the defensive rushers from reaching the quarterback and "sacking" him—tackling him before he has a chance to throw. When this pass blocking breaks down, the passer is forced to scramble or be buried. Football is rarely more entertaining than when a passer leads the defensive rushers on a merry chase through the backfield, all the while searching for a receiver. But the quarterback is usually more effective if he can remain in the protective "pocket" of blockers and throws quickly. His receivers (the ends, flanker, and running backs are allowed to receive a pass) are running carefully timed and coordinated patterns, and they usually break into the clear for just an instant. A quarterback must be ready to deliver the ball just then. If he waits (or is forced to wait while avoiding tacklers), the pass defense has a chance to recover and perhaps to intercept his pass.

A pass that is thrown sideways or backward is considered a lateral. A lateral may be thrown anywhere on the field and to any member of the team. When a lateral is incomplete, however, the ball remains in play and, like a fumble, may be recovered by the defensive team.

In most cases the offensive team will punt if it fails to gain 10 yards in its first three downs. The ball is snapped by the center directly to the punter, who is usually lined up about 10 yards behind the line of scrimmage. A team will occasionally "quick kick," that is, punt on the third down in hope of catching its opponent off guard.

PLAYING TIME AND TIMEOUTS

The actual playing time in college and pro football games is 60 minutes, but most games last from 2½ to 3 hours because of timeouts and intermissions. The game is divided into two 30-minute halves with a 15- to 20-minute rest period, or halftime, between them. The two halves are in turn divided into two 15-minute quarters, at the end of which the teams change sides. High school football games are 48 minutes long, 12 minutes to each quarter.

High school and college teams are allowed four timeouts per half, professional teams three. The clock automatically stops for an injury, a score, an incomplete forward pass, a play that ends out of bounds, a penalty, a touchback, or a team's allowing a punt to roll dead or the other team's falling on, or downing, it. The clock is also stopped to mark the last two minutes of each half. In all these cases the clock does not start again until the ball is snapped for the next play. The game officials may stop the clock at any other time at their discretion.

SCORING

There are four kinds of scores in football: a touchdown; a point after touchdown, or conversion; a field goal; and a safety.

A touchdown is worth six points and is scored by advancing the ball into the end zone. After scoring a touchdown, the scoring team attempts the point after touchdown. The ball is placed on the 3-yard line, snapped to a kneeling "holder," who positions the ball on the ground for the kicker as the kicking tee does for him on the kickoff. The kicker then tries to place-kick the ball between the uprights for the point. In college and high school football, running or passing the ball into the end zone on the conversion scores two points, in the pros one. A field goal, worth three points, is scored by place-kicking the ball over the crossbar between the uprights.

A safety, worth two points, is scored when a ball carrier is tackled or forced out of bounds in his end zone. After a safety, the team that has yielded it must kick the ball to the opposing team. Taken from the 20-yard line, the kick may be either a place kick or a punt. In all other respects, this kickoff follows the rules for the kickoff at the beginning of each half.

STRATEGY

It is obvious that certain plays will do better than others against certain defensive alignments. A quarterback who is anticipating a hard rush from the defensive line and one or more of the linebackers (a "blitz") may call for a quick pass over the middle to capitalize on the area vacated by the onrushing linebacker. A hard pass rush by the defensive line is often negated with a screen pass (a short pass tossed over onrushing linemen) to a receiver who then moves downfield behind a screen of blockers, or a draw play (a delayed handoff to the fullback after a deceptive pass drop by the quarterback). The smart quarterback must be able to "read" defenses and counter with the play that will succeed against them. Often, a quarterback calls a play in the huddle and then comes up to the line only to find that the defensive alignment is geared to stop the very play he has called. The smart quarterback will then call an "automatic," shouting signals at the line of scrimmage that redirect his players. Many defensive teams now have automatics of their own. If a middle linebacker suspects that the quarterback has changed to a different play, he too can realign his defense to anticipate the quarterback's strategy. The offense's strategy seems to be deception—disguising passing plays as running plays, and vice versa; the defense's strategy is reaction—"reading" the play and moving to stop it.

OFFICIALS

There are four officials in high school football, five in college, and six in professional. Each official has a special area of responsibility, though all have equal authority to call any penalty at any time.

The referee is the official who has overall control of the game. He determines whether the ball is dead or in play, indicating his decision by blowing his whistle. His position at the start of each play is behind the offensive team.

The head linesman is responsible for determining the forward progress of the ball and for supervising the "chain gang," the three men who manage the first-down equipment. His position at the start of each play is at one end of the line of scrimmage.

The umpire is responsible for supervising play in the line and calling fouls that occur there. His position at the beginning of each play is behind the defensive line.

The field judge is responsible for keeping time during the game. He positions himself for each play at the end of the line of scrimmage, opposite the head linesman.

The back judge is present only in college and professional games. In college games he lines up behind the defensive line and is generally responsible for supervising action when play moves beyond the line of scrimmage. In pro games he stands 10 to 15 yards behind the offensive team and watches for infractions in the backfield.

The line judge is present only in professional games. His position at the start of each play is in the general vicinity of the field judge. His main responsibility is to assist the umpire in watching for infractions in the line.

Opposite: *Most running plays employ the handoff, the safest way to transfer the ball.* Top and bottom right: *Franco Harris and O. J. Simpson scoot around end.*

PENALTIES

Many a thundering football stadium has been silenced by the sight of a yellow flag fluttering to the ground. That flag signifies that one of the officials has spotted a foul and that after the play is completed justice will be done. For the players, the thing to do is to complete the play. Yet, try as one might, it is difficult to become absorbed in watching such a play; a penalty flag makes a football play as exciting as a court verdict subject to appeal, because that is exactly what it is. After the play, the referee explains the infraction to the captain of the offended team. The captain then has the choice of having the play nullifed and the penalty assessed or allowing the play to stand and ignoring the infraction. If the captain chooses to nullify the play, the referee usually returns to the line of scrimmage, paces off 5, 10, or 15 yards against the offending team, places the ball at the new line of scrimmage, and signals to both sides of the field what the foul was. If a team is penalized so that the ball would be placed in its end zone, it is penalized half the distance to its goal line instead.

Of the many penalties, the most common are offsides (being past the line of scrimmage when the ball is snapped) and illegal procedure (the offense moving illegally before the snap). Both infractions are penalized 5 yards. More serious fouls, such as personal fouls (unnecessary roughness) are penalized 10 or 15 yards. Perhaps the most exciting and controversial call is pass interference—a pass defender interfering with a pass receiver or vice versa while a pass is in the air. If the pass defender is judged guilty, the offense gains a first down at the spot of the foul (or at the opponent's 1-yard line if the foul is committed in the opponent's end zone). If the offensive player commits pass interference, his team loses 15 yards from the line of scrimmage.

Canadian Football

Canadian football, like the American game, has its roots in rugby and soccer. It is, in fact, quite similar to American football, though it has a few major differences.

The game is played on a field 110 yards long between goal lines and 65 yards wide. The end zones are 25 yards deep, and the back line of the end zone is called the dead-ball line. The goalposts are set on the goal line.

A Canadian football team consists of 12 men. The extra man, the flying wing, usually plays in the backfield, though he may play as an end. The other positions more or less correspond to the positions in American football. In the backfield are the quarterback, the left halfback, the right halfback, the center halfback (fullback), and the flying wing. The line consists of the snap (center), the right and left inside wings (guards), the right and left middle wings (tackles), and the right and left outside wings (ends).

Each team is given three downs to advance the ball 10 yards. Members of the offensive team may not block farther than 10 yards downfield from the line of scrimmage. On punts, the receiver's teammates may not block for him, and he may not call for a fair catch. If the ball is kicked into the end zone, the receiver may choose not to return it, but there is no touchback in Canadian football. If the punt receiver is tackled in the end zone, or if he chooses not to return a punt that he catches in the end zone, the kicking team is awarded one point, called a rouge. A rouge is also scored when the ball is kicked through the end zone and over the back line—the dead-ball line.

With the exception of the rouge, scoring is identical with the American system. For the point after touchdown, called a convert, the ball is spotted on the 10-yard line.

Gaelic Football

Gaelic football is an extremely rough sport that is played almost exclusively in Ireland, though there are some teams in the United States and other parts of the world. It began hundreds of years ago in Ireland and seems to have developed independently of other types of football. The early form of the game was played between church parishes. In these contests, as in the early forms of field hockey, the number of players per side was unlimited and the playing area sometimes covered several miles.

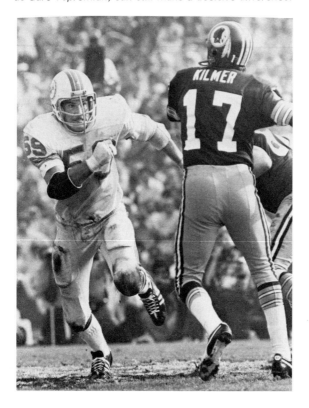

In 1884, there was a particularly brutal battle between a 32-man team from Waterford and a 32-man team from Tipperary. After the contest, a group of spectators and players decided that it would be wise to make the game less violent. Led by Michael Cusack and two brothers, Daniel and Maurice Davin, a group met in Thurles to draw up a set of rules. This group standardized the rules and also founded the Gaelic Athletic Association, which remains the ruling body of the sport.

The game is played on a level, grassy field, similar to a football or soccer field. There is a goal, constructed from two goalposts and a crossbar, at each end of the field. The goalposts extend well above the crossbar, and the area of the goal from the crossbar to the ground is enclosed by netting. The ball that is used is similar to a soccer ball.

The players advance the ball by kicking it as in soccer, punting it as in American football, dribbling it as in basketball, and punching it with the fist.

Scoring is accomplished by punching or kicking the ball through the goal. If the ball goes over the crossbar and between the uprights, one point is scored. If the ball goes into the netted area of the goal, three points are scored.

Games consist of two 30-minute halves.

The Gaelic football season extends through the summer months. During this time, competition is among county teams. Each county in Ireland has a number of teams, which play in various classifications. At the end of each season, each county picks an all-star team from players in the highest (senior) classification. These all-star teams then compete in a single elimination tournament for the National Cup, emblematic of the all-Ireland championship.

GLOSSARY

Aerial: A forward pass.

Audible; automatic: A play called at the line of scrimmage.

Backfield in motion; illegal motion: An infraction that carries with it a five-yard penalty. Only one back may be in motion at the beginning of a play. His motion must be parallel to or away from the line of scrimmage.

Blitz; red dog; shooting the gap: A tactic used by defensive linebackers and safeties. As the ball is snapped, one or all of them rush the quarterback, ignoring pass defending responsibilities.

Bomb: An extremely long pass.

Bump and run: A method of pass defense. The defender attempts to hold up or knock down the pass receiver at the line of scrimmage and then shadows him for the rest of the play.

Clipping: Illegally blocking an opponent from behind. The penalty for clipping is 15 yards from the spot of the foul.

Clothesline: To brutally tackle a fast-moving offensive player by stiffening and extending the forearm so that it catches him around the chin and sends him sprawling. Clothesline tackles are used against blockers as well as runners.

Double reverse: The quarterback handing the ball to a running back or end moving in the opposite direction and then this new ball carrier handing the ball to a running back or end moving in the opposite direction from him.

Down and out: A route taken by a receiver. He sprints straight downfield a predetermined distance and then cuts sharply toward the sideline.

Face masking: It is illegal to grab the facemask of an opponent for any reason. This infraction usually occurs when a defender is attempting to tackle the ball carrier. The penalty is 15 yards in college football. In pro football, the penalty is 5 yards and an automatic first down, unless the foul is flagrant, in which case the penalty is 15 yards, and possibly, disqualification of the offender.

Fair catch: When a punt receiver sees that he has no chance of advancing the ball, he may call for a fair catch by extending one arm into the air. Once he has done this, members of the opposing team may not tackle him, unless he muffs the ball in his attempt to catch it.

Fly pattern: A route taken by a receiver who sprints straight down the field in an attempt to outrun the defenders.

Free kick: A kick taken without pressure from the defenders, such as a kickoff. After a fair catch, the offensive team has the option of a free kick. After a safety, the team that has been scored on must make a free kick from its 20-yard line; this kick is usually a punt.

Holding, defensive: Although defensive players may use their hands to ward off blockers, they may not hold. The penalty for doing so is 5 yards. In professional games, the penalty carries with it an automatic first down for the offensive team.

Holding, offensive: An offensive player holding a defender or blocking with his hands away from his body. A 10-yard penalty in the pros.

Hole: An opening in the line for a runner.

I-formation: An offensive formation in which the quarterback stands right behind the center, and two or three of the other backfield members stand behind the quarterback in a line perpendicular to the line of scrimmage.

Illegal procedure: Any of several rules infractions, such as motion in the offensive line before the snap, failure by the offensive team to have seven men on the line of scrimmage, or a team having more than eleven men on the field. The penalty is 5 yards.

Pass interference, defensive: The penalty called when a pass defender prevents a receiver from catching a pass by playing the receiver rather than the ball once the pass has been thrown. Defender and receiver have equal rights to the ball, but neither may interfere with the other. The penalty for defensive pass interference is a first down at the spot of the infraction. If it occurs in the defensive team's end zone, the offensive team is granted a first down at the 1-yard line.

Pass interference, offensive: Once a pass has been thrown, a receiver may not block or tackle the defender in order to prevent him from intercepting. The penalty for this infraction is 15 yards from the line of scrimmage and loss of down.

Line of scrimmage: An imaginary line from sideline to sideline, separating the teams before each play and passing through the forward tip of the ball.

Onside kick: An attempt by the kicking team on the kickoff to kick the ball short and recover it after it has gone the required 10 yards.

Penalty: When a team is guilty of an infraction of the rules, it is penalized by having the ball moved toward its own goal. Most penalties are 5 or 15 yards. A penalty may not exceed half the distance to the goal. In the case of most penalties, the down is played over. If a penalty occurs on the last play of the first half or on the last play of the game, the down is replayed only if the defensive team committed the infraction.

Personal foul: There are a number of specific personal fouls, such as clipping, but officials may call a personal foul for any act that seems unnecessarily rough. The penalty is 15 yards.

Post pattern: A pass route taken by a receiver who sprints straight downfield and then cuts toward the goalpost.

Roughing the kicker: Once the punter has kicked the ball, no defender may block or tackle him. The penalty for doing so is 15 yards.

Shift: A change of formation, usually in the offensive backfield, before the play begins.

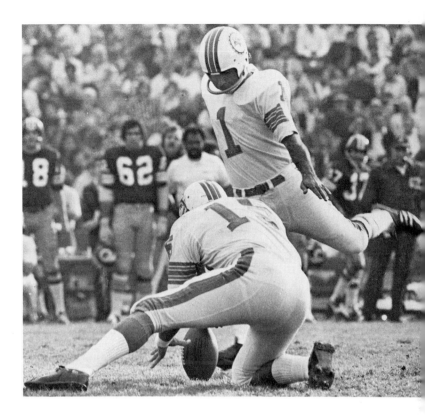

Snap: The exchange of the ball between the center and the quarterback, center and punter, or center and holder for a placekick. The snap starts each play.

Strong side: The side of the offensive line on which there are more men before the snap.

Stunt: A defensive lineman's maneuver just before the snap of the ball. The lineman quickly switches his position and, at the snap of the ball, charges against a different offensive lineman than he normally would. By this tactic he hopes to confuse the offense and allow a teammate to break through.

T-formation: An offensive formation, often modified, in which the quarterback stands right behind the center, and the three other backfield members stand behind the quarterback, parallel to the line of scrimmage. The center and quarterback are in a line that forms the shaft of the "T"; the backs are in a line that forms the top of it. Two common variations of the T-formation are the wing T, in which one back lines up on the flank instead of behind the quarterback, and the wishbone T, in which the fullback stands slightly in front of the other two backs, thus forming a curved top of the "T."

Turnover: The offensive team losing the ball to the defensive team by means of either a pass interception or a fumble.

Weak side: The side of the offensive line on which there are fewer men before the snap.

Zone defense: A type of pass defense in which each defender is responsible for guarding a particular area of the field rather than a particular receiver.

Frisbee

Not long after the end of World War II, students at Yale and Princeton could be seen sailing pie tins at each other. These tins came from the Frisbie bakery in Bridgeport, Connecticut. A man named Fred Morrison saw the commercial possibilities of these flying objects and sold his idea to the Wham-O toy company of San Gabriel, California. First called the Wham-O Pluto Platter, then the Wham-O Flying Saucer, it finally was sold under the name of Frisbee. The Wham-O product, with its patented ridges, comes in many varieties, including the Mini Frisbee, the Regular Frisbee, the Pro or Sport Model Frisbee, the All American Frisbee, the Moonlighter Frisbee (for night play), the Master Frisbee, and the speedy Fastback Frisbee.

Frisbee was originally one of the purest of sports—a simple, graceful pastime without rules. At one time it seemed as if it were the national collegiate sport. The colorful discs could be seen floating across almost every campus in the country. And it was probably inevitable that the more skillful players would invent Frisbee games.

COMPETITION

The first International Frisbee Tournament was held in 1958 in Eagle Harbor, Michigan. The tournament consisted (as it still does) of three events: distance throwing, accuracy, and guts Frisbee. In guts Frisbee two 5-man teams face each other, standing roughly fifteen yards apart, and throw the Frisbee at each other. The throwing team scores one point for each toss the other team fails to catch on the fly. Games are won with 21 points and must be won by at least 2. The winner of guts Frisbee receives Frisbee's highest award, the Julius T. Nachazel Memorial Trophy, which is made of a coffee-can lid and tin cans.

Frisbee has become so popular that today it even has its own organization, the International Frisbee Association (IFA), which is run by the Wham-O Corporation. The IFA has organized a National Junior Frisbee Championship. Winners compete in the national championship.

Golf

Anyone who doubts golf's extraordinary popularity need only take a sunrise journey to the local golf course on any weekend. At an hour when not even the roosters are up, he is likely to find a mass of people (many of them still half asleep) waiting to hack their way through several miles of golf course. At 6 A.M. on a summer Sunday morning, the waiting time at the local public golf course in a major city is sometimes as long as five hours.

To understand just how remarkable this early morning mobilization is, it is best to follow an average, 30-handicap golfer around the course. After having waited two and one-half hours or more just to play, he has what seems to be a truly miserable time. After each mighty yet ineffectual swing sends his ball into another unfortunate location, the duffer lets loose a litany of epithets. He spends half his time trudging through woods, weeds, and even swamp. He loses four or five balls. And he gets drenched in a sudden thunderstorm.

Nongolfers must wonder why anyone accepts the challenge of knocking a little white ball into a hole. But the duffer walks off the eighteenth green smiling serenely. His score of 102 swings is two strokes lower than his previous best, and he'll do even better next Sunday, he says.

As the duffer demonstrates, golf is one of the few sports in which the essential battle takes place inside the individual. The real opponent is not one's partner but the golf course and one's nerves. Each course is different and each hole presents a unique challenge to the golfer's composure as well as to his skill.

Hale Irwin, the 1974 United States Open champion and a former football standout at the University of Colorado, has said that golf is a more demanding sport than football. A golfer walks more than five miles in a normal round, but the mental strain is the most brutal. Ben Hogan, one of the greatest golfers ever to play the game, was finally forced to quit competitive golf when the emotional strain of standing over important putts had become so great that he literally could not properly strike the ball. Hogan was only one of the more notable casualties of "the yips." Even the weekend duffer who plays for pin money can understand why some of those four- and five-foot putts are called "character builders."

For all its nerve-racking intensity, golf is an impartial sport. The sandlot baseball player may bat .300, but he'll never know how he would have done against major league pitching. The golfer has no such unanswered questions. Although courses vary in difficulty, golf is basically the same sport for Jack Nicklaus as it is for the 30-handicap duffer.

Perhaps the strongest bond between hacker and hero is the nightmarish situations that plague all golfers, even the pros. Bobby Cole, tied for the lead in the 1974 Professional Golfer's Association (PGA) Championship on the seventy-first hole, actually missed his ball completely while trying to hit it from under a tree. On the last hole of play in his victory in the 1974 British Open, Gary Player

Frisbee is a game for the young and light-hearted, opposite; golf for the older and more serious, above. Lee Trevino is as good-natured a golfer as there is, but even he can become grim watching a putt.

was forced to take a left-handed slap at the ball with his putter after having smacked the ball over the green and against a wall underneath the clubhouse balcony.

The physical measurements of some of golf's greats are also a source of comfort to the average player. Certainly Jack Nicklaus and Tom Weiskopf are big and strong, but Chi Chi Rodriguez stands about 5 feet 7 inches and weighs less than 140 pounds. Gary Player, one of the most enduring stars, is 5 feet 6 inches tall and admits to wearing black because "it makes me feel stronger." For older golfers there is inspiration to be found in observing Sam Snead, who in his sixties is still a contender in the tournaments he enters.

Inspired by such heroes more than they are frustrated by their own blunders, men and women, celebrities and amateurs, spend more than $200 million each year on the game.

HISTORY

There are written records of golf dating back to 1457, and it is probable that the game originated in Scotland in the twelfth century. The seaside dunes where the early Scots played golf were called links, a name that is still applied to golf courses. The first golf club, the Honourable Company of Edinburgh Golfers, was founded in 1744. The oldest golf club in existence today is the Royal and Ancient Golf Club of St. Andrews, Scotland, which was founded in 1754. The original golfing code of 13 basic rules

was composed there that year. Windswept St. Andrews, with knee-deep rough and "bombcrater" bunkers that are typical of the old British seaside links, is still regarded as one of the world's finest courses. It was the site of the 1970 British Open.

The equipment used in the early days of golf would be considered primitive by today's standards. The original ball resembled the high-compression, liquid-center balls of today only in that both were round. Called a feathery, the first balls consisted of a leather casing tightly stuffed with feathers. Around 1848, the feathery was replaced by the gutty, a solid ball made from gutta-percha, the latex from the tree of the same name. By 1919, the A. G. Spalding Company had devised a rubber-cored ball with a mesh cover design similar to the present dimpled golf ball.

Clubs were carved from wood and were much more cumbersome than the sleek, aluminum- and graphite-shafted models of today. The old clubs also had intriguing names. The modern set of golf clubs are simply referred to by their numbers: one through four wood, and one through nine iron. In the old days the five iron was called the mashie, the seven iron the mashie niblick, and the nine iron the niblick. The one, two, and three woods were called, respectively, the driver, the brassie, and the spoon.

Although the United States Golf Association was formed in 1894 and the first United States Open held a year later, it wasn't until 1913 that American golf became famous. In that year a

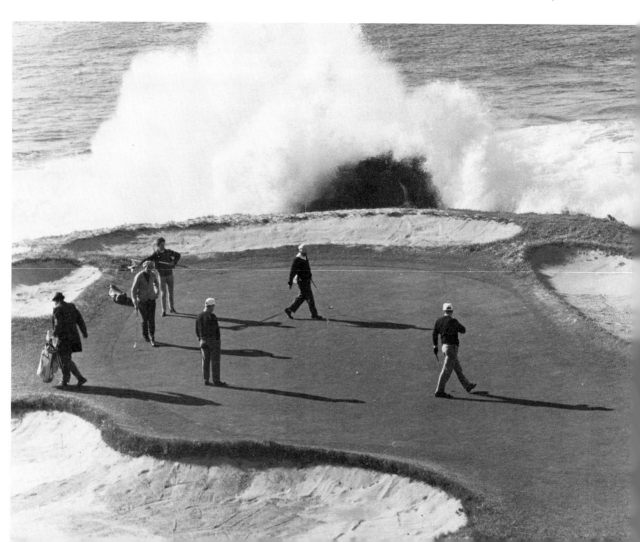

skinny, 20-year-old former caddie named Francis Ouimet challenged the British and European champions of the game in the 1913 United States Open in Brookline, Massachusetts. Ouimet happened to live across the street from the course. His familiarity with the course helped him to a playoff victory over six-time British Open champ Harry Vardon and Ted Ray, an upset that made the front pages of newspapers across the country.

A parade of golf greats followed. Walter ("the Haig") Hagen, who as a 20-year-old himself had been tied with Ouimet at the halfway mark of the 1913 Open, went on to win five PGA Championships. Then came the twenties, "the Golden Age of Sport," and Bobby Jones, who must rank with Babe Ruth and Jack Dempsey as a star of the era. Jones played his entire career as an amateur, but before he retired at the age of 28, he won 13 major championships (second only to Nicklaus). In 1930, his final year, Jones won in succession the four most difficult championships of the time: the British Open, the British Amateur, the United States Open, and the United States Amateur—the Grand Slam.

Ben Hogan came closest to winning the modern version of the Grand Slam. In 1953, Hogan won the Masters, the United States Open, and the British Open, but he decided not to enter the PGA championship. Although Hogan was the dominant

Opposite: *Part of the charm of golf is that it can be played in marvelous settings. At Pebble Beach, in California, a golfer can see, hear, even feel the ocean spray. (The ocean breezes make for tricky golf, too.) Top left, top right, above right: old-time greats Babe Didrickson, Ben Hogan, Bobby Jones.*

force in golf during the forties and fifties, he was by no means the only great player. Byron Nelson, Gene Sarazen, Jimmy Demaret and, of course, Sam Snead were some of the players who challenged Hogan's supremacy and became stars in their own right.

Golf's popularity continued on the upswing during the forties and fifties. The increase in prize money brought more and more good players into the public eye, and the public responded by taking up the sport in large numbers. In 1948, the Junior Amateur for Boys was started, and the next year a similar tournament was held for girls. Professional women golfers began to organize, and in 1946, the first women's Open championship was staged. Women golfers such as Babe Zaharias, Louise Suggs, and Mickey Wright became stars in a previously all-male sport.

Golf was still far from the big money sport it is today, however. Sam Snead was the top money winner in 1950 with $35,000. Then in the late 1950s, a young, ruddy-faced pro from Pennsylvania burst upon the scene with a flamboyant, go-for-broke style of play that attracted millions of fans to the game. Arnold Palmer won his first of four Masters titles in 1958, but it was his dramatic come-from-behind victory in the 1960 Masters that started the legend of the "Palmer charge." Trailing by six strokes at the start of the final round, Palmer sizzled over the course in sixty-six strokes, taking the title by two strokes. It was one of many times that Palmer was to explode on the final day of play and steal a tournament.

Such heroics brought Palmer a horde of followers, soon dubbed "Arnie's Army," who cheered the Palmer charges with the enthusiasm of baseball bleacherites. Palmer won $75,000 that year and his charisma attracted larger and larger crowds around the country, guaranteeing larger purses for all the touring pros. In 1963, Palmer became the first golfer to win more than $100,000 in a single year, and in 1973, the top money figure had bulged to more than $300,000.

As Palmer's domination of the sport ebbed, a new name emerged as heir apparent to the title of world's greatest golfer. Jack Nicklaus' second-place finish in the 1960 United States Open as an amateur had been overshadowed by another dramatic Palmer victory. But Nicklaus soon proved that he was no perennial runner-up. In 1962, at the age of 22, Nicklaus tied Palmer for the United States Open Championship at Oakmont, Pennsylvania, and then won the playoff by three strokes. His collection of major titles grew quickly. He won the Masters and the PGA in 1963. His score of 271 in the 1965 Masters shattered Ben Hogan's long-standing record of 274, and two years later he broke Hogan's mark for the United States Open with a score of 275. In 1973, Nicklaus established himself as the premier golfer of our time by winning his fourteenth major championship, one more than the legendary Bobby Jones.

GOLF COURSE

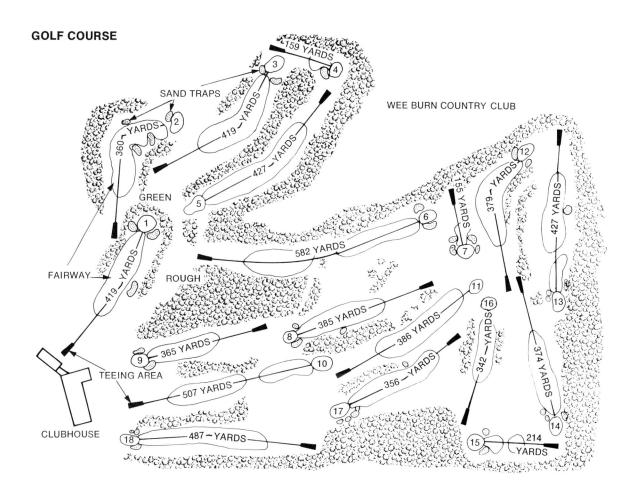

SAND TRAPS

WEE BURN COUNTRY CLUB

159 YARDS

419 YARDS

427 YARDS

360 YARDS

GREEN

155 YARDS

379 YARDS

427 YARDS

582 YARDS

FAIRWAY

ROUGH

385 YARDS

386 YARDS

342 YARDS

374 YARDS

365 YARDS

TEEING AREA

507 YARDS

356 YARDS

CLUBHOUSE

487 YARDS

214 YARDS

Arnold Palmer, opposite top, *and Jack Nicklaus,* opposite bottom, *were the golf superstars of the television age, when the sport found a mass audience and began to shed its image of a rich man's game. Above: Ben Hogan starts the journey from tee to green.*

GOLF COURSES

No two golf courses are exactly the same, but they are all similar. A full-size golf course consists of eighteen holes. The end of the eighteenth and the beginning of the first are both near the clubhouse, the home base for the course. The first nine holes are called the out, or front, nine; the final nine holes are called the in, or back, nine. The average course is about 6,300 yards long (the sum of the lengths of each of the holes) and covers an area between 100 and 200 acres. Championship, or tournament, courses may extend more than 7,000 yards.

Most courses have a par of 70, 71, or 72 strokes. That is, it should take that many strokes for the golfer to complete the course. The regulation number of strokes, or par, for each hole is based on its length. For holes up to 250 yards long, par is usually three strokes; from 250 through 450 yards, par is four. Par-five holes usually range between 450 and 600 yards. The average course consists of four or five par-three holes, three or four par-five holes, and the rest par-four holes. In computing the par for a hole, it is assumed that it should take a player one stroke to reach the green (the short, cushionlike grass near the hole) on a par three, two

strokes to reach the green on a par four, and three strokes to reach the green on a par five. Two strokes are then allotted for "holing out" on the green.

It is important to remember that par is only a standard, not a scoring system. It is an estimate of how many strokes a given hole or course requires, but changes in weather conditions can render par meaningless. Tournaments have been won with scores well above par and lost with scores well below.

A score of one less than par on a hole is called a birdie. A two-under-par score on a hole is an eagle. Eagles are quite rare, but even rarer are double eagles, or a three-under-par score for a hole. A double eagle is not a hole-in-one on a par-four hole. The way to shoot a double eagle is to hole out the second shot on a par-five hole. In the 1935 Masters Gene Sarazen was trailing Craig Wood by three shots as he prepared to hit his second shot on the par five, 485-yard fifteenth hole. Instead of playing his ball close to the green, which was protected by a menacing pond, and then hitting safely over the pond with another shot, Sarazen decided to gamble and go for the green. He took out his number-four wood and slammed the ball 230 yards right into the hole. It was a fantastic shot and a critically important one, as well. Sarazen finished in a tie for the championship and then beat Wood in the playoff.

More familiar to the weekend golfer is a score of one over par for a hole, or a bogey. A score of two over par is a double bogey, three over par a triple bogey.

FROM TEE TO GREEN

A complete hole starts from the teeing area, usually called simply the tee, an area about 10 yards wide and slightly elevated. Most golf courses have marks from which different levels of golfers should begin the hole. There is a forward position for women golfers, a medium position for the average golfer, and a rear tee for tournament competition.

Usually, the golfer hits his first, or tee, shot with a driver, or one wood. This is a long-stemmed club with a wooden clubhead. With his tee shot the golfer hopes to place his ball in the fairway, a strip of medium-length, well-kept grass about forty yards wide that extends from the teeing area to the green. Most fairways have a marker about two hundred yards from the tee to help the golfer judge the distance to the green. An inaccurate tee shot will often wind up in the rough, the area on either side of the fairway. The grass in this area is allowed to grow much higher than the fairway grass—sometimes as high as six inches—and it is much more difficult to hit a good shot from this area than from the fairway.

A bad tee shot may find an even worse resting place than six-inch-high grass, however. Plenty of other hazards—woods, lakes, and streams—can swallow an errant drive. The only solution for the golfer who finds his ball in an undesirable location

Shots from the fairway usually require an iron—a lower-numbered iron for less loft and greater distance (top), a higher-numbered iron for more loft and less distance. Hitting a ball buried in a sandtrap, above, a golfer uses an iron with the most loft of all.

Top: *Hale Irwin hits a short approach shot to the ninth green at the 1974 U.S. Open, which he won.* Left: *Gary Player's classic putting stroke.* Above: *Sam Snead's unorthodox one—the croquet mallet approach.*

is to get the ball back into the fairway as best he can and only then try to approach the green.

Before hitting his shot from the fairway to the green, the golfer first estimates how much distance remains to be covered, because this measurement will dictate which club he will use. A distance of more than two hundred yards usually calls for a three- or four-wood shot, but a well-hit tee shot on the standard par four will usually require only an iron shot to get the ball on the green. (An iron is a club with a shorter stem than a wood and an iron hitting surface.) The lower the number of the iron, the less loft, or angle, there is to the club's hitting surface. Consequently, the lower-numbered clubs hit the ball lower and farther than the higher-numbered clubs, which have the greater loft. In order to make the proper selection for the shot, each golfer must discover for himself how far he usually hits with each club.

If his choice of club is wrong, the golfer might find his ball in one of several bunkers, or sand traps, which often surround the green (and sometimes line the fairway). Traps are filled with loosely packed sand, so when a hard-hit golf ball enters, it is often buried. Weekend duffers sometimes spend much of their time on the course becoming acquainted with the difficulties of shooting, or "exploding," a covered ball from a sand trap.

Once the golfer gets his ball on the green, he begins the business of putting, crouching over the ball and tapping it with the putter, a club that has no angle to its clubface and hence no loft at all. Putters come in many styles, but most are simply shafts connected to a flat metal surface. Golfers are constantly experimenting with new styles of putters in search of that "magic wand." Some of the more extreme variations are almost comical—the tuning fork putter, for instance, emits a different note depending on the force of the stroke.

The green consists of very well tended short grass. Greens vary in size and shape and are often surrounded by an area of slightly longer grass, called the apron, or the "frog hair." The cup, which has a diameter of four and one-half inches, may be located anywhere on the green. Inside the cup rests the pin, a long metal pole on which a flag bearing the number of the hole is attached. The pin must be removed from the hole when the golfer is putting on the green, lest the ball strike the pin (a two-stroke penalty).

Any professional golfer will attest to the wisdom of an old saying in golf: "You drive for show but you putt for dough." The great majority of tournaments are won and lost on the greens. Each putt is different and each must be closely studied for the proper speed and direction. The slope of the green and bend in the grass will often cause a putt to curve, or break, leaving the ball far from its intended destination unless the golfer has compensated sufficiently for the break. On the first hole of the 1974 United States Open, Jack Nicklaus tried a 25-foot birdie putt. When his ball had finally stopped, it was 28

feet on the other side of the hole. Putting is by no means an exact science, even for the best players.

SCORING

The rules of golf are long and detailed, but the basic idea is simple: to get the ball from the tee into the hole with no assistance other than the 14 clubs allowed in a golf bag. The common phrase is "play it as it lies." There are exceptions, times when a player may be allowed to improve the resting position, or lie, of the ball, but these cases are strictly defined and more often than not will add one or more penalty strokes to the golfer's score.

The goal in competitive golf is to get around the course in as few strokes as possible. There are, however, two distinct forms of tournament play—match play and medal play.

In match play the golfer or team that takes the fewest strokes on a hole wins that hole. (In best-ball match play only the lowest score for each team is counted on each hole.) The golfer or team that wins the most holes over the eighteen hole course wins the match. Often it is unnecessary to play the full course. If, for example, one team has won four more holes than its opponents and there are only three left to play, the losing side cannot catch up and the match is ended. The leading side has won four and three—four holes up and three left to play. The United States Amateur Championship uses a match play format, and there is a World Match Play championship held every year in Great Britain. The PGA Championship was a match play tournament until 1958, when it was changed to medal play.

In medal play the winner is the golfer who uses the lowest total of strokes to play the tournament (usually four rounds of 18 holes each). The large majority of tournaments today are medal play.

HANDICAPS

In amateur golf most players are awarded a handicap—a certain number of strokes that they may deduct from their score in medal play. The handicap varies from player to player; the better the player, the lower his handicap. The purpose of the handicap system is to allow players of different skill to compete against each other on an equal footing.

A player's handicap is figured by taking the average of his 10 lowest scores in his last 25 rounds and subtracting par. The player's handicap is all or part of the difference. For example, if his average is 80 and par is 72, his handicap will be 8 or less.

There are particular rules for deducting the handicap from the score. It is not permitted simply to tally the final score and deduct the handicap from it. Instead the player must deduct one stroke on each of as many holes as he has handicap strokes. If his handicap is 10, he deducts 1 stroke on each of the 10 most difficult holes. (The score-card lists the holes in order of difficulty.) If his handicap is 18 he deducts 1 stroke on every hole. If his handicap is more than 18, he may be permitted to deduct 2 strokes on some holes.

Gymnastics

To the Greeks, no man who neglected his body was considered a complete person, so the ideal education trained both the mind and the body. *Gymnasia,* where men exercised (without clothes—from the word *gymnos,* meaning "naked"), were also places where one could listen to lectures. The gymnastic exercises were quite different from our own. Their main purpose was to prepare athletes for the important contests in running, jumping, and wrestling. Gymnastics was not simply a means to an end.

HISTORY

Modern gymnastics, which we think of as exercises performed on different types of apparatus, was cre-ated in the last two centuries. Two distinct schools developed: the Swedish system of Hjalmar Ling (1820–86), in which rhythmic floor exercises were stressed, and the German system, pioneered by Friedrich Jahn (1778–1852), in which muscular strength was developed on crude pieces of equipment that were the forerunners of today's apparatus. In the late 1800s, there was much wrangling over which was the better method, and in the 1920s, the Federation Internationale de Gymnastique (today responsible for international events) blended the two systems.

Gymnastics has never been as popular as competitive team sports in the United States. Until

Gymnastics, an important sport in many parts of the world, escaped from obscurity in the United States when Olga Korbut, an impish, innovative gymnast from the Soviet Union, charmed American television viewers with her routines at the 1972 Olympics. Later, she made a triumphal tour of America.

Women gymnasts compete in four events, including the ballet-like floor exercises (performed to music), top, and the balance beam, above, a 16-foot-long wooden shaft on which the contestant stands with her hands as often as with her feet.

recent years it was practiced here mainly by European immigrants, who founded their own *Turnvereins* (gymnastic schools) and were the major force in the building of school gymnasiums. From time to time there have been spurts of interest in gymnastics, especially at the end of the major wars, when the military released statistics showing the deplorable physical condition of young American men. The sport is still far less important in the United States than in many other countries, particularly in Europe, where gymnastics is a major part of the physical education curriculum. American gymnasts have rarely done well in international competition since 1932.

Japan is the model of a nation with the dedication necessary to excel at gymnastics. In the gymnastic competitions at the 1936 Olympics, the Germans won practically every event, the Japanese nothing. No one was surprised because the Japanese were considered too small to master some of the apparatus. But the Japanese made films of the competition and studied them carefully. They knew that success in gymnastics comes only from constant practice and repetition of movement, and they had the patience not to attempt difficult skills until they had mastered the basic ones. Having compensated for physical limitations with agility and control, Japanese gymnasts have become, after years of effort and learning, some of the most skilled in the world.

COMPETITION AND EQUIPMENT

In essence gymnastics is not a competitive sport. The gymnast's performance is measured against a standard of excellence, or perfection, not against the performance of others. Gymnasts are probably in better condition and exercise better control over their bodies than any other type of athlete. According to a study done at a recent Olympics, the gymnasts there had less fat on their bodies than any other group of athletes. Gymnasts must watch their weight almost as carefully as jockeys.

A chief function of gymnastic competition is to advance the sport. Top gymnasts are constantly inventing original, more difficult movements that set new standards. For example, in the 1964 Olympics Haruhiro Yamashita performed a difficult new vault on the long horse. Immediately dubbed the "Yamashita," this vault was used by the first three medalists in the 1968 vaulting competition.

In the 1972 Olympics, there was not only a new routine unveiled, but also a new image for gymnastics. Olga Korbut, a tiny Russian teenager, won three gold medals with, among other new stunts, a backward somersault on the uneven parallel bars. Even more important, Olga brought a gaiety and charm to her routines that delighted the crowds and television viewers. And she thrilled the spectators with her ups and downs. When she was working well, she smiled exuberantly. When she flopped—

as she did disastrously once—she burst into tears. The crowds were captivated by the show, and in the end, when Olga emerged victorious, she became an instant celebrity. She proved that gymnasts, who had previously been thought severe, even cold, could be as spectacular as any athletes.

In international and national competition, men compete in floor, or free, exercises; pommel, or side, horse; long horse, or vault; parallel bars; rings; and horizontal bars. Women used to compete on the same equipment as men, but they now work on apparatus that requires less strength. The four women's events are floor exercises, the side horse for vaulting, the balance beam, and the uneven parallel bars.

Each competitor performs twice in each event—one set of compulsory exercises and one optional exercise that the gymnast plans himself.

MEN'S EVENTS

Performed on a padded mat, the floor exercises are usually done first to give the competitors a chance to warm up. Starting in a stance of attention, the contestants perform tumbling movements such as handsprings, cartwheels, somersaults, dive rolls, and movements demonstrating balance and strength. The dynamic movements must be rhythmic, and the static movements should be held for at least two seconds.

The pommel horse is of ancient origin. The

Among the six men's events are the horizontal bar, above left; floor exercises, top right; and the side, or pommel, horse, above right. A contestant competes in all the events, and the winner is the one with the highest composite score.

113

Romans used it for the very practical purpose of training soldiers to mount horses. Some suggest it was used even earlier, by the bull dancers of Minoan Crete. Jumping over bulls by doing springs off the animal's horns, these dancers surely must have practiced on something a little tamer than a live bull. Today, the pommel horse events are less exciting. The gymnast performs intricate leg-swinging movements while supporting his weight on his hands, which are either grasping the pommels or lying flat on the leather of the horse. As he swings his legs so that one follows, or "shadows," the other, the gymnast demonstrates strength, balance, and timing. Exercises such as single or double leg circles and scissors must be done continuously and in both directions. The pommel horse is difficult to master and not a favorite among gymnasts; they call it "the beast."

The long horse is the same piece of apparatus as the side horse, with pommels removed. The gymnast vaults the length of the horse from a slanted springboard. With a carefully measured stride, the vaulter starts slowly and reaches top speed three to five steps before reaching the board. He plants his hands on the horse and vaults over it in an explosion of spins, somersaults, and twists. He is given two tries to vault successfully.

The parallel bars are two wooden, somewhat springy bars about one and a half feet apart and mounted level with each other, usually about 5.2 to 5.6 feet off the ground. The gymnast supports himself with his hands and performs a continuous series of movements, vaults, handstands, shoulder stands, and somersaults.

Of all the apparatus, the rings require the most strength. They are made from wood, are about seven inches in diameter, and are suspended about eight feet off the ground by cables and straps. The gymnast must perform certain movements while holding the rings in a steady position (that is, with-out swinging). In addition, he undertakes such impossible-looking maneuvers as crosses, in which the body is held vertically in the shape of a cross, handstands, and levers, in which the arms are straight up and the body horizontal to the floor.

The horizontal bar event is the flashiest and the most dangerous. The horizontal bar is a polished steel bar anchored atop two uprights about eight feet from the floor. The gymnast moves in large swinging circles on the bar, body fully extended. His vaults, turns, and somersaults require that he occasionally release the bar. The momentum of the gymnast's swing can generate up to five G's of centrifugal force, so anyone who miscalculates is in trouble.

WOMEN'S EVENTS

Women's floor exercises are performed to music and emphasize grace rather than strength.

The side horse vaulting event for women differs only slightly from the men's event. The horse is 3.6 inches shorter, and women vault over the width of the horse rather than over the length.

The balance beam is mounted about four feet off the ground. It is wooden, about sixteen feet long and only four inches wide. The competitor who performs on the balance beam shows not only balletlike grace and beauty but courage and confidence as well. Her exercises include walkovers, splits, leaps, stands, squats, poses, headstands, cartwheels, and even forward and backward handsprings. The exercises are forever becoming more spectacular and dangerous, and the gymnast who is to execute them must do so without looking at her feet.

The uneven parallels are similar to men's parallel bars except that one bar is set higher than the other—about seven and a half feet to five feet. The gymnast performs a series of swings, vaults, reverses, and body rolls, moving freely between the two bars. The most spectacular part of this event is often the dismount from the bar, which can be very dangerous.

JUDGING

A panel of four judges evaluates the gymnasts. The high and low scores are disregarded and the two middle scores averaged. Performances are scored on a 10-point scale in increments of one-tenth of a point. Thus a perfect performance would net 10.0, a near perfect would net 9.9, and so on. In the compulsory exercises the judges award 10 points on the basis of how well the gymnast has executed his exercises. In the freestyle section for men, 4.4 points are awarded for execution, 3.4 for difficulty, and 1.6 for technical value. In the freestyle section for women, 5 points are awarded for the composition of the exercise and 3 points for execution. That leaves .6 points for bonuses—.2 each for risk, originality, and virtuosity.

Finally, a gymnast's scores for all the events are totaled to select an all-around champion.

The long horse is the same piece of apparatus as the pommel horse, except that the pommels have been removed.

Handball

All you need is a ball and a wall. And, if you're feeling competitive, someone to play against. These are the essentials of handball, a simple sport played by large numbers of Americans, especially those who live in the cramped urban areas. As played by top competitors, handball is an especially grueling sport. Players have been known to sweat off six pounds in one match. But the game can be played enjoyably on many other levels as well. A visitor to a city park will find all levels of handball players and a variety of matches.

HISTORY

Handball in its modern form comes from Ireland. Called "fives," the Irish game is played with a very fast, hard ball, and with both feet as well as hands. The Irish players were (and still are) phenomenally well coordinated.

An Irish whiz named Phil Casey brought handball to the United States (or at least to Brooklyn) around 1883. Because there were no other facilities for the game, Casey built his own four-wall court. "Casey's court" in Brooklyn was the site of many early handball contests that were avidly followed by heavily betting fans. (Betting has always been one of the attractions, and one of the seamier aspects, of handball.)

Around the turn of the century, kicking became illegal, the court was made shorter, and a softer, slower ball was introduced. With these major changes handball became accessible to a greater number of people and made the transition from spectator to participant sport.

COURT AND EQUIPMENT

Handball can be played on one-, three-, or four-wall courts. In New York City, where there are more players than anywhere else in the world, indoor and outdoor courts are common. In the rest of the country, handball is strictly an indoor sport. In an attempt to attract spectators, some recently built four-wall courts were designed with galleries that can seat one thousand viewers.

Tournament handballs are made of hard black rubber and are hollow. They are 1⅞ inches around and weigh 2.3 ounces. Many players prefer a softer, pink ball. With the black ball, gloves are an absolute necessity, for unless one's hands have been toughened, playing fast handball without gloves could result in severe bone bruises.

The one-wall court has a 16-foot wall and a court 20 feet wide and 34 feet long. The short line, a line running parallel to the wall, is 16 feet from it, and the service line is 9 feet behind the short line.

The four-wall court is 20 feet wide and 40 feet long. The three forward walls are 20 feet high. The back wall is 12 feet high. The short line divides the court in half, and the service line is 5 feet in front of it. The three- and four-wall courts are identical, except, of course, that the three-wall has no back wall.

THE GAME

In both singles and doubles play, the rules are quite simple and basically the same for one-, three-, and four-wall. The server, standing behind the service line and in front of the short line, bounces the ball once and hits it on the fly directly against the front wall. The ball must then land past the short line and not reach the back wall (if there is one) before bouncing. If it bounces in front of the short line or if the server crosses the short line while serving, a fault is called and the server gets one more chance to serve properly. If he muffs both serves, he loses the chance not only to serve but to score points, since points can only be scored on service. The winner of the game is the player or team that first scores 21 points. A match is normally best two of three games.

The receiver must wait behind the short line before hitting the ball, either on the fly (volleying) or after one bounce. His return must hit the front wall on the fly. In three- and four-wall handball, the ball may bounce off any combination of walls and ceiling, but it must hit the front wall before hitting the floor.

After the first return, players alternate hitting, again returning the ball either by volleying or by hitting it after the first bounce. In one-wall handball each shot must land within the court or on one of the lines marking the boundaries, unless the returner chooses to volley.

Handball serves as a recreational pastime or a high-level sport. Athletes use it to stay in shape; non-athletes to get in shape. Good handball demands good conditioning.

ONE-WALL HANDBALL COURT

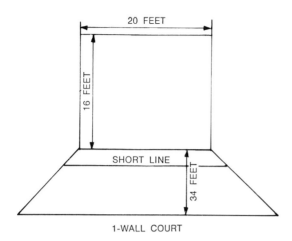

1-WALL COURT

Simple, then: just keep returning the ball to the front wall. There is, however, one tricky aspect to handball—the rule about "hinders." Stated simply and straight from the rule book, it says that each player must get a "fair chance to see and to return the ball." If a player violates this rule by not moving to allow his opponent to reach the ball, by blocking his view, or by being struck by his return, his opponent calls a hinder. It must then be decided whether or not the hinder was "avoidable." A server who makes an avoidable hinder loses his service; the receiver who does so loses a point. Unavoidable, or "dead ball," hinders are simply played over. In championship matches there is an official to decide these and other questions, but in recreational handball, where there is no official, differences of opinion about whether or not a hinder was avoidable can turn a friendly game into a shouting match.

The rule for hinders in the one-wall game is somewhat different from the three- and four-wall rule. So long as the player remains completely still, either in front of or beside the player making the shot, he is not hindering.

The athletic abilities and stamina required for handball are considerable. The ability to make backward, forward, and side bends, quick starts and stops, and overhead shots should be in every player's repertoire. In addition, unlike most sportsmen, handball players must be able to use both hands. The aspiring player has to develop his "off" hand, or he will lose consistently. It's not surprising, then, that handball is a favorite conditioning sport among professional athletes.

THE STROKES

The three basic strokes are the underhand, sidearm, and overhead. The "natural" stroke, the underhand, is the simplest and the one fledglings first attempt. With the fingers slightly cupped, the player strikes the ball with an underhand motion like that of a softball pitcher. For the sidearm stroke, the power stroke in handball, the body is low and the swing parallel to the floor. The ball is met around knee level. At the beginning of the stroke, as in tennis, the shoulder is facing the front wall; at the end the body faces the front wall and the player is poised on the balls of his feet for the next shot.

The overhand stroke is best employed to hit the ball to the ceiling in the three- and four-wall games. The shot then rebounds high off the front wall, bounces back very high toward the back of the court, and is difficult to return.

For virtuosos, there is the punch shot—a shot made with a closed fist. Like a punch shot in volleyball, it is powerful but difficult to control.

STRATEGY

The strokes for the one- and four-wall games are basically the same, but the games themselves are quite different. In general one-wall play is more defensive, since the player must keep the ball within the court. Control is important. Four-wall is a more intricate game. The ball may follow an endless variety of routes as it ricochets around the court, requiring the competitor to have equal amounts of physical and mental agility.

The winning handball player usually dominates center court, facing the front wall, cutting off the angles, and forcing the other player to hit past him.

The point-making shot in handball is the kill shot. A properly executed kill is hit low into a corner formed by two walls or the wall and the floor. At its best it rolls onto the floor, impossible to return.

Paddleball

The rules for paddleball are the same as those for handball. The game is played on both four-wall and one-wall courts. Games are for 15 points and are scored like squash, points being scored only by the server. Paddles are of hardwood, usually 3-ply glued, and are 14¾ by 7½ inches. Balls are similar to those used in handball.

Racquetball

The rules and regulations for racquetball are the same as those for handball. Racquetball is also played on one-, three-, and four-wall courts, and again, the court dimensions correspond exactly to those for handball. The prime difference, of course, is the racquet. It measures 11 inches in length and 9 inches in width, has a maximum handle length of 7 inches, and is strung like a tennis racquet. The ball is 2¼ inches in diameter and weighs 1.40 ounces.

As in handball, the object of the game is to prevent the opponent from successfully returning a shot. Only the serving side can score; if the serving sides loses the point, it loses only the serve. A score of 21 points wins the game.

Horseracing

"An-n-nd they're off!" To the more than fifty million Americans who go to the racetracks, these words are magic. These fans and the billions of dollars they wager at more than one hundred tracks across the country (to say nothing of the money bet off-track, both legal and illegal) make thoroughbred, or flat, racing far and away the most popular spectator sport in the country. But to call thoroughbred racing just a "spectator sport" is not quite apt. Trying to outwit all the other gamblers by picking a winner, the bettor is more than just an observer of the action. Without him and his never-extinguished hopes, the sport wouldn't exist, for it is the bettors' money that supports racing.

Horseracing has been called the "sport of kings," and with good reason—only those of royal means can afford to breed and race horses. The

chances of a thoroughbred growing up and winning enough races to recover the cost of rearing him are fairly slim, so people in this country's "horsey set" come from monied families—the DuPonts, Phippses, Vanderbilts, Whitneys, Morrises, and Mellons. Undeterred by the cost, they breed horses that have admirable bloodlines. (The stud services of Secretariat, the great Triple Crown winner, were syndicated for more than six million dollars.) But there is no sure way to produce a champion, no way to predict where the next Man O'War, Whirl-away, Sea Biscuit, or Kelso will come from.

HISTORY

One of the most important men in the history of racing was not quite a king, just the brother of one. In 1764, William Augustus, the Duke of Cumber-

From afar racehorses seem to be all gliding grace, but watch them up close, at the start of the homestretch, and you'll discover their enormous, thumping power.

land and brother of King George III of England, mated a beautiful mare with an ugly but rugged sire and produced Eclipse. Eclipse wasn't a pretty horse, but he was much faster than the other horses of his day, always outdistancing the rest of the field. More than ninety percent of the thoroughbreds racing today descend in the male line from Eclipse, himself a descendant of the famous Darley Arabian, one of the three Arabian male ancestors of all thoroughbred racehorses.

In the United States racing was mostly a gentleman's affair at first; horse owners raced their animals and bet among themselves. After the Civil War, the sport evolved into its modern form, with widespread betting done through professional brokers, or "bookies" (then legal). The races that form the American Triple Crown were all first run in this period—in 1867, the Belmont Stakes; in 1873, the Preakness Stakes; and in 1875, the Kentucky Derby. To date, only nine horses have captured the Triple Crown.

Ironically, thoroughbred racing grew most rapidly when most people could not afford to bet, during the depression years. Seventeen states passed racing laws, and there was a flurry of racetrack construction. The states desperately needed a form of revenue, and the unemployed people who went to the track found something to hope for.

Today racing is legal in thirty states, but the true mecca of horseracing is New York, which has probably the best racing in the country. There are a number of thoroughbred racing associations in the United States, but the chief authority is the New York Jockey Club, founded in 1894 and custodian of the Stud Book, in which all racehorses must be registered. Like the founders, the present members of the club were never jockeys, but they are some of the most powerful and wealthy men in America.

THE TRACK AND THE RACE

Most races in this country are run on oval, dirt tracks that are a mile or a mile and one-eighth long. The racetrack unit of measure is the furlong, equal to one-eighth mile. Tracks are usually marked by posts along the inside railing at intervals of one-sixteenth mile. Races vary in length, but in the United States they are usually between five and ten furlongs. Races of less than one mile are considered sprints. Most tracks also have a turf, or grass, course directly inside the dirt course. At least one of the nine races on a typical day's race program will usually be run on the turf.

At all large tracks, horses are lined up in a starting gate as the starting, or "post," time approaches. Each horse is enclosed in an individual stall. At the start of the race, a bell rings and the front door of each stall springs open. Once the horses are on their way, no horse or jockey may interfere with another horse or jockey. If the race officials detect a foul, they have the power to disqualify the horse. Jockeys used to get away with much mischief. They would slow down another horse by grasping its saddle cloth, and they would whip and deliberately jostle each other. But in the 1930s, races began to be filmed and the stewards could detect more fouls.

Another use of the camera—at the finish of the race—has improved the sport. As the horse passes under the finish wire, a camera snaps a picture that will usually resolve any arguments over who won a close, or "photo-finish," race.

TYPES OF RACES

Every track wants its races to be as close as possible; otherwise the bettors may lose interest. Horseracing officials have developed a number of ways of

The Triple Crown won by Secretariat, the first since Citation won it in 1948, began with the start of the 1973 Kentucky Derby, opposite top. *(Secretariat is 1A, third from right). The triumph came just after the final turn at the Belmont Stakes,* opposite bottom, *about a month later.* Above: *The hazards of a hurdle race.*

classifying horses to make races competitive. The most widely used is the claiming race. Approximately seventy-five percent of the races run in this country are "claimers."

In a claiming race the race officials set a claiming price for all entered horses. When an owner enters a horse, it is immediately for sale, and any other owner registered at the track may buy the horse for the claiming price before the race begins. For example, in a $10,000 claimer, any horse entered may be bought for that price. An owner who enters a valuable horse against an inferior field is likely to lose the horse before it has a chance to run.

Just as claiming races are designed to keep fast horses out of races for slower ones, sweepstakes, or stakes, races are designed to exclude slower horses from a top-level field. The owners of the entered horses put up a portion of the prize money in entry fees. The slow runners are kept out because no owner will risk a large fee unless his horse has a realistic chance of winning.

Horse races are equalized in many other ways. In an "allowance" race some horses are allowed to carry less weight than others, according to a formula based on each horse's past performance. The worse a horse has been running recently, the less weight it has to carry. In a handicap race, horses carry different amounts of weight, too, but it is the track secretary, using his own judgment, who determines how much weight each horse should carry. In addition there are "maiden races," held for horses that have never won before.

Jockeys (and their gear) are weighed twenty minutes before each race and immediately after a winning race. No jockey may bet on any horse but his own.

JOCKEYS

The jockey's lot is not easy. Controlling a thoroughbred racehorse—more than one thousand pounds of animal moving at about forty miles per hour—takes strong arm, back, and leg muscles. And the sport is dangerous. Almost every jockey is injured during his career, some fatally.

A good jockey has to know the ability of his horse and pace it to run the best possible race. It takes a keen sense of timing to know if a horse is running faster or slower than usual. For the top dozen or so jockeys, the pay is quite good. They generally receive ten percent of the purse and may earn as much as $300,000 a year.

Since 1969, women jockeys have been racing at American tracks, making racing the only professional sport in which women and men compete together. This breakthrough may have occurred in horseracing because these days few American men are light enough (about one hundred ten pounds) to be jockeys.

Jockeys take their orders from the horse's trainer, who is hired by the owner to supervise every aspect of the horse's preparation for racing. A good trainer is important to a horse's success, and a trainer with the best reputation has no trouble earning a living.

The uniforms that jockeys wear are called silks, though the material used nowadays is usually nylon. The silks are furnished to the jockeys by the owners and each set of silks bears the owner's colors—a particular color scheme on the jersey to distinguish one stable from another. The jockey's uniform also includes a riding cap, long boots, a hand whip, and, for a muddy track, goggles.

FLAT TRACK RACECOURSE

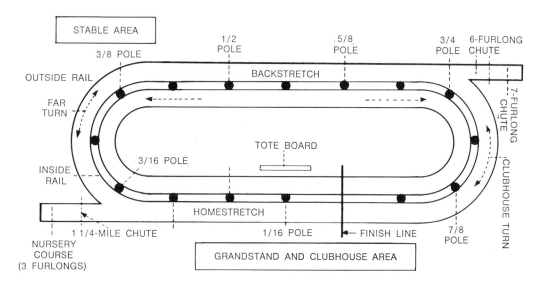

BETTING

Racetracks use the pari-mutuel system, in which all the money bet on a specific race goes into a pool and the odds on each horse are determined by the amount of money bet on it. After each race, the track takes a percentage of the wagered money (about 5 percent for itself, about 11 or 12 percent in taxes for the state) and divides the rest among the bettors holding winning tickets.

Racing's scoreboard is the "tote board," located on the track's infield. Connected to an electronic computer called the totalizator, it shows the amount of money bet on each horse and the odds for each.

Bettors can risk their money in a variety of ways. The three basic methods are bets to win, place, and show. A bet to win ("on the nose") pays off only if the horse comes in first; a bet to place wins (somewhat less) if the horse comes in first or second; and a bet to show pays (even less) if the horse comes in first, second, or third. Horseplayers can also bet "across the board"—that is, bet that their horse will win, place, or show. (This is also a low-risk bet and thus doesn't pay off well.)

In an effort to lure betting dollars, most tracks offer other combination bets. The most popular is the "daily double," in which the players try to pick the winner of the first and second races. In the "exacta," or "perfecta," the bettor must pick the win and place horses in the right order of finish. In the "quinella" he must pick the first two finishers regardless of order. In the "triple," or "trifecta," the bettor must pick the first three finishers in proper order. The chances of winning such bets (especially the triple) are low, so payoffs are quite high.

How does a horseplayer go about picking a winner? To those not betting whimsically, the *Daily Racing Form* is the Bible. This newspaper contains a multitude of information on each horse running that day at the various tracks in season, including detailed information on past performances. Scientific bettors "handicap" all the horses in a race to decide which have the best chances. But the number of factors in any race make betting hazardous even to the most trained and analytical horseplayers. Most veteran horseplayers will admit that in the long run it's a losing game.

Harness Racing

Harness racing is an original American sport developed in the late 1600s by well-off farmers who raced their carriage horses. Today, most harness racing takes place at night so as not to conflict with daytime flat racing.

The two varieties of harness racing are trotting and pacing. Trotters move opposite legs in unison; pacers move the legs on the same side in unison. The driver sits behind the horse in a lightweight sulky, or "bike." The drivers' weights in harness racing have a negligible effect on the race's outcome since all the horses are pulling a relatively heavy vehicle and not carrying the weight dead on their shoulders. Harness horses race in classes based on sex, age, and previous performance.

Betting is on the pari-mutuel system, as in thoroughbred racing. Trotters and pacers usually run truer to their past records than thoroughbreds do, but the betting is still risky. For example, a trotter or pacer can break from its gait and thus disqualify itself even though it may lead the field across the finish line.

A closely bunched field in a harness race can create quite a jumble. These are trotters, because they move the front leg of one side in unison with the back leg on the other. Pacers move front and back legs on the same side in unison.

Horseshoes

HISTORY

No one knows for certain how the game of horseshoes started. Most authorities agree, however, that it probably originated as an imitation of one of the ancient Olympic games—the discus throw. Since the average Greek was too poor to have his own discus, he used some sort of metal ring. This, like the discus, was thrown for distance, but later, stakes were driven into the ground as targets, and accuracy rather than strength became important.

The practice of shoeing horses to protect their hooves was begun by the Greek and Roman armies a few centuries after the birth of Christ. The discarded shoes were picked up and thrown. At first they were hammered closed and then thrown, but later the shoes were hurled as they were. Evidently the Norman invaders brought the game to England. English colonists brought the game to the New World. It wasn't until 1899, when a club was formed in Meadville, Pennsylvania, that an organization was given to the sport.

The game grew in popularity, and matches began to be played between clubs. In 1914, the Grand League of the American Horseshoe Pitchers Association was formed and some important rules were adopted. The real revolution in the sport came in the early 1900s, when the "open shoe" throw came into use. Until then, ringers were considered hard to throw, so instead players tried to score by throwing as close as possible to the stake. Today, most championship winners throw an average of eight ringers in 10 tries.

THE COURT AND EQUIPMENT

A regulation horseshoes court is on level ground. The stakes are 40 feet apart and lean slightly toward each other. Stakes should be 23 inches high, and the area around them should be of moist clay to keep the shoes from bouncing when they land. Regulation horseshoes are no more than 7¼ inches wide, 7⅝ inches long, and 2½ pounds. The opening should not exceed 3½ inches.

THE GAME

Players pitch two shoes each, alternating pitches for an inning. A shoe must land within six inches of the stake to score. There are two types of scoring— the cancellation method and the count-all method. In cancellation scoring the closest shoe to the stake scores one point, two shoes closer than the opponent's best shoe scores two points, and each ringer scores three points. An equal number of points scored by each side in an inning cancel out each other, and only the difference between the scores of an inning counts toward the final score. A game is fifty points. In the count-all method of scoring all ringers count three points and every shoe that lands within six inches of the stake scores one point; the game lasts for 50 throws by each player (25 innings).

Doubles horseshoes is the same as singles, with partners throwing from opposite ends of the court.

Horseshoes tournaments are governed by rules set forth by the National Horseshoe Pitchers Association, formed in 1921 and incorporated in Ohio. World championships are held each year in the United States.

Pitching horseshoes is not just a matter of a casual toss. For one thing, at two and a half pounds, horseshoes aren't all that light. It takes some strength for this big a windup and delivery.

Ice Hockey

More than any other team sport, ice hockey is a game of motion. There is motion even when nothing happens. In other sports a whistle stops the motion; in hockey it stops the play but only changes the motion from frenzy to flow. Then, as the flow subsides but never quite stops, as the players reach their faceoff positions but rarely rest there, the puck is dropped and the frenzy begins again.

It takes a practiced eye to make sense of this never-ending motion, to distinguish the mainstream of the game from the eddies that adorn it. For example, coaches are forever telling their players that skating in graceful circles is no substitute for hard, ice-scarring stops-and-starts, and no practice session is complete without a drill on this lesson. But like the referee with his whistle, coaches can only pattern, not stop the movement. Ice hockey never stops moving.

The newcomer is apt to complain that the game is hard to follow. He is right, of course. But once you are afloat in the stream of hockey, either as a spectator or player, rushing along and navigating dangers or anticipating new movements in an instant, you can be transfixed by the motion. The proof comes every spring when the motion addicts of hockey, emotionally drained just from watching the Stanley Cup playoffs, turn to the languorous sport of baseball and wonder how they will survive the long, slow summer.

HISTORY

Man had been ice skating and playing hockey for a long time before he began to do both at the same time. The first ice skaters were probably Northern Europeans in the Middle Ages; the first hockey players were North American Indians. They played a game French explorers called *hoquet*, French for shepherd's crook, the type of stick the Indians

Ice hockey likes to call itself the fastest game. It may not be, but it is a sport of perpetual motion. Bobby Orr controlled perhaps better than any other player the shifting speeds of the game.

123

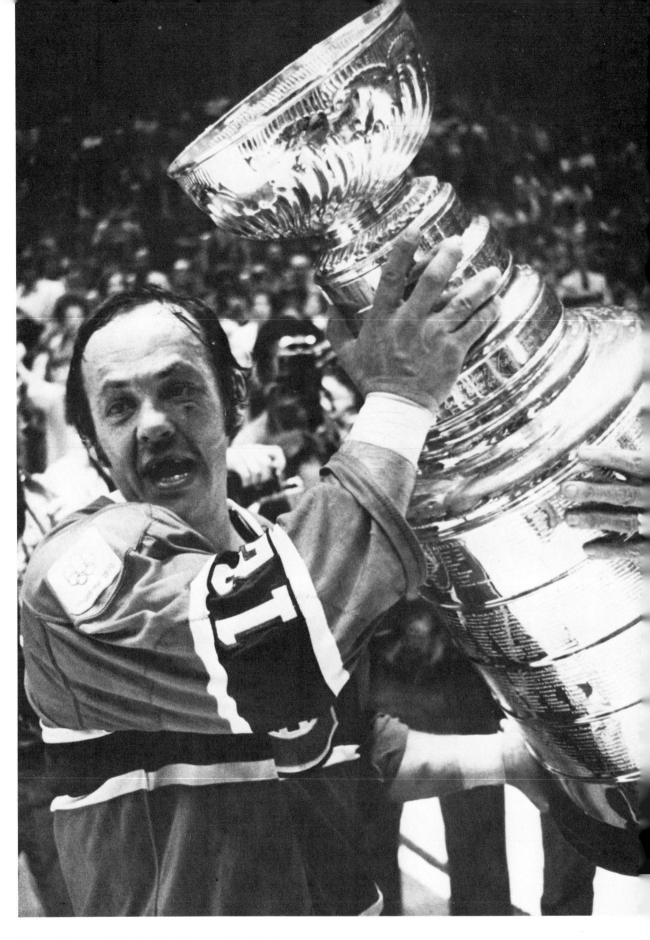

The most treasured trophy in hockey—and, hockey fans
say in all of sports—is the Stanley Cup, presented
each year to the winner of the playoffs in the National
Hockey League. In 1976, the Montreal Canadiens won the
cup, as they had many times in the past, and their
captain, Yvan Cournoyer, posed proudly with it.

used. But who was the mastermind who combined ice skating and hockey? If there was one, he has long been forgotten. Baseball had its Cartwright and Doubleday, basketball its Naismith, tennis its Wingfield. Ice hockey had no such founder. Historians can only speculate that the first ice hockey players were field hockey enthusiasts pursuing their passion during the winter.

In 1862, a London newspaper denounced ice hockey players for disturbing the proper and sedate Londoners who wished to use the city's frozen ponds merely for a leisurely skate. So from its very beginnings, ice hockey has had a reputation as a game for rowdies. The English would surely have turned up their noses had they realized that in the Queen's Dominion of Canada, where ice hockey was finding a home in the late nineteenth century, some of the first hockey pucks were nothing but frozen horse dung. But one needn't have been priggish to disapprove of ice hockey—the first games were truly wars on ice. Even after rules were passed limiting the number of players to a side, mob rule was common. There was no netting to enclose the goal, and the hapless goal judge, standing behind the goal and signaling when a goal had been scored, had to be as pleasing to the crowd with his decisions as he was nimble in dodging the puck. Often he lost on both counts.

Ice hockey was an unruly game, but as it spread throughout Canada, for the most part still an unruly land, even the governor general took notice. Lord Stanley of Preston donated a huge silver bowl and directed a board of trustees to oversee its presentation each year to Canada's best team, starting in the 1893–94 season. Today this Stanley Cup is the most prized trophy in professional hockey (even in all of professional sports, say some hockey partisans). The trophy cost Lord Stanley the American equivalent of $48.50. In 1973, the cherished Cup was stolen but, to the traditionalists' relief, soon returned.

Professionalism found its way into ice hockey as it did into most other major sports. Entrepreneurs (Canadian dentist J. L. Gibson was the first) began buying up the best amateurs and creating superteams that fans rushed to see. The self-righteous outrage of the owners of amateur teams was quickly overcome (after all, these owners were making money from the services of unpaid players), and soon Lord Stanley's cup was the permanent possession of the professionals. The great amateur players of the day—Cyclone Taylor, Hod Stuart, Newsy Lalonde—led the flight to professionalism, earning as much as $500 per game (not including bets). The players' exorbitant salaries reduced a few of the early professional leagues to bankruptcy, but the idea of playing for pay was too hardy to fail. By the start of World War I, there were two major professional leagues in Canada: the National Hockey Association (NHA) in the East, and the Pacific Coast Hockey Association (PCHA) in the West. The two were constantly feuding because the

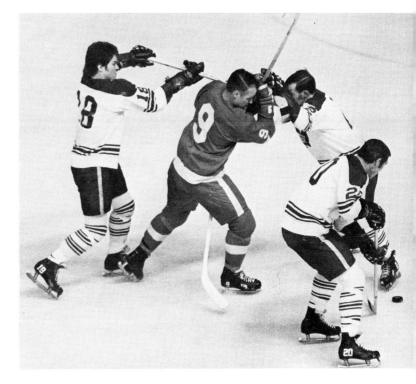

The big men of the fifties and sixties, when hockey discovered the big shot and the big scorer—top: Maurice ("The Rocket") Richard; middle: Gordie Howe (9); bottom: Bobby Hull, "the Golden Jet."

heads of the PCHA, the wily Patrick brothers, had established their league by the now-classic method of luring away players from the established league with fat salaries. But in another ten years, the Patricks themselves became the victims of such tactics, and in 1926, they sold the remainder of their failing league to the NHA's successor, the National Hockey League (NHL). A half century later, the NHL is still pro hockey's premier league.

The Patricks were innovators as well as businessmen. Even before the brothers sold their league, the NHL had accepted many of their ideas. The Patricks divided the ice into thirds with two blue lines and permitted forward passing within each zone. Such a rule seems stodgy today, when passes zing all over the ice, but at that time it was revolutionary: the rules had not permitted forward passing before. The Patricks also introduced (and the NHL later instituted) end-of-season playoffs, a clever money-making proposition that many pro sports have adopted. Today's Stanley Cup champion is not the champion of the season play but instead the winner of a special postseason tournament, the Stanley Cup playoffs, for which the three top teams in each of the NHL's four divisions qualify.

With the interleague wars settled, the NHL survived the economic strife of the thirties and the world war in the forties as basically a six-team league, with franchises in Toronto, Montreal, Boston, New York, Chicago, and Detroit. The owners

were mostly tight-fisted, conservative men, whose players had no choice but to work hard for relatively little pay or be gone, back to the tiny, mostly poor Canadian towns they had come from.

In the late forties and fifties, while football gained the bomb and basketball the towering center who could score seemingly at will, ice hockey acquired the booming slap shot and with it the game's greatest scorers yet: Maurice Richard, Gordie Howe, and Bernie ("Boom Boom") Geoffrion. A bit slower but bigger and more powerful than the former stars, they could blast the puck into the net at a prodigious rate. In 1944–45, Richard scored 50 goals in 50 games—the first and still the only man to complete a full season at a goal-per-game pace.

In the sixties the trend toward such power hockey continued, but in the seventies a new style of play, from an unlikely source, startled the hockey world. The Russians, relative newcomers to the game, had perfected a style of short passing and rigidly disciplined checking. Nevertheless, the mavens of the North American pro game hardly took seriously the Russians' supremacy in Olympic hockey and other amateur competition. Then in 1972, the Russians finally met a team of top NHL professionals in a series of eight games. The result was thrilling hockey, and only a game-winning goal in the dying seconds of the final game gave the Canadians the edge in the series.

As if their problems with the Russians had not been embarrassing enough, the NHL found itself

ICE HOCKEY RINK

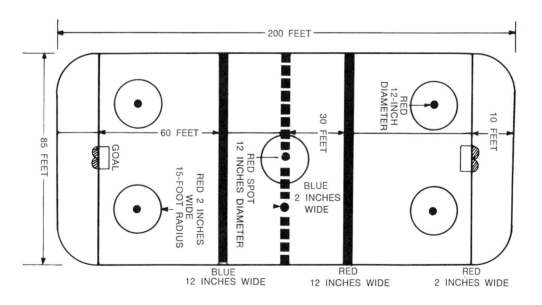

Opposite: *Goaltenders, those heavily padded, masked creatures, have the hardest job—stopping pucks blasted at speeds of as high as 100 miles per hour. It's enough to make Ken Dryden jumpy.* Top: *A hockey rink seems to be a spacious place, but when bodies are hurtling all around, it can get quite confining.*

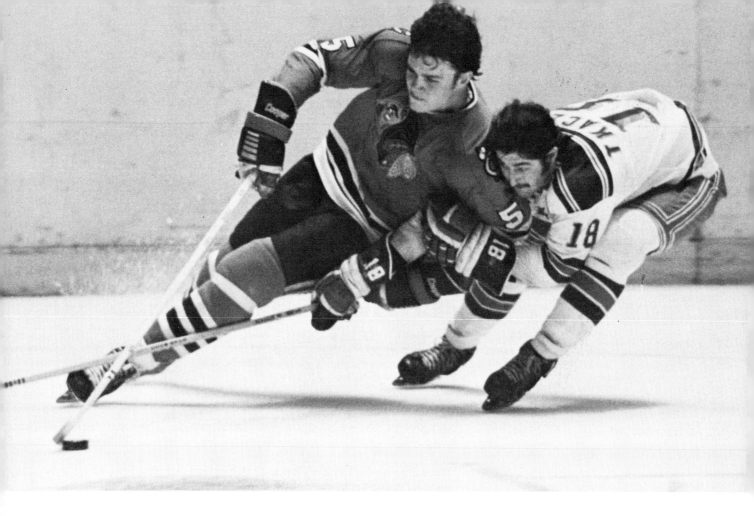

rivaled by a new league in 1972–73, the World Hockey Association (WHA). The NHL had doubled in size in 1966–67, won a rich national television contract, and added six more teams through 1973–74. Nonetheless, the WHA organizers believed the public would support still more hockey. With the birth of the new league, suddenly the pay scale for hockey players jumped to the tremendous levels of other major sports. Through 1975, the WHA was in shaky financial condition, but pro hockey was still growing. As the two leagues continued to battle, rumors were heard of expansion to Europe. Perhaps London newspapers will once again carry accounts of this rowdy sport arousing the citizenry.

EQUIPMENT

The goaltenders, the two men who move the least in this free-flowing game, are the most heavily protected by their equipment and by their teammates, who regard body contact against their goalie as a declaration of war. All hockey players wear padding underneath their uniforms of jerseys, long stockings, knee-length shorts, and padded gloves. In addition the goalies strap a chest protector underneath their jerseys, and on each leg a long, wide, leather pad that covers the leg from the top of the knee to the top of the skate. With his legs held together and the blade of his stick resting on the ice against the front of his skates, the goalie forms a shield that protects his goal as well as himself. The

stick he holds has both a wider blade (3½ inches compared to 3) and a wider bottom of the shaft than does the regular hockey stick. Unlike the other players, he usually grips the stick with only one hand, the other being occupied with catching the puck in a deep, floppy mitt similar to a baseball first baseman's mitt. A stylish goalie handling his stick has the aplomb of an orchestra conductor waving a baton, but the goalie's stick is far more than a stylish accessory. The goalie relies on his stick. He uses it when he moves behind the net to stop a skittering puck for his defensemen or when he neatly caroms a puck off the boards away from a charging opposition forward, or, in extreme cases, when he slams the puck the length of the ice to save his team's disorganized defense. And he may use it as a sabre—for slashing at the ankles of an opponent who ventures too close to the goalmouth.

Today, almost all goaltenders wear masks, though 15 years ago masks were considered not only unmanly but, remarkably enough, even hazardous. Critics said they limited a goalie's vision. Then in 1959, an innovator and master goalie, Jacques Plante of the Montreal Canadiens, was hit in the face with a shot. It took seven stitches to close the gash that resulted. He returned to the ice wearing the crude mask with which he had been experimenting in practice. The Canadiens won the game and their next 10 with the masked goalie. When asked if wearing the mask meant he was afraid, Plante replied, "If I jump out of a plane without a parachute, does that make me brave?"

A controversy as heated as the one over goalies' masks was the question of curvature in the blade of the sticks. Until recently the only dimensional requirements for a nongoalie's hockey stick were that its shaft be less than 55 inches long and that its blade be no more than 12½ inches long and between 2 and 3 inches wide. Then Bobby Hull and Stan Mikita of Chicago accidentally discovered that a curved blade (that is, a blade that still rests flat on the ice but curves in depth from heel to tip) gave their shots a vicious dip and, after they practiced some, allowed them to carry a puck better. The curved stick craze was on, but before long the goaltenders were pounding their (totally uncurved) sticks in protest. Bombarded with shots of 100

Opposite: *The speed and momentum of a skater can make some incredibly awkward positions seem quite natural.* Below: *Play begins after every stoppage with a faceoff. The players usually try to swipe the puck back to their teammates.*

miles per hour and faster, high hoppers, fluttering floaters, and tricky rollers, the goalies protested that it was too much to expect them to confront these fiercely dipping shots. The rulesmakers listened, and today a hockey stick's curvature is limited to one-half inch.

One of the few pieces of equipment that hasn't recently been a source of controversy is the puck, a black rubber disc, three inches in diameter, one inch thick, and weighing between 5½ and 6 ounces. It is frozen before the game to make it bounce and roll more truly.

The blades of hockey skates are shorter than those of figure skates but are razor sharp and capped at the back with safety tips. Players sometimes repair to the dressing room during a game for a quick skate sharpening.

The last piece of equipment is for use after the game—false teeth. Most hockey players lose their real teeth early in their careers, so to keep their flashing smiles, they acquire dentures. Another problem of the trade (for goalies, who are more likely to retain their teeth), is not watching television and going to the movies. The netminders say it ruins their vision.

THE RINK AND THE GAME

Emile Francis, formerly the coach and general manager of the New York Rangers, once compared a hockey rink to a bull ring. He was suggesting that the barrier that encloses the playing surface—the three- to four-foot-high boards topped with Plexiglas sheets—leaves the players no refuge while they are on the ice. In football or basketball a harried player may escape a threatening situation by stepping out of bounds. In hockey, if the 200-by-85-foot playing surface isn't big enough, a player has to reconcile himself to being mashed into the boards. Some players find it hard to accept this basic fact of the game; others eagerly take advantage of it by saving their hatchet work for the tussles along the boards, particularly in the rounded corners, where it is difficult for the referee to spot fouls. Many a brawl has begun after someone has been crushed along the boards. There is a penalty for boarding— violently checking an opponent into the boards rather than "riding him off" along them—but like all penalties in hockey, it curbs but does not eliminate the abuse. Generally, any man carrying the puck along the boards is fair game to be slammed into them.

There are nine faceoff spots, each one foot in diameter, on the ice: one in the center of the rink, two near each goal (one on either side of the goals), and four between the blue lines (two near each, on opposite sides of the rink). The ones near the goals and the one at center ice are enclosed by restraining circles. Whenever play stops for a goal, for the end of a period, for a penalty, for a puck "frozen" in a jumble of players along the boards or at the goalmouth, for a goalie holding the puck, or for an infraction, it begins again with a faceoff, usually in

one of these nine circles. Two opposing players stand on either side of the circle, their sticks on the ice in front of them, their backs to their goals, and their teammates even with or behind the faceoff circle (and outside the restraining circle if there is one). When the official drops the puck between them, the two faceoff men usually try to shovel it to a teammate. Hockey experts claim that the team that wins the most faceoffs usually wins the game, and recently hockey statisticians have taken to keeping faceoff records as conscientiously as they count shots on goal. Whether by trickery or simply with uncanny hand-eye coordination, some players have a special knack for winning faceoffs. Watching Chicago's Stan Mikita facing off holds about as much suspense as observing a master safecracker picking a lock.

A goal is centered on each of the two goal lines, which span the width of the rink 10 feet from the ends. The goalposts are two hollow iron bars that rest on stakes set into the ice six feet apart. A crossbar connects the tops of these four-foot-high goalposts, and netting, braced by a flat rod down the middle and anchored by metal at the base, encloses the goal. This is the enclave the goaltender guards. Each time the goaltender fails in his efforts and the puck passes completely over the goal line between the goalposts, a goal is scored. To alert the referee and the spectators to the fact that the puck has entered the net, a goal judge, who sits in a tiny booth in the stands immediately behind the goal, presses a button that lights a red goal light, mounted on the Plexiglas above him.

Usually the red goal light only confirms what everyone already knows. The attacking team has raised its sticks in triumph; the defenders have wheeled away in resignation; the goalie has slammed his stick in frustration. It is all too clear that the puck has gotten behind him, even if it got there so fast that most of the spectators are really not sure how. But sometimes that obscure man in the glass-enclosed booth becomes the star witness in a hotly disputed case. In the second game of the 1974 Stanley Cup semifinal playoffs between New York and Philadelphia, New York goalie Ed Giacomin sprawled along the goal line with one hand desperately extended behind him smothering the puck. His hand was partly behind the goal line, but was the puck completely behind it? Not even the television cameras, much less the referee, whose decision is final, could tell. But the goal judge stoutly maintained that the puck had crossed the line, and despite vigorous protests from Giacomin and his teammates, it was the goal judge's ruling that the referee accepted.

Finally, there are the most important markings on the ice, the three center lines. Between the goal lines, the ice is divided in half by a center, dashed red line (in professional hockey only; in amateur play there is no red line) and into thirds by two unbroken blue lines. Understanding the functions of these three lines is the key to understanding hockey. The two linesmen, the officials who assist

Scoring a goal, particularly a big one, sets off a passionate celebration. Phil Esposito, who scored 76 goals one year for the Boston Bruins, proves you never score too many.

the referee on the ice, use these lines to determine the common infractions of offside and icing.

A game lasts for three periods of 20 minutes each. If the game is tied at the end of regulation play, there may be an overtime period. (In the Stanley Cup playoffs, all tie games are resolved in sudden-death overtime periods, as many as necessary to determine a winner.) The clock stops for all infractions, for the puck being hit out of the rink, for goals, and of course for the two intermissions (usually 15 minutes long) between periods. With all the clock stoppages, the game takes more than two hours from start to finish.

In addition to the goalie, each team fields two defense men (right and left) and three forwards (right wing, center, and left wing). The unit of three forwards (three or four units to a team) is called a line. If it is successful, a line will become as permanent as a good double-play combination in baseball and perhaps earn itself a catchy nickname (the Punch Line, the Production Line, the GAG—goal-a-game-line—for example). A more common fate for a line is to be shuffled. Like a losing card player always shuffling the deck to change his luck, an anxious coach will use as many different combinations on this forward line as he can devise. With 11 or 12 forwards to use, he has many possibilities, but

a good coach remembers that linemates are not likely to succeed unless he allows them the time to become accustomed to each other's style.

One of the fascinating and unique aspects of hockey is the line change "on the fly," or when play is in progress. At a relatively safe moment, as many as three and occasionally even more players skate toward their bench, and when they are almost there, their replacements leap over the boards into the fray. It takes fine coordination not to be caught in a bad position or, even worse, with too many men in the play, which results in a two-minute penalty. Every hockey player, particularly defensemen, can tell horror stories of being "caught on a change."

ICING

Icing is the tactic of shooting the puck from one's own half of the ice across the opponent's goal line (but not on the goal). As soon as any member of the opposing team but the goalie touches the puck, a whistle stops the play and the puck is returned to the offending team's end of the ice, where a faceoff is held in one of the two faceoff circles near the goal. Icing is usually a defensive tactic. When the play is so threatening that the defending team senses it cannot begin a rush of its own when it gains control of the puck, it simply bats it down the ice

Stickhandlers usually don't have the luxury of looking at the puck, as Gilbert Perreault (one of the trickiest and best) does, opposite right. *Curt Bennett,* opposite left, *keeps his head up.* Above: *Action around the goal is often the roughest.*

and uses the halt in play to reorganize. The often-time Stanley Cup champion Toronto Maple Leafs of the 1960s were famous for this style of play. To the mounting frustration of the opposition and all but their own fans, the Leafs would ice the puck constantly, breaking the momentum of the attack and transforming the game into a slightly faster version of shuffleboard.

In amateur and international hockey, in which there is no center red line (and, incidentally, only one linesman), icing occurs when a team shoots the puck from behind its blue line across the opponent's goal line. The whistle is blown as the puck passes the goal line, not when an opposing player retrieves the puck. Also unlike most professional hockey, in which icing is permitted to a team that is playing with fewer men than its opponents because of a penalty, amateur hockey penalizes icing whenever it occurs.

OFFSIDE

Offside is an infraction more common even than icing and more difficult to explain. Indeed many fans, though they may have learned the numbers of every player in the league and who has beaten up whom how often, don't fully understand the offside rules. There are really two kinds of offside, the blue

line offside and the two-lines-pass offside. The blue line offside rule reads simply enough: no member of the attacking team may precede the puck across the opponent's blue line. A linesman straddles the blue line to rule on the question of offside. As the attacking team passes the line, he judges the attacking players' position by their skates. If one or both skates of the attacking players are on the blue line or to the center ice side of it as the puck passes toward the goal, the play is onside. Once the puck is on the goal side or inside the blue line, the attacking players may move wherever they please, but if the puck comes outside the blue line, they must likewise move outside the line and on their next thrust again follow the puck across the blue line toward the goal.

One of the tense moments in any hockey game comes when an attacking team is struggling to keep the puck inside the blue line and the defenders are fighting to knock it out. Both teams and all the spectators know that the attack will be thwarted if the puck passes the blue line (because then the attackers will be forced to retreat and regroup in center ice), so the blue line becomes to hockey what the first-down yard line is to football: it marks the progress of the attack.

The tricky part of the blue line offside is the so-

133

called "delayed offside." When the attacking team is offside, play is not necessarily stopped. The linesman simply raises his hand to indicate the offside, but he blows his whistle to stop play only if an attacking player actually touches the puck inside the blue line or if the defenders clearly fail to control it there. Perhaps one attacking player has passed the puck across the blue line to a teammate who has preceded the puck across the line. The receiver is offside, but before the pass reaches him, a defender intercepts. The linesman raises his hand to indicate a delayed offside, but if the defender moves the puck back across the blue line to center ice, the linesman lowers his hand and the offside is forgotten. However, if the defensive player loses the puck inside the blue line, the linesman blows his whistle and play is stopped, even though some time has passed since the puck first crossed the blue line with a player offside. Hence the term "delayed offside."

For the most blue line offsides, a faceoff is held at the closest of the two faceoff spots just outside the blue line.

The two-lines-pass offside is a rule that limits forward passing in professional hockey. A player who stands inside his blue line may not pass to a receiver standing across the red line. The linesman then halts the play, and a faceoff is held at the spot where the pass originated. However, if the pass receiver is standing on his side of the red line when the pass is made and the puck precedes him across the other lines, then he may receive the pass as far

forward as he likes. In other words, long lead passes are permitted if the receiver starts only a zone away from the passer. There is no "basket hanging" in hockey.

Now it is perhaps clear why many fans don't bother to learn the offside rules fully—they are not easily learned. These fans just accept the whistles without explanation and concentrate on the more easily understood and more visually appealing aspects of the game. Perhaps they don't realize that once the offside rules are mastered, hockey becomes almost as simple as bashing a puck with a stick into a net—which is, after all, the object of the game.

PENALTIES AND FIGHTS

In very few sports are fouling players even sent from the field, but in ice hockey they are virtually sent to jail, to a little cell called the penalty box. Hockey seems to prefer its transgressors to be locked up, and with good reason: once a player has been ordered from the ice for two minutes or more, he would prefer nothing more than to have an opponent accompany him. And so he usually seeks to cruise about stirring up more trouble. With a pen-

alty box and the rule that commands any player to proceed directly to it after he is penalized, the referee and linesmen can better keep law and order.

A player may find his way to the penalty box, or "cooler," or "sin bin," for a variety of fouls—hooking, tripping, spearing, high-sticking, slashing, boarding, roughing, elbowing, interference (checking a player who doesn't have the puck)—all of which are wholly within the referee's discretion to punish or ignore (assuming he sees them in the first place). Sometimes he is so strict that the players fall down constantly, trying to convince him to penalize the opposition; sometimes he is so lax that bodies litter the ice like streamers and balloons after a score. Either way, ice hockey is not always a game played on skates.

The referee's object is to avoid the brawling that hockey-fight fans love and pure-hockey lovers despise. Fighting is still an important part of professional ice hockey—most players believe it is necessary to fight to gain respect—but since the institution of the "third-man-in" rule, the NHL has curbed team warfare. This rule orders the referee to banish for the remainder of the game the first player to intervene in a two-man fight. The referee's more

Opposite: *A lot of weird things happen along the boards during a hockey game.* Above: *Bobby Clarke, left, is one of the grittiest (some say the dirtiest) of superstars.*

135

common sentences are two minutes (a minor penalty for infractions such as tripping), five minutes (a major penalty for fighting or a particularly vicious instance of what would normally deserve just a minor penalty), and ten minutes (a misconduct penalty for any particularly abusive behavior).

When fighting does erupt, the two linesmen usually attempt to separate the combatants while the referee watches impassively, totaling the charges to be relayed to the penalty timekeeper.

If two opposing players receive major penalties at the same time or if any player receives a misconduct, his team may replace him in the play. For all other penalties, including those to the goalie, who never serves them himself, the team skates less one man. However, a team may not play with fewer than four players, so if a team is already playing two men short and it is penalized again, the newly penalized player goes to the penalty box but does not begin serving his penalty until one of his teammates has finished serving his. Until that time, the newly penalized player may be replaced.

A team with a manpower advantage is said to have a power play. The great teams are particularly adept at scoring on the power play. The Montreal Canadiens of the fifties were so proficient that on some power plays they scored a flurry of goals, deciding a game within two minutes. A majority of

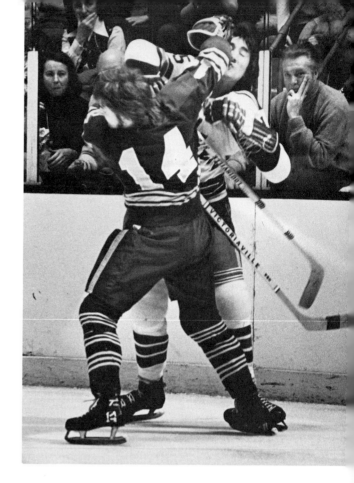

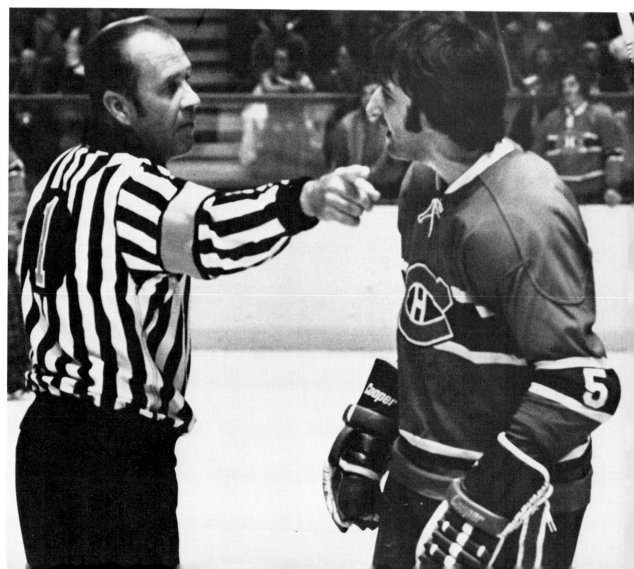

the rulesmakers (that is, the executives of the clubs that were being blitzed) suddenly developed great compassion for the punished. So they passed hockey's parole rule: if a team scores on a power play, the penalized player is deemed to have suffered enough and unless he has committed a major penalty he may return to the play.

With so much stress on penalties and fighting, it is sometimes forgotten that ice hockey demands superbly conditioned athletes. They are tested not so much by the game's scuffling and fouling but by the sheer speed and the sometimes terrifying injuries that result from men moving so quickly. Ice hockey players have an extraordinary and much-vaunted capacity to recover from injury and endure pain. But like all athletes, they can with experience only delay, never arrest the deterioration of their bodies. Eventually, the legs simply no longer can pump as hard as they must.

AMATEUR HOCKEY

At all levels amateur hockey has grown with the pro version. Most pro hockey players are still bred in Canada's extensive training network. But despite a woeful shortage of rinks, ice hockey leagues for youths have recently begun to sprout in the United States, and no longer are America's top college hockey teams stocked as heavily with Canadian imports.

An offshoot of the hockey boom has been the resurgence of roller hockey—the pavement version of ice hockey—and decades ago a popular pastime in big Eastern cities. Today roller hockey is flourishing among urban youth, who play the game on the cities' cement, bedecked in store-bought versions of the big ice hockey stars' uniforms. Only the wheels on their skates and the grating of roller skates against cement distinguish the city youths from their ice skating couterparts in suburbs. An amateur roller hockey tournament is held each year by the Roller Skating Rink Operators of America, located in Lincoln, Nebraska.

As if to authenticate the hockey boom in America, the United States won the bronze medal in ice hockey at the 1972 Winter Olympics. In 1960, the Americans had shocked the world (and particularly the Russians) by winning the gold medal, but since then the Soviets had reigned and the Americans declined. As one vivid demonstration of the difference between the two countries' teams, the Russians shelled an American goalie with 68 shots in one game.

The referee in a hockey game doesn't see all the fouls and doesn't penalize all those he does see. The result is much heavy hitting, some of it illegal (opposite top), *protest* (opposite bottom), *and frequent fights* (above).

Ice Skating

When does an athlete become an artist? There are moments in every sport when the beauty of an athlete's performance makes us forget we are watching a competition. In figure skating grace is more than a by-product of athletic endeavor; it is the reason for it. The figure skater strives not only to be graceful but to make his movements seem effortless. Despite the look of ease, expert figure skating requires much effort and stamina that comes only after much training and practice.

HISTORY

The first skaters, thousands of years ago, could not have been so graceful. Tying bones to the bottoms of their feet, they used sticks to pole themselves across the ice. Over the centuries bone was replaced by wood, wood by iron, and iron by steel. The use of skates changed, too. At first simply a practical method of transportation, they were later used for pleasure.

Skates were developed and used mostly in the icy, northern European countries—Norway, Sweden, Finland, and especially Holland. But one of the most important contributions to the development of skates came from England, where a blade shorter than the Dutch blade was developed. Turns could then be made in a smaller area. In 1742, the first skating club was established in Edinburgh, Scotland, and with it the first proficiency test. To join, one had to be able to skate a circle with either foot. It was a man's sport, partly because women's garb of the period gave women little freedom of movement.

Figure skating was shaped largely by Jackson Haines, the American ballet master. He took his dancing skills to the ice and almost singlehandedly created modern figure skating. Like many American artists, Haines was better appreciated in Europe than in his native land. In 1864, he went to England, where he gave exhibitions of free and breezy elegance. The English, whose skating style was confined, were outraged. Rebuffed, Haines moved to Vienna and became an instant success. The Austrians were especially delighted by his waltzes on ice.

Haines's compatriots in the United States were looking to more practical matters. The Philadelphia Humane Society dedicated itself to saving people who had fallen through the ice. In 1861, when the Humane Society merged with the Skaters' Club of Philadelphia and became the Philadelphia Skating Club and Humane Society, the by-laws of the new organization required members to carry rope with them whenever they went skating. In 1869, 259 rescues were made, some of which may have been unnecessary—the $12 reward may have encour-aged bogus rescues. Such heroics would become unnecessary with the invention of the artificial rink. In America the first indoor rink was opened in 1879 in New York's Madison Square Garden. Many hotels put rinks on their rooftops, and in 1915, at the Hippodrome playhouse in New York City, forty European skaters put on a show called "Flirting at St. Moritz," a harbinger of today's Ice Capades.

Figure skating has been in every Olympics since the 1908 Games in London, 16 years before the Winter Olympics were instituted. Free skating was not as exciting then as it is today—the men performed some fine jumps and spins, but the women were more inhibited. In fact, in 1920, the American Theresa Weld was marked down for the unladylike leaps she used in her program.

In 1928, 15-year-old Sonja Henie rid figure skating of such stuffiness. Her unparalleled mastery of technique and graceful, ballet-trained movements took the skating world by storm. She had begun skating at the age of six and throughout her career practiced many hours every day, preferring skating to eating, she said. Her single-minded dedication set a pattern for training that championship skaters have followed ever since. Today, anyone with the desire to become a champion figure skater must be willing to make skating his life from the time he can strap on a pair of skates.

EQUIPMENT

A skate has two parts—a leather boot and the blade. Figure-skate boots should be strong, very well fitting, and, for maximum support of the ankles, rather tight when laced. The blade is slightly curved and should be screwed to the boot where the body weight is greatest, at the inside of the center line running from heel to toe. Maneuverability rather than speed is the figure skater's prime concern, so the blades are usually shorter and thicker than hockey or racing blades. Unlike hockey blades, figure-skate blades are "hollow ground"—that is, there is a slight groove that runs the length of the blade, creating two edges. When their edges wear down, blades must be sharpened to prevent slipping. At the end of each blade on a figure skate are sawlike teeth that make up the toe rake, or toe picks—used mainly by advanced skaters in spins, jumps, and other movements.

TECHNIQUE

Figure skaters skate on the edge of the blades and propel themselves with thrusts from the side of the blade, not the front edge. Movements or figures are described with abbreviations that identify which foot a skater is skating on, in which direction he is going, and which edge of the skate he is using. Thus

the abbreviation "RFI," for example, means the skater is using the right skate (R), is moving forward (F), and is resting on the inside edge (I). The foot the skater is using is known as the skating, or employed, foot, the other as the free, or unemployed, foot. An imaginary line down the center of the body divides the body into "skating" and "free" categories. Thus, if the skater employs the right foot, the right arm is the skating arm and the left is the free arm.

The rank beginner, of course, doesn't skate on the edges of the blades. Happy enough to be standing and not sprawled on the ice, he makes tentative, short steps, skating with the blade flat. Such a skater will have difficulty turning because turns are best made on the edges of the skates.

Looking pretty on ice skates takes strength and stamina, acquired during many years of practice. Peggy Fleming, like all champion skaters, began her training when she was a child.

COMPETITION

Individual figure skating competition consists of three parts: the compulsory figures—geometric designs traced on the ice—a short free skating program in which each competitor links seven movements—jumps, spins, and step sequence—and a long free skating section. Over the years the compulsory figures have become less important. Once the major part of the competition, they now account for only 30 percent of the score. If some skaters had their way, they would be eliminated entirely. These critics consider the compulsory figures an arid exercise of technique that must be mastered only because it helps them to perform better in freestyle. Proponents of the compulsory figures claim that the

compulsories provide a uniform basis of comparison in competition.

For the compulsory figures section, competitors must perform several figures drawn by lot from the standard figures. The figures—all based on the figure "8"—must be traced in the ice three times for three-lobed figures, six times for two-lobed figures. The judges then scrutinize these tracings for symmetry. Although the tracings should be as close together as possible, a skater is well advised to correct a mistake from the first tracing the next time around. Besides examining the exactness of the tracings, judges weigh factors such as graceful body carriage and smoothness of execution.

Free skating is always the most popular part of any competition, for it is the ultimate test of a skater's skill. Skating to music, competitors perform programs they have devised, replete with leaps, spins, pirouettes, and dance steps, skated over the entire ice surface. The more original and difficult the program, the better, yet all movements must blend well with the music. Good choreography is very important to the competitor's score.

Judging is often controversial because the judges' opinions vary widely, but the large number of judges used helps to even the scoring. Ideally, judges should be knowledgeable enough to recognize a difficult movement even when it is performed so well that it looks easy.

Pair skating is skating performed by men and women in couples. Skating to music, the pair must synchronize their movements. The man is usually taller than the woman and strong enough to lift his partner as their routine demands.

ORGANIZATIONS

The world governing body for amateur figure skating is the International Skating Union. In the United

States the governing body for amateur figure skating is the United States Figure Skating Association (USFSA), founded in 1921. The USFSA provides opportunities for skaters to take proficiency tests (there are nine levels), which form the basis for entry into qualifying competition on the regional, sectional, and national levels.

Speed Skating

Speed skating is simply racing on ice—competitors even refer to what they do as "running." Speed skates have a long blade, extending well past the toe and heel of the boot, so that racers can make longer, stronger glides. The blades are flat on the bottom and extremely thin. The boots must be especially light and comfortable for maximum

Opposite: *Speed skating is nothing but a race on ice. The United States has consistently produced champion speed skaters, such as Sheila Young.* Below: *In pair figure skating, the contestants are judged on how well they work together, among other things. The judging in figure skating is imprecise and controversial.*

speed. Speed skaters flash over the ice at thirty miles per hour in short sprints. A track runner, aided only by his sneakers, would finish a miserable second in a race with a speed skater.

As in track, speed skating events cover a variety of distances; there are sprints, intermediate-distance, and long-distance races. Strength is most important, especially in the longer races, held on oval, banked tracks. The skater bends from the waist on the straightaway and, hands behind his back, skates as straight a line as possible to save time. On turns a good, consistent cross-over leg motion is important. Shorter races are held on the track's straightaway.

American speed skating events are man-to-man or woman-to-woman. The first racer to cross the finish line wins. In international competition, races are run against the clock, in heats. Two racers, who must stay in assigned lanes, compete in each heat. After all the races are run, the skater with the fastest time wins.

All national and international speed skating championships in North America are sanctioned by the Amateur Skating Union of the United States and the United States International Skating Association.

Jai Alai

Ninety percent of the world's jai alai players come from the region where the game probably originated—the Basque country, a small region along the Pyrenees mountains in northern Spain bordering France. There, at a very young age, the players go to special schools, where they train several hours a day to learn the demanding skills of the game we call jai alai. At the age of sixteen or so, the best players go to such cities as Miami, Las Vegas, Mexico City, Manila, Milan, and Madrid to play in arenas, or *frontons*. They play their stunningly fast game for the entertainment of spectators whose main interest is betting. Americans can now attend jai alai schools in Miami. There are more than twenty American pro players.

Although the Basques have always called the game *pelota*, the Spanish word for ball, the sport also came to be known as jai alai, the Basque words for "merry festival," since important games were nearly always scheduled to take place at festivals.

Jai alai is a super-fast version of three-wall handball, but instead of gloves, players use two-foot-long, curved wicker baskets called *cestas*. Strapped to the player's arm, the *cesta* becomes a part of it. The player uses the cesta to catch the ball as it comes off the wall, and then in nearly the same movement, he flings it back to the front wall. The ball, two inches in diameter and 4½ ounces in weight, has a hard rubber core and a goatskin covering. Handmade and very expensive, balls must be able to withstand the high-speed impact against the granite front wall.

Jai alai courts vary in size, but the Miami courts are usually 176 feet long by 55 feet wide. Spectators, protected by a wire screen, sit in a gallery where the fourth wall would be and cheer on their favorites.

The game may be played with one, two, or three players per team. The server hurls the ball against the *frontis*, or front wall. His opponent, catching the ball on the fly or after one bounce, must return the ball to the front wall again. A point is scored by the winner of each volley.

The bettors favor the quiniela, a betting form that started with jai alai. Teams or individuals are given a tote number, and the first to score a designated number of points pays off. Past performance records for each player are available to help the bettors decide how to wager.

The jai alai professional possesses amazing stamina, courage, and agility. The ball may travel as fast as 150 miles per hour and the rallies sometimes last for two or three minutes. Most men can't continue the game after they reach thirty-five years of age. Their reflexes just aren't fast enough, and the cost of a sluggish reaction can be more than the game. Players hit in the head by a speeding ball have been fatally injured. Yet many of these proud men have scorned the safeguard of helmets. One player, insulted by the mere suggestion, said, "Would a bullfighter enter the ring in a tank?" However, helmets are now mandatory for all jai alai players in the United States and for front court players in Spain.

JAI ALAI FRONTON

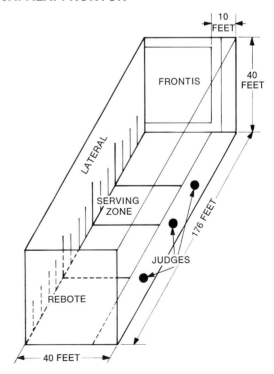

Top: *In jai alai two players slam a hard ball around a three-walled court.* Opposite: *The essence of judo is to move with an opposing force rather than try to resist it.*

Judo

Judo is that rarity among sports—the creation of one man. Based on *jujitsu,* the martial art of the medieval samurai warriors, judo was invented by Professor Jigaro Kano. Kano, frail as a youth, studied many different methods of *jujitsu,* a sport that was often vicious. He improved some of the movements and became so successful with his new methods that he was able to defeat the most accomplished *jujitsu* students. Judo was officially established in 1882, when Kano opened his own school, called the Kodokan, in Tokyo.

The essence of judo, which means "gentle way," is often said to be, "Pull when pushed; push when pulled." Kano believed that in physical combat, as well as in life, one should not resist an opposing force but rather move with it, maintain equilibrium, control it, and redirect it. In its physical aspect judo is a way of using the momentum of one's attacker against him by breaking his balance while retaining one's own. It is self-defense with a vengeance and, as such, popular among smaller people.

COMPETITION

In formal competition, judo is a violent sport, and to prepare for it, contestants undergo rigorous training, an important part of which is learning to fall properly. To win in competition, one must throw one's opponent or hold him immobile on his back for thirty seconds. A fighter may cause his adversary to submit by choking or by exerting pressure on sensitive joints. The loser may acknowledge defeat with two quick slaps, either on the mat or on the victor's body. Or he passes out.

Not all fights are won on the mat. A contestant can win one point, or *ippon,* and the match by throwing his opponent cleanly on his back—with proper technique, of course. A successful but sloppy throw gains only part of a point. If the time limit (usually no more than 15 minutes) for the match expires before either opponent has scored a point, the judges award the match to the contestant who has scored the most or, if neither has scored, to the fighter they judge to be superior.

Contests are held among students, or *judokas,* of the same level. Practitioners advance from one level to the next by passing examinations. Colored belts show the students' degree of skill, ranging from beginner's white to expert's black. Black-belt wearers are rated in 10 categories of excellence.

Judo is now an Olympic sport, dominated by the Japanese. Competitions are held in several weight categories and in one open category. The theory once was that weight categories weren't necessary since a smaller man can, after all, throw a larger one—a theory that was disproved in 1961 when Anton Goesink, a huge Dutchman, beat all the Japanese entered in the world championship fights.

ORGANIZATIONS

In 1954, the Judo Black Belt Federation of the United States was organized. It is now known as the United States Judo Federation. The world technical center for judo remains Kano's original Kodokan of Tokyo, sometimes called the Judo Institute. Member nations also affiliate with the International Judo Federation (IJF) for most competitive and technical aspects of the sport.

Karate

Although in Japanese *karate* means "empty hand," no adept practitioner of the art is truly empty handed. Developed in seventeenth-century Okinawa by rebellious peasants forbidden the use of all weapons, karate is one of the most deadly forms of unarmed combat. The true *karateka* uses his skill only when he must, for his scientifically placed punches and blows can kill.

Science is an important part of karate, as of all the Asian martial arts. Blows are struck with the closed fist, the edge of the hand, the fingertips, and the elbow. Kicks are made with the ball of the foot or its outside edge. The usual targets are the most vulnerable parts of the body—eyes, temples, nose, throat, groin, or knees.

Karate involves more than just the body, though. Americans, like most Westerners, are impressed by the flashier, physical aspects of the sport—the breaking of stacks of bricks or boards, for instance. But the spiritual part of karate is just as important. Breaking a board with the side of one's hand is an act of will as well as of strength; only someone who believes he can do it actually can.

There are two basic areas of training: *kata* and *kumite*. The *kata,* or forms, may be performed alone or in a group and involve a series of moves, including turns, leaps, blows, and kicks. *Kumite,* or sparring, consists of practicing these moves with a partner, either real or (as in shadow boxing) imagined. Because beginners often can't control their punches, some karate masters won't allow their students to spar with real partners until they've studied the sport for a while and become competent.

Competition usually includes events in both *kata* and *kumite.*

In the United States, *kumite* is divided into two types, contact and non-contact. The non-contact is the most common type of sparring competition. Blows have to be softened, or "pulled," at the last instant. Even so, slight miscalculations can result in broken ribs. Participants must have faith in the ability of their opponents to control their kicks and blows. Young and old, beginning and advanced students may engage in this type of competition in relative safety. The audience appeal is somewhat limited, however.

Experts—almost always black belts—judge the matches. In *kumite* a blow that would have been

lethal or disabling (had it not been pulled) scores one point and wins the match, a less serious blow one-half point.

Contact karate is emerging as a competition form for the *karateka* of great physical capacity and experience. Actual full-power blows are struck and the match is scored similarly to boxing. The audience appeal is very high and it appears that if karate develops into a professional sport, full contact will be the match format.

Practitioners wear a *gi,* a loose-fitting, two-piece garment similar to a judo costume but lighter. As in judo, the colored belt around the fighter's waist indicates his degree of accomplishment, beginning with white, followed by yellow, green, brown, and black. The contact fighters wear pads on their feet and hands.

There are several karate schools, each with its own style and emphasis. *Shotokan,* founded by the recognized father of karate, Funakoshi Gichin, is the original style formulated in Okinawa. It balances speed with power. The *shito-ryu* form, founded by Kenwa Mabuni, emphasizes speed and mobility. The *kyoku-shinkai,* founded by Korean Mas Oyama in 1923, is based primarily on strength. Two other styles are *goju-ryu,* derived from the Japanese words *goken* (strong fist) and *juken* (soft fist), and *wado-ryu,* a style similar to *shotokan* but incorporating various throws.

Most of these subtle variations of Korean and Okinawan karate are blended together in the thousands of karate schools that have blossomed over the last ten years in this country. Beginning students are taught the basic kick, thrust, and block moves with little mention of the spiritual and meditative aspects of the sport until they are well into their training. The original concept of the Oriental martial arts was as a method of combat. Over many generations these martial arts evolved through contact with Zen Buddhism and other religious and philosophical systems into a vehicle for developing the overall human capacity, physically, emotionally, and morally. Today's interest in violence, both in everyday life and in the movies and television, has made the sport again synonymous with pure aggression in the eyes of the general public.

Many schools also teach kung fu with karate. Begun in Canton, China, kung fu was a term to describe many different methods of Chinese fighting, but the recent wave of karate exploitation films and television shows has blurred the distinctions between kung fu and karate. Kung fu is considered a deadlier weapon than karate and more difficult to learn. Grips with names such as the *praying mantis*

and the *tiger claw* are used in the attack, which is less direct than the basic karate attack of straight-ahead punches and thrusts.

The basic rules for karate competition are set forth by the World Union of Karatedo Organizations (WUKO), which was established in Japan in 1970. Seventy nations presently belong to the Union, and world championships are held every other year. In this country the AAU United States Karate Championships are held each year, as well as the annual grand national championships staged by the United States Karate Association. Competitions are held in both belt and weight categories for men and women and in age categories for boys and girls. If the popularity boom for karate continues, it may soon join judo as an Olympic sport.

Karate trains a person in both the mental and physical aspects of combat. Opposite: *It permits a woman to be as deadly an assailant as a man.* Right: *It makes it possible to resist blows to some of the most vulnerable parts of the body.*

Lacrosse

A fast, fluid game resembling hockey, lacrosse is, along with basketball, the only sport North America can claim as all its own. Originally an Indian game called *baggataway*, it was dubbed *la crosse* by a French cleric who thought the hook-shaped stick the Indians used resembled the crozier carried by Catholic bishops.

HISTORY

Modern lacrosse is a rough sport involving lots of blocking, shoving, and other body contact, but compared to the old Indian game, it is positively gentlemanly. *Baggataway* was a war game—the Indians even called it the "little brother of war"— played by young braves to toughen themselves for combat. Any number could play, and often entire tribes would play each other, with as many as a thousand men taking part. The object of the game was similar to its object today—to carry a ball held in a web at the end of a stick across a goal line. But the strategy was a bit different. With so many players on each side, the opposition literally had to be attacked. Each team did its best to eliminate as many of the other side as it could, often using the sticks to deliver crippling blows. As the day wore on and numbers became more manageable, the warriors would stress the game's finer points.

On one occasion a game of *baggataway* set the stage for a real massacre. In 1763, Indians who were enraged by their treatment at the hands of the British developed a game plan. They decided to celebrate the birthday of King George III with an exhibition of *baggataway* just outside the gates of the British Fort Mackinac. The British were so entranced by the game that they opened the gates of the fort to see better. At that point the Indians dropped their sticks, and grabbing tomahawks concealed by their squaws, they massacred the soldiers.

The whites continued to find the game attractive, though, and often fielded teams against the Indians (at first permitting themselves more players, as a precaution as well as a handicap, perhaps). The free form of the wild Indian game was not to their taste, however, and in 1867, the Montreal Lacrosse Club drew up rules. A net was placed at the center of the goal line, the field was given definite boundaries, and the number of players was restricted.

THE FIELD AND EQUIPMENT

A lacrosse field is 110 yards by 70 yards. The triangular goals are 80 yards apart, with 15 yards of playing territory behind each of them. In the United States each team has 10 men: three defensemen, three midfielders (who both attack and defend), three attack men (who play closest to the opposition's goal), and the goalie. The 18-foot-diameter crease surrounding the goal is the sole territory of the goalie.

When the Indians played, they usually wore no more than a breech cloth. Modern players, not such stoics, are well protected with helmets, facemasks, shoulder pads, padded gloves, and cleated shoes.

The hard rubber ball is about the same size as a tennis ball (between 7¾ and 8 inches around) and weighs between 5 and 5¼ ounces. It is a solid object, heavy enough to inflict bruises on a hapless goalie or any other player who blocks a hard shot.

The stick, or crosse, is between three and six feet long, depending on the position of the player using it. Attack men, who have to make short, quick shots on goal, need shorter sticks. Defensemen use longer sticks to intercept the ball more easily. The face of the stick, used for catching, throwing, and carrying the ball, is a rounded triangle with a netting of gut, leather, nylon, or clock cord. Faces vary from 7 to 12 inches across; only goalies may use sticks with 12-inch faces. The pocket cannot be too deep or have any attachments designed to hold the ball better. A contestant particularly adept at carrying the ball sometimes arouses suspicion and is taken aside for a stick check.

THE GAME

The game is 60 minutes long and is divided into 15-minute quarters. At the start of each period and after each goal, play begins with a "face." Two players place their crosses on the ground, parallel to each other and about an inch apart. The referee balances the ball on top of the two crosses, and as soon as he blows his whistle, the two players scramble for possession.

The object of the game is to score goals, each worth one point. Each team keeps four men on its side of the field at all times, three men in the attacking zone, and the others roaming freely. The ball is advanced by quick passes from stick to stick but may be batted with the stick or kicked. Body checking, similar to checking in ice hockey, is allowed on anyone within five yards of the ball, as are checks with the stick.

It is a brutal game. Lacrosse is a favorite of college and high school football players, who play it during their off-season. There's plenty of need for brains and agility. Teams usually employ man-to-man defenses, so quickness and deception are necessary. And it is axiomatic that the team speedy enough to recover the most ground balls (a statistic recorded for each game) will win. Stamina is another important quality. Jim Brown, the famous

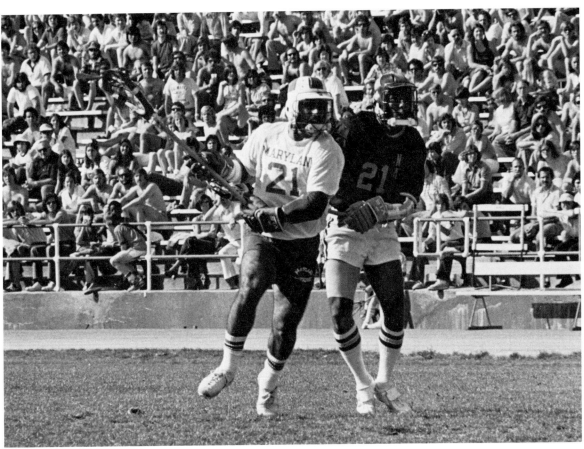

Above: *Lacrosse is a rugged game, for which the players wear gloves like those of hockey players and helmets even more protective than those for football players.* Top: *Scores are made by flinging the ball past the goalkeeper and into the net.*

college and pro football running back, played lacrosse midfielder in high school and college and found that lacrosse demanded more endurance than football.

Playmaking—the use of preplanned strategy—is possible in lacrosse, but it is more difficult than in basketball, for instance, because the players are farther apart and the play much less patterned.

The best way for the attacking team to score is by means of a "feed" play. A player, usually in back of the goal, passes to a player in front who shoots before the goalie can position himself properly. To foil the feed play, the goalie yells "Check!" whenever he thinks he sees the play in progress, and the defensemen all strike the sticks of the men they are covering.

As in ice hockey, a penalty box confines players penalized for such personal fouls as illegal checks, slashing, and unnecessary roughness. Technical fouls such as pushing, illegal blocking, and touching the ball with the hands result in 30 seconds in the box if committed by a defensive player, or loss of possession if committed by an offensive man. The referee, assisted by a judge, detects these fouls and sentences the offenders.

COMPETITION

Today, lacrosse's popularity is very much on the rise. In the United States the game is played mostly in prep schools, high schools, and colleges in the East (including the Ivy League schools). The National Collegiate Athletic Association conducts a championship tournament each year, as does the United States Intercollegiate Lacrosse Association. There is also an annual North-South Classic, featuring the top collegiate players in the nation. There are some who say that lacrosse will eventually replace baseball as America's spring sport, at least in the schools.

WOMEN'S LACROSSE

In 1876, Queen Victoria witnessed a game between some Iroquois and Canadians and wrote in her diary that it had been "pretty to watch." Thereafter, the English developed a noncontact version of the game for women. Women's lacrosse, like field hockey, allows no blocking and except for the goalkeeper is played without padding. The game is shorter, played in two 25-minute halves separated by a 10-minute break.

LACROSSE FIELD

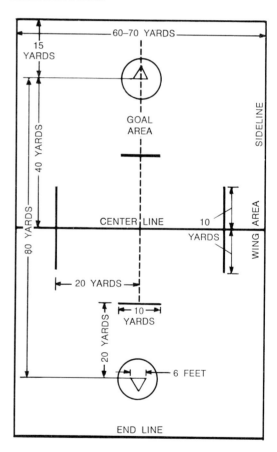

An indoor form of lacrosse, professional "box" lacrosse, which was even rougher than the outdoor, amateur version of the game, was begun in the early seventies.

Motorboat Racing

Racing a motorboat can be expensive, and prize money, when there is any, is modest, but there is no lack of speed demons eager to zoom over the lake and sea courses in competition.

Not surprisingly, the motorboat is said to have originated in France, the cradle of automobile racing. The auto engine was adapted to fit small boats, which were then raced. One of the first races was for the British International Trophy, offered by Sir Alfred Hainsworth in 1903. The winning boat hit a speed of about nineteen miles per hour. Today, boats built specifically for setting speed records travel close to three hundred miles per hour.

COMPETITION

Motorboats race in a variety of classes. For inboard and outboard craft, the fastest types are the hydroplanes—boats that entrap air under the bottom to skim over the water instead of pushing through it as conventional boats do. The hydroplane in motion touches the water at three points: two running surfaces, or sponsons, and the propeller.

The oldest and probably the most important race in the United States is the Challenge Cup, usually referred to as the Gold Cup, sponsored by the American Power Boat Association. The first Gold Cup was held in 1904 and was won by a 59-foot craft, the Standard, which averaged 23.6 miles per hour. Modern Gold Cup races are run by unlimited hydroplanes. There are minimum requirements for a boat's length and weight, but no maximum length, weight, or engine size. In recent years top competitors have averaged more than 107 miles per hour for the sixty-mile Gold Cup race.

A hardy breed of drivers competes in offshore racing on the open sea, a form that makes strenuous demands on boats and drivers. It is a participant sport by its very nature, for there are few vantage points for spectators. Accompanied by a mechanic and a navigator, the offshore driver rides standing up, his knees absorbing the jolts of riding at high speed over ocean waves. One of the top offshore events is the Miami-Nassau Race from Florida to the Bahamas. It is so tough a race that just finishing is an accomplishment.

A fairly new development in the sport is motorboat drag racing. The boats accelerate from a standing start and their speed is electronically measured over the last 132 feet of the one-quarter-mile-long course. The top drag boats exceed two hundred miles per hour, reaching that speed from standstill in a few seconds. Boats race in classes determined by their engine size. There are about fourteen such classes ranging up to the X, or unlimited, class.

ORGANIZATIONS

Most motorboat racing in this country is controlled by the American Power Boat Association (APBA), formed in 1903. The National Outboard Association, founded in 1952, controls some aspects of outboard motor racing. (An outboard craft is one with its motor attached outside the stern, whereas an inboard has its own engine within the hull.) The world governing body of the sport is the Union of International Motorboating (UIM), founded in 1922. The UIM regulates international racing and sanctions all world records.

The fastest motorboat races are those for hydroplanes, because these boats skim over the water instead of through it. They leave an impressive spume of water in their wake.

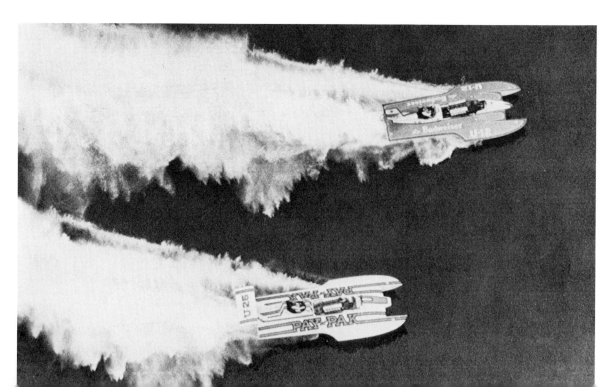

Motorcycling

There are few things more thrilling than flying along a highway on a motorcycle. The rider experiences a sense of speed and freedom no automobile ride can give. However, the casualty rate of motorcyclists is grim. On the basis of miles traveled, the chances of a fatal crash are twenty times greater for a motorcyclist than for an automobile driver. Motorcycle organizations point out that most automobile-motorcycle accidents are the fault of the car driver, not the motorcyclist. Those that the motorcyclists cause can be laid to operator inexperience rather than to any unavoidable danger in motorcycling. In any case, Americans are riding motorcycles more than ever before. It has been estimated that there are ten million motorcyclists in this country.

With the increase in motorcyclists of all kinds comes an increase in competition. The variety and number of events is dizzying: road racing, flat track racing, motocross, trials, enduros, observed trials, and indoor short track racing are but the most important. The American Motorcycle Association (AMA) sanctions more than six thousand events each year in the United States.

Besides raw courage a cyclist must have athletic ability and stamina, for he needs his entire body to control the machine. The top professionals have more diversified skills than their auto-racing counterparts, in part because the national championships consist of several types of events, all requiring different bikes and riding skills.

COMPETITION

Motorcycle road racing, like automobile road racing, is European in origin and essence. The most prestigious and oldest TT (tourist trophy) race in Europe is the sensational Isle of Man race. In the seven-lap race, each 37¾-mile lap has 219 bends, plus hills and jumps. Although the contestants

Above: *Riding a motorcycle, not to mention racing one, can be an exhilarating experience. It feels, and, from a certain angle, even looks like flying.* Opposite top: *Road racing uses the most powerful bikes.* Opposite bottom: *Motocross pits the cyclists against each other over natural but rugged terrain*

know the course, 99 have died on it since 1907.

More in the American grain is flat track racing. In 1974, 50 percent of the AMA's Grand National Trail races were flat track races, run at speedways on mile, half-mile, and quarter-mile oval tracks. The machines are designed for these tracks and lack such "frills" of road racing bikes as fairings (covering that makes the machine look sleek), fenders, and shock absorbers. The secret of winning is to take the turns fastest and remain upright. For example, to turn left, the racer must stick his left "hot shoe" into the dirt while his machine slides hard to the right. The spectators enjoy such action enormously, much like stock car racing fans.

Motocross is perhaps the fastest growing branch of the sport and some say one of the most strenuous sports in the world. It takes place on a course of basically natural terrain, studded with steep hills, sharp turns, dips, jumps, and water hazards.

The cross-country endurance races, called "trials," are events for daredevils verging on masochists. The contestants must maintain a speed of between 23 and 26 miles per hour as they race their bikes for two to six days over trails, through woods, across streams, over sand, and up and down hills. Special tests are incorporated in the race to test each rider's ability to go fast as well as to maintain a speed average. However, speed is relatively unimportant; finishing is what matters. And finishing 150 miles over brutal terrain is not easy.

In the United States, road races are at least 75 miles long and most are held on special paved courses. The most important road race is the Daytona 200, whose 3.8-mile track is the fastest in the world. Its banked corners allow drivers to roar around at top speed of 175 miles per hour and more. Most contestants don't.

Enduros are similar to trials but without the special tests. A portion of the course is often public roads. In this event the better riders not only finish, but manage to maintain speed averages only seconds away from their targeted averages.

Observed trials are the slowest competition. Contestants have to maneuver over rough terrain without putting a foot down for balance. It seems impossible, but a good cyclist's balance is so exquisite that he can often climb all over his bike without having to steady himself by touching the ground.

Indoor short track racing, done with relatively small bikes, has flourished recently in such arenas as the Houston Astrodome, where the 1976 AMA Camel Pro Series event attracted a two-night crowd of seventy-five thousand people.

In the United States, drag races, or speed trials (Europeans call them sprints), are held at the Bonneville Salt Flats in Utah and at other drag racing facilities around the country. In recent years speeds of about two hundred miles per hour have been reached. Contestants race in different classes. For a moderate entry fee, an amateur can buy a chance to break a record.

At least two million minibikes have been sold since 1967. Boys and girls aged four to twelve compete on them in AMA-sanctioned events. Although relatively safe, the sport has been criticized for the often fierce, tense competition it produces. Critics call it a Little League on wheels, in which parents are often more interested in their children winning than the children themselves. About two thousand minibike tracks attest to the popularity of this form of motorcycling, which may be breeding tomorrow's champions.

151

Polo

These days there is hardly a sport that doesn't like to call itself "most popular," or "fastest growing," or at the very least "the sport of the future." In such a boastful world, the game of polo is a refreshing exception. No one claims that it is a sport of the many; it is a sport of the few who can afford to contribute to the training and upkeep of a string of polo ponies.

Yet from its cradle in the eastern United States, polo has spread to all parts of the country and embraces players from all walks of life. When Texas cowboy Cecil Smith arrived in big-time polo, Will Rogers went so far as to say that polo had "moved from the drawing room to the bunkhouse."

HISTORY

Some historians have suggested that polo was played as far back as 2000 B.C., in Persia, but others charge that at that time the horse had not yet evolved into an animal strong enough to carry a man. Whatever its origin, the modern sport was one of those games (badminton was another) imported from India by British army officers. The Indians called their game *pulu,* meaning "willow root," because the ball was made of willow. The British cavalry officers mispronounced the name but nevertheless enthusiastically adopted the game.

By 1876, polo was fairly well established in England. James Gordon Bennett, a millionaire American newspaper publisher, saw the game there, liked it, and brought home with him mallets and balls. (He got the ponies from Texas.) America's aristocrats favored the new game and were soon pursuing their pleasure at such bastions of privilege as New York's Polo Grounds (later moved uptown for the more common sport of baseball), Long Island's Meadow Brook Country Club, and the Westchester Polo Club.

In 1886, the Americans decided to test their prowess at the sport against the British champions. The British accepted the Americans' challenge, soundly defeated the challengers on the challengers' turf, and returned to England with the first International Polo Challenge Cup. In later years the Americans more than avenged their defeat. In 1909, they surprised their former tutors at the sport by completely changing its style into a fast, long-hitting, wide-ranging game. While the Americans raced about (and even rose from their seats to whack the ball), the British made a futile attempt to preserve decorum by playing their traditional short-hitting game.

FIELD AND EQUIPMENT

Outdoor polo is played on a level, grassy field 300 by 200 yards. Sometimes an 11-inch-high board runs the length of the field on either side, in which case the field is narrowed to 160 yards. There is a goal at each end of the field, consisting of two posts 24 feet apart. The posts are made of a light, flexible material so as to prevent injury to a horse or rider that crashes into them.

Mallets, made of a bamboo head and a bamboo-cane shaft, vary in length depending on the player's size, his horse's size, and the style of play. Players who sit fairly erect when they shoot need longer mallets. Most mallets are between 48 and 53 inches. They vary as well in "whippiness," or flexibility. Near the top of each shaft is a webbed loop, which the player wraps around his wrist to ensure that he won't lose the mallet in a skirmish.

THE GAME

A game lasts for six 7½-minute periods, or chukkers. After each chukker, players have four minutes to change horses. In a hard, fast game, like those played on the international level, a pony will be exhausted after one chukker. (One of the ponies of the great American player, Tommy Hitchcock, died of a ruptured heart during a match.)

The game begins when the umpire bowls the ball between the two 4-man teams lined up at the center of the field. The object is simply to score goals, each worth one point, by driving the ball between the goalposts. A player is allowed to hook from behind the stick of someone who is swinging for the ball, but he may never reach with his stick in a way that might trip the horse. Blocking is allowed if the horse, not the rider, does it. Such a maneuver, called "riding off," usually results in a collision and may not be used against an opposing player who is following the line of the ball. Fouls are penalized by free shots.

In general the four men on a team have certain duties. The number-one man plays nearest the goal and attacks. The number-two man, often the strongest and "best-mounted" player, assists him. The number-three man (usually the best player on the team) or pivot, feeds the ball to the attackers from the number-four man, who defends the goal.

THE PONIES

Strictly speaking, the polo pony is not a pony but a horse. Before 1916, the rules permitted only ponies no more than 14.2 "hands" high (a hand is four inches) and about 600 to 650 pounds. Today's "ponies" are thoroughbred horses weighing about

Polo is much rougher on the horse than on the rider. Without a good mount, all a player's skill is useless. Nevertheless, it takes a great deal of skill to be able to control a ball with a mallet while galloping about at full tilt.

1,100 pounds. A good pony is about 60 percent of the game, for without a fast, intelligent, quick-turning mount, all a player's skill is useless.

It may take a few years to train a horse for polo. A horse must first become used to mallets swinging around him. Then he must be trained in riding off without fear, without hesitation, and often. And he must be just as adroit at stopping instantly to avoid a collision. Such a horse is a prized possession of a polo enthusiast.

HANDICAPS

Because some polo players are better than others, there is a handicap system to even the play. Each player is rated on a scale of −1 to 10 goals. The better players merit the higher ratings, or handicaps. In a game played under this handicap system, the handicaps of each team are totaled and the difference between the totals is the starting score for the lower-ranked team.

In this country, the United States Polo Association assigns handicaps. It lists the handicaps of about thirteen hundred players, about fifty percent of whom are listed at 0. No more than three or four percent are at 5 or more.

POLO FIELD

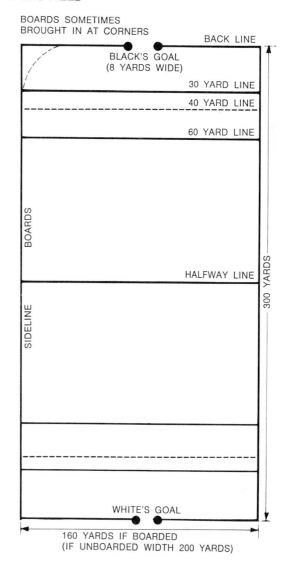

BOARDS SOMETIMES
BROUGHT IN AT CORNERS

BACK LINE

BLACK'S GOAL
(8 YARDS WIDE)

30 YARD LINE

40 YARD LINE

60 YARD LINE

BOARDS

HALFWAY LINE

300 YARDS

SIDELINE

WHITE'S GOAL

160 YARDS IF BOARDED
(IF UNBOARDED WIDTH 200 YARDS)

Rodeo

The sport of modern rodeo is far removed from the cowboy roundups of the Old West. Professional cowboys, many of whom learned their skills at special schools and perfected them in competition, resemble professional athletes everywhere. But the romantic cowboy mythology dies hard in America, and much of it remains in rodeo. Whether because of the nostalgia it presents or the more tangible thrill of men risking their necks, rodeo draws more spectators each year.

The first tests of riding and roping skills were informal contests among heavy-betting cowhands. Not until the late nineteenth century, after the cattle drive had given way to the cattle train and the old breed of cowboy had died off, did the forerunner of today's rodeo appear. Towns in the West and Southwest, realizing the tourist potential of such events, began to compete with each other in staging rodeos.

Every year about three thousand rodeos take place in the United States. About six hundred of these qualify as professional events and attract members of the Professional Rodeo Cowboys Association (PRCA), formed in 1936 to provide rules and safeguards for the sport. Most of the prize money for rodeo comes from the cowboys' pockets, from entrance fees. Although some top professionals, such as Larry Mahan and Tom Ferguson, have earned more than $60,000 annually in prize money, rodeo hardly pays the X-ray bills of many of its participants. And the competition gets tougher every year.

A few of the major PRCA-sanctioned rodeos are the Pendleton Roundup, in Pendleton, Oregon; the Frontier Days, in Cheyenne, Wyoming; and the Calgary Stampede, in Calgary, Alberta, Canada. The National Finals are held each year in Oklahoma City, Oklahoma.

COMPETITION

A rodeo may consist of several novelty and comedy events, but the five standard events are saddle bronc riding, bareback bronc riding, calf roping, steer wrestling, and bull riding. In most rodeos contestants are allowed two or more attempts in each event. The winner is the contestant with the highest score or the lowest time.

SADDLE BRONC RIDING

In this event the cowboy mounts a horse in the chute and waits for the gate to open. When it does, the horse bolts from the chute and the cowboy rakes his mount with the spurs on his boots. He tries to maintain a smooth spurring motion from the horse's neck to the cantle of the saddle. The harder the horse bucks, the better the cowboy's chances of performing well and impressing the judges. He must stay on until the buzzer sounds, a long eight seconds after the horse leaves the chute. The cowboy rides with one hand in the air, the other holding the rein. If he "pulls leather," that is, touches the saddle with the free hand, or wraps the rein around his hand, he is disqualified.

BAREBACK BRONC RIDING

This is the most physically demanding event in rodeo. The rider must stay on his horse for eight seconds, during which time he is tossed and jerked about like a rag doll. A man's body must be supple for this punishment.

Again, the cowboy rakes the horse with his spurs, but this time he tries to lean back and spur over the horse's shoulders. At the finish of the ride, two mounted pick-up men help the cowboy off the horse, if he hasn't already flown off.

STEER WRESTLING

Bill Pickett was a cowboy who used to delight onlookers by jumping off his horse onto a running steer, grabbing the animal's horns, twisting its head, and then seizing its upper lip in his own teeth—hence the nickname for steer wrestling, "bulldogging." The modern event is similar but without the biting. Contestants race against a clock to force an animal to the ground so that all four legs extend in the same direction. A good dogger, provided with a smart horse, can accomplish the feat in less than five seconds.

CALF ROPING

In this event the cowboy rides after a calf, ropes it, fastens the rope to the saddle of his horse, dismounts, throws the calf, and ties three of its legs together. His horse must be well trained, stopping as soon as the rider jumps off and backing up to keep the rope, or lariat, taut. The instant the cowboy finishes, he throws both hands in the air and a judge makes sure the tie is secure. A good rider takes 10 seconds or less to subdue the calf.

BULL RIDING

This is the last event in most rodeos, a real crowd pleaser, and quite dangerous. The cowboy must hold on with one hand as he rides the bull for eight seconds. When he jumps—or flies—off, he must quickly get away from the snorting animal, for a bucking Brahma bull, unlike a horse, will try to trample a man. Rodeo clowns (many of them former professional cowboys themselves) distract the bulls and often save lives.

In addition to his skill, the cowboy depends on the specially bred rodeo animals. He studies them much as a batter in baseball may study the pitchers he will face throughout the season. In the riding events cowboys are paired with animals by blind draw, so many pros keep notes and trade information on the characteristics of the animals. Even with this aid, rodeo professionals must be daring men.

Rodeo matches man against beast. In steer wrestling the cowboy tackles the steer from his horse and pins it to the ground on its back, all in only a few seconds.

Roller Skating

HISTORY

Roller skating, the story has it, was first thought of by a frustrated Dutchman who loved ice skating so much that he wanted to skate the year round. So he attached large wooden spools to his ice skates. But this "land skate" did not work well.

Records show that the first man to apply for a patent for a roller skate was Joseph Merlin, an inventor and violinist. He exhibited his invention at a fashionable party in England, skating among the dancers while playing his violin. His skates could not turn, though, and Merlin skated into a large, expensive mirror, hurting himself and his violin, and smashing the mirror.

In Paris in 1847, attention focused on roller skating when roller skates were used in an opera to imitate ice skating. This caused a sensation, and people came to see the opera just for the skating scene.

The man who gets credit for inventing the modern skate was an American, James Plimpton, of New York. His skate, introduced in 1863, was able to turn, but its wooden wheels cracked often, causing accidents. It wasn't until the 1880s, when the Richardson ball-bearing skate with metal casters was introduced, that the sport became truly popular. Roller skating became a fad, helped by a ballet master and ice skater named Jackson Haines, who performed graceful dance movements on skates. Today, figure roller skating is an important aspect of the sport.

EQUIPMENT

There are two types of skates. One, mounted on ball-bearing wheels, is clamped to the shoe, and a strap is tied around the ankle. The other type is a shoe skate, with wooden, fiberglass, or plastic wheels on rubber cushions. This type of skate is used by accomplished skaters and in indoor roller rinks.

COMPETITION

Roller skating competition in this country on an amateur level is supervised by the United States Amateur Confederation of Roller Skating (USAC), located in Lincoln, Nebraska. National finals are held each year, with events in speed skating, artistic skating, and roller hockey. In the speed competition, men's events are races of five miles, two miles, one mile, and 880- and 440-yard sprints. Women race two miles, one mile, and 880 and 440 yards. Competition in artistic skating consists of events in pairs, freestyle singles, dance, and figures.

Roller Derby

Roller skating became very popular in the United States in the 1930s. In 1935, Leo Seltzer, a Chicago promoter of the dance marathons and bicycle races that were popular during the depression years, read in a magazine that roller skating was the sport with the greatest number of participants in the United States. This fact was enough to get him started. At first he had no real game—only a marathon test of endurance. One day, Seltzer was sitting with Damon Runyon, the famous writer, when a fight broke out among some of the skaters. Runyon thought that this added excitement to the sport. His reaction inspired Seltzer to create the modern version of roller derby. It was born in 1938.

THE GAME

The rules for roller derby are fairly simple. The game is played in two halves. Each half has four 12-minute periods. In alternate periods men skate against men, women against women.

To begin play in a period, all ten players, five from each team, start bunched together on the track, forming what is called the pack. On each team are two blockers (white helmets), two jammers (striped helmets), and a pivot man (black helmet), who is usually the captain and star of the team. As the pack begins to move around the track, a "jam" begins. A jam is a 60-second period during which jammers try to pull out of the pack, circle the track, and catch up to the back of the pack. For each member of the opposing team they pass after circling the track, jammers score one point. The lead jammer may call off the jam by placing his hands on his hips.

Almost any kind of block is legal in roller derby, but penalties of one or two minutes are sometimes called against players, forcing their team to skate short-handed.

Today's game of roller derby, watched on television by some twenty million fans, is a blend of rough competition and entertainment. Although there may often be some suspicion that the games have been rigged, there is no doubt about the degree of skill and endurance of the competitors. Skaters can sometimes attain speeds of thirty miles per hour. Skating is usually done in a five-stride—five steps and a coast through the turn. The track is usually from 100 to 200 feet around, but may be made smaller to fit in a particular auditorium, and it is usually steeply banked. On an average night, the women on a team may skate 28 miles, the men 33 miles.

Rowing

Some of the first crew teams were composed of galley slaves. Chained to their seats, sometimes five or six men to a heavy oar, they propelled heavy Roman warships into battle, generally under the eye of a man with a whip. The modern oarsman is under no such compulsion, but he must still be amazingly strong and be able to ignore the pain of straining muscles. In top competition an oarsman pulls about a hundred pounds per stroke, thirty to forty times a minute for several minutes.

HISTORY

Although rowing has a long history—it is at least as old as the ancient Greeks and Romans—a good starting date for the modern sport is 1716, when several ferryboat oarsmen competed for the Doggett's Coat and Badge. Thomas Doggett, a comedian of the day who wanted to contribute something more lasting than his jokes, decreed that the race be run "forever after," and so far it has been.

Modern rowing is mostly an amateur, college-based sport. In England, Oxford and Cambridge universities held their first regatta in 1829. The first Harvard-Yale regatta took place in 1852 and was won by the Harvard eight. By today's standards their preparation for the competition was less than vigorous. Before the event, the men rowed together only a dozen times "for fear of blistering their hands."

Over the years rowing has experienced many minor revolutions. Innovators have consistently found more efficient ways to row and have put their theories into practice with winning crews. Steve Fairbairn introduced a technique that depended on strong leg thrust, and with this method as his basis, he coached many winning teams for Cambridge.

EQUIPMENT

Rowing has two basic varieties: sculling, in which usually one, two, or four men compete, each using two oars; and crew, in which from two to eight men per boat compete, each man rowing with both hands on one oar.

There are no specifications for the size, shape, and weight of the crafts (shells) used in crew or in sculling. They are, however, light, long, and narrow, scarcely resembling common rowboats. An important feature of these racing boats is the sliding seat, first used in 1870 in an American race. Before its invention, oarsmen sat stationary and swung their bodies to give power to their strokes, pulling back hard and finishing each stroke in almost a horizontal position. The sliding seat allowed oarsmen to slide back and forth with each stroke and thereby to gain more power from their legs.

The oars used in sweep rowing are generally about 12 feet long, and in sculling (sculls) they are usually about 10 feet long.

COMPETITION

Traditionally, the single sculler has been the rower most likely to win glory. In addition to being a master of technique, the winning single sculler must be strong and big. Most weigh approximately two hundred pounds.

In crew racing all the oarsmen must work in perfect unity. In crew, teamwork is an axiom. An oarsman whose timing is imperfect, no matter how strongly he rows, will destroy team coordination.

The most popular and prettiest event is the eight-oars race, usually run over a 2,000-meter course. A coxswain is seated facing the oarsmen in the back of the craft. He steers the boat with a rudder and, in combination with the "stroke" oarsman, sets the rhythm for the team's stroking. Physically, the coxswain must be light; mentally he must know the strength of his oarsmen so as to set a pace that will not exhaust them. If he guides his team to victory, his reward is a dousing (and sometimes a dunking) at the hands of his oarsmen.

WOMEN'S ROWING

At least one coach, Gus Constant of the Vesper Boat Club, has said that because women are more graceful than men they are better natural rowers. At one time grace was the only requirement of an oarswoman. In 1897, at the University of Washington, bloomer-clad oarswomen marched down to the water, entered their boats (that had been carried there by men), and rowed—gracefully, since they were judged only by aesthetic standards.

Today, there are more than 75 women's crews and rowing associations in the United States, and women compete in the same lung-bursting style as men. 1976 was the first time women's crew teams competed in the Olympic games.

ORGANIZATIONS

Rowing has been an Olympic event since 1900. It is governed internationally by the Federation Internationale des Societes d'Aviron. In 1962, the World Championships were founded, to be held every four years. But the most famous rowing event in the world today is the Henley Royal Regatta, an international competition held annually on the Thames River in London.

Amateur rowing in the United States is governed by the National Association of Amateur Oarsmen, formed in 1872.

Rugby

HISTORY

Like most sports, rugby began by accident. One day in 1823, William Ellis, a student at the Rugby School in England, succumbed to frustration during a soccer game, picked up the ball, and ran with it. Such "handling" was a shocking breach of the rules (for which Ellis's captain apologized), but it demonstrated a way to speed up the game. For a long time this new version of soccer was played strictly in schools, but by 1871, there were enough amateur clubs in England to permit the formation of the Rugby Football Union.

Working-class men such as miners and mill workers took to the game enthusiastically. But in order to play, they had to take time off from work, time for which they were not paid. They demanded compensation from the Rugby Union, but the officials of the league were shocked by this specter of "professionalism" and refused. So in 1895, the first semiprofessional league was formed, the Northern Rugby Union, today called the Rugby League.

Although rugby league (professional rugby) is still confined to the English midlands, rugby union (amateur rugby) is played throughout the British Isles and in Ireland, France, and Australia as well. It is also especially popular in New Zealand and South Africa, where there are no other major sports to distract the populace. Amateur rugby has been gaining favor in schools in the United States, and some Americans prefer the informality of it to the serious American business of football.

THE GAME

Rugby union is a much more continuous game than American football, its child. By passing, kicking, or running with the ball, two 15-man teams try to advance down the field and over the opposition's goal line. The teams play on a flat, grassy field, a maximum of 75 yards wide and 110 yards from goal line to goal line. On each goal line stands a set of goalposts 18½ feet apart, connected by a crossbar 10 feet above the ground.

The ball is similar to the American football but more nearly round, weighing between 13½ and 15½ ounces. Although the play is rough, the players wear no padding—just jerseys, shorts, and cleated shoes.

Each team has seven backs and eight forwards. The forwards are generally defensive men, who attempt to capture the ball from the opposition and pass it to the backs, whose duty is to score.

Games consist of two 40-minute halves broken by a 5-minute rest. There are no substitutions for injured players or players who foul out.

Play begins with a kickoff from midfield to the receiving team, which is lined up behind its 10-yard line. Any member of the team may advance the ball, but no member may be in front of the ball carrier. Passes must be lateral or backward.

Only the ball carrier may be tackled or blocked. He is permitted to use the palm of his hand to "hand off" would-be tacklers—a maneuver resembling the old football stiff arm. He is considered tackled when the ball touches the ground or when an opponent puts him into a position from which he cannot play the ball. When tackled, he must immediately let go of the ball, whereupon either team can take possession.

Play is stopped only for a score, an infraction,

RUGBY FIELD

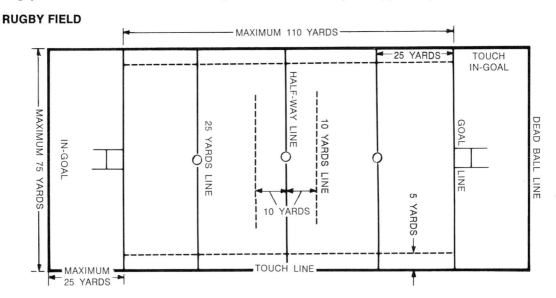

158

Opposite bottom: *If a soccer player picked up the ball and started to run with it, the reaction of the defense might be to jump on him. That's not far from the way rugby got started.* Opposite top: *A lineout, the means by which play is restarted after the ball goes out of bounds.*

or the ball going "in touch," out of bounds. When the ball goes in touch, as it frequently does, play resumes with a "lineout." The two sets of forwards line up at right angles to the touchline, or sideline, and parallel to each other. The ball is tossed between the two lines (the toss must be at least five yards) and the teams then battle for possession.

A scrummage, or scrum, occurs when the referee stops play for any infraction. The scrum consists of the two sets of forwards packing themselves together with arms interlocked. Into the tunnel formed by this bizarre formation, the referee tosses the ball, and the forwards then try to kick it out to one of their backs.

The two basic scoring plays are the try and the goal. A try is worth four points and occurs when a player advances the ball past the opposition's goal line. It can be converted to a six-point play by a placekick or a dropkick over the crossbar (similar to the point after touchdown in football). A referee will award a team four points in the rare instance when he feels that a try would have been achieved had a serious violation not been committed. This score is called a penalty try, and it too is followed by a two-point conversion.

The various types of goals are each worth three points. They include the "dropped goal," in which a player while advancing up the field drop-kicks the ball through the uprights; the "penalty goal," which is a free placekick awarded by the referee after an infraction; and the "fair catch goal" (similar to a fair catch in football), which is scored when a player signals while the ball is in the air his intention to try for a placekick. The spot where he signaled is marked, and the player is given 10 yards of free space to get the kick away.

The rules for the professional game, rugby league, are somewhat different. Only 13 men play on a side, and two substitutions per game are allowed. A team is allowed the ball for only four tackles (a rule resembling the "four downs" of American football), after which a scrum is formed. In general rugby league is a tougher game, more formal and specialized than rugby union, and closer to American football. It is still played mostly by English coal miners and mill workers.

Shooting

HISTORY

Strange as it may seem, the rifle was for a long time a less accurate weapon for killing a man or an animal or for hitting a target than the bow and arrow. Firearms put an end to archery's use in warfare not because they were more accurate but because they didn't require the years of training necessary to master the bow and arrow.

Today's precision guns make accurate shooting easier, but to become a true sharpshooter—by modern standards that means someone who almost never misses—one needs absolute, unflappable concentration and steady, consistent technique. In competition the marksman must be nerveless under pressure. He must have no thought other than to hit the target he is aiming at, forgetting all past mistakes. Developing such skill takes a lot of practice, and in shooting that means money. Guns, ammunition, and targets are expensive.

In the United States organized target shooting contests began in the 1860s. In 1871, members of the New York National Guard, disturbed by the poor marksmanship of the North's forces during the Civil War, founded the National Rifle Association (NRA).

Today, it has more than one million dues-paying members and regulates virtually all rifle and pistol competition in this country. In addition the NRA is an extremely powerful political organization that in recent years has been the most influential in defeating legislation to regulate the sale and ownership of guns.

International events are regulated by the International Shooting Union. Shooting events have been part of the Olympics since 1896.

TARGET SHOOTING

In the United States shooters usually compete in classes with other shooters of comparable skill. Contests are held using a variety of firearms, from the high-power military rifles to pistols, .22 caliber rifles, and even precision air rifles and pistols.

Competitors in high-power rifle competition usually shoot from prone, sitting, kneeling, and standing positions at distances between 200 and 1,000 yards from the target. For smallbore or .22 caliber competition, the distances are from 50 to 100 yards. Some matches are fired just from the prone position, others from all four positions—

prone, sitting, kneeling, and standing. Some small-bore matches require metallic sights; others allow telescopic sights.

In pistol shooting contests, competitors generally fire at targets set 25 and 50 yards away. Shooters normally fire a specified number of shots from 50 yards and two sets of shots from 25 yards. The first set of shots is slow fire, the second somewhat faster (5 shots in 20 seconds), and the third rapid fire (5 shots in 10 seconds).

TRAPSHOOTING AND SKEET SHOOTING

There are more than twenty million Americans who hunt with guns. Since much hunting is done with shotguns, trapshooting and skeet shooting, which also employ shotguns, are very popular shooting sports. Indeed for many, skeet shooting and trapshooting are sports in themselves. Both are shotgun competitions that use "clay pigeons."

Trapshooting started in England in the early nineteenth century. Farmers held competitions in which they released small birds from wooden traps. One English club, founded in 1832, was called the "High Hats" because it staged contests in which the shooter put a live bird under his hat, lifted the hat on a given signal, then shot at the fleeing bird. Catching birds for use in such a sport soon proved tedious, so artificial birds were designed. One of the more notable designs was a glass ball stuffed with feathers that were released in a shower when the ball shattered. In time a "clay pigeon," composed of river silt and pitch, became the ideal target.

Trapshooting today is done mostly with 12-gauge shotguns. The target is thrown by means of a trap machine in a direction away from the shooter, with only slight variation in the angle of flight. Shooters fire from five different stations. If a handicap system is used, the better shots move farther back from the trap.

Skeet shooting was invented to provide real practice for game shooting. Targets are released from two houses, a high house on the shooter's left and a low house on the right. Competitors shoot from seven different stations at clay pigeons, so a great variety of angles of flight are included.

Target shooting encompasses a variety of firearms, from high-powered rifles to pistols. Opposite: Smallbore rifle shooting. *Right:* Pistol shooting, part of the pentathlon event.

In both skeet shooting and trapshooting (or any shooting involving moving targets), marksmen must be skillful in calculating the right amount of lead. That is, depending on a variety of factors—distance from the target, angle of target to shooter, speed of the shot, and wind velocity—the marksman must shoot ahead of the target to compensate for the distance the target will travel while the shot heads toward it. The targets in both skeet shooting and trapshooting travel at about thirty miles per hour.

Skiing

The thrill of skiing defies analysis or even description, so it is perhaps not surprising that skiers talk endlessly of equipment and technique and much less about the beauty and exhilaration of skiing. Ski talk evidently brings the slopes closer, but once the skier actually reaches the slope, it is best forgotten—there is too much else to enjoy.

The wobbly-kneed beginner snowplows uneasily down the bunny slope on a pair of rented, scratched-up skis that don't seem to belong on his feet at all, but even he experiences an elation that easily equals that of the spectacular downhill racer.

Their styles are worlds removed, but skiing can satisfy the novice as fully as the expert. Plenty of people become bored or frustrated after attempts at other sports, but almost everyone who tries skiing falls in love with it. At its best it's a first-class tour of a glistening wonderland, and even a fall can be fun (provided that one is in the proper frame of mind to enjoy it—and that no bones are broken).

If it were not for the great expense, skiing might attract thirty million enthusiasts instead of the present three million. Unfortunately, clothing, equipment, lift tickets, transportation, and lodging all add up to a fearsome expenditure. Even a fanatic skier considers himself quite lucky to make 20 outings a year, and these at a substantial cost in money and dedication. Skiers follow the snow as devotedly as surfers follow the sun.

HISTORY

It has taken a long time for skiing as a sport to acquire a wide and dedicated public. In Siberia and the Scandinavian countries, archeologists have found skis that are at least 4,500 years old. Those first crude skis were used for transportation. All skiing was cross country, and skis often played an important role in war, moving soldiers across snowy terrain much faster than the soldiers could march through it. For centuries skis were a necessity in northeastern Europe.

Originally, the boots were attached to the skis tightly enough to keep them from falling off but too

SLALOM COURSE

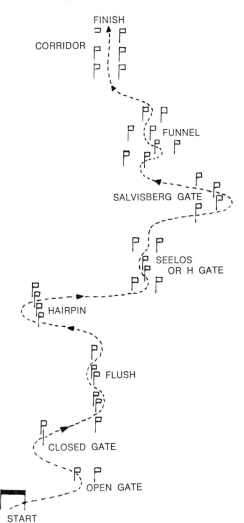

Opposite: *Downhill racers hurtle down a mountain as fast as 60 miles per hour. In the straightaways, they crouch in an "egg" position to keep wind resistance to a minimum.* Above: *Slalom racers go much slower, in order to be able to negotiate the gates on their course. Giant slalom, shown here, is a sort of compromise between downhill and slalom.*

loosely to allow the skier to turn. Skiers raced, but only on a straight course. Not until the 1850s, when Sondre Norheim of Norway devised stiff bindings that allowed skiers to make turns, was the modern sport born.

Skiing progressed gradually and unspectacularly in the decades following as skis, bindings, and boots were improved. But downhill, or alpine, skiing as well as cross-country skiing remained sport only for the hardy few. The alpine skier first had to reach a ski trail and then spend most of his time climbing it. The introduction of rope tows and ski lifts in the 1930s solved part of the problem, but it was not until the 1960s that going skiing became as easy as taking a ride to the country. Suddenly a skiing boom gripped the United States; everyone was skiing, from swinging singles to stay-together families, and developers rushed to meet the demand. They began carving up mountainsides at such a rate that conservationists worried when and where the craze would end (though many of them were skiers themselves). Today, there are more than one thousand ski areas in the United States, with some in such unlikely areas as the Midwest.

EQUIPMENT

The theories and principles behind today's complex and varied ski equipment would challenge a physicist. The wooden skis of former days have given way to metal skis and to skis of plastic-coated fiberglass with metal edges. They vary in length and width with the skier's experience and with the type of skiing to be done: downhill, slalom, giant slalom, hot-dogging, cross-country, or jumping. One of the latest theories to hit the skiing world is the Graduated Length Method for learning to ski. By this method the beginner may switch skis as often as each time he skis. He begins on short, maneuverable skis only a few feet long and advances to longer ones as he becomes better able to handle them. A few years ago it was thought that beginners needed the stability of long skis, but skiing is a sport that changes quickly, and it is littered with discarded theories and fashions.

In general most skis are from six to eight feet long and three to four inches wide. The front tips of the skis are pointed and curl upward. A slight arch, or camber, in the ski at the point where the foot rests raises that part of the ski a half inch to an inch and a quarter from the ground and helps distribute the skier's weight.

The most sophisticated boots today are rigid, high-backed, plastic models that can be fitted very precisely to the foot. Because they allow almost no room for ankle "play," they have changed the style of skiing from the time when skiers moved more freely in their boots, and with their bodies in general.

To the beginner, the binding may well be the most important item of equipment. The purposes of the binding are to attach the boot to the ski and to release the skier from the ski in the event of a fall.

Opposite: *Soaring hundreds of feet through the air on skis, a ski jumper seems to be a most daring fellow. But compared to the freestyler, or "hotdogger,"* left, *who thinks nothing of a somersault on skis, the traditional ski jumper seems stable.*

There are many types of bindings, including one kind that attaches only to the heel of the boot, leaving the toe free and the unwary skier a bit nervous. Properly adjusted, all bindings should release the skier when his foot twists or wrenches. Then a simple, thin safety strap from boot to binding keeps the ski from sliding away. Despite the advances in bindings, the many fractured legs in skiing suggest that the foolproof binding has not yet been designed.

The simplest item is the poles, made from tubular steel or aluminum. The poles help the skier to maintain balance, gain speed, turn, stop, and rise after falling. Each pole has a handgrip and a strap at the top, a point at the bottom, and, slightly above the bottom a ringlike device called a basket that keeps the pole from jabbing too deeply.

Care of the skis is a high art, best appreciated by competitive skiers. For sharp turning, the edges of the skis must be kept sharp with constant filing. Because all skis today have fast, plastic running surfaces, the recreational skier need no longer wax his skis to help them go faster. But the racer, to whom even a slight advantage is important, has his skis hot waxed as a matter of course.

At one time the purpose of ski clothing was simply to keep the skier warm and dry. But anyone who has been to a modern-day ski lodge has observed the less practical dictates of ski fashions. Recreational skiers often strive to look like racers. They wear skin-tight stretch pants with sweaters or ski parkas, and on their heads, stocking caps and tinted goggles. Too poor or too rebellious to accept this uniform, many youngsters have devised their own—jeans, short or long. And on particularly warm spring days, male skiers may be favored with the sight of a beautiful young female cruising down the slopes in a bikini.

COMPETITION

The early days of skiing competition were marked by some wondrous novelty events. In one, the bag-snatching race, competitors skied down a course, snatching paper bags hanging from ski poles. The racer who finished in the least time with the most bags was the winner.

Another form of downhill race was the roped race. Two skiers roped together (supposedly for safety, strangely enough), skied down the course together.

Today, the frills have been mostly eliminated, but there is still some novelty skiing, called "hot-dogging." The best hot-dogging is performed in formal competitions, but the more frequent, less skilled type, takes place on the spur of the moment at all ski areas. It's called showing off. Most competition today has a less romantic object—pure and simple speed.

DOWNHILL

The fastest skier is the downhill racer, who will negotiate a course at sixty miles per hour with nothing to protect him but his crash helmet, his skill, and a strong ego. Winning is a matter of only a fraction of a second, and each contestant knows he will have to ski as fast as he can, pushing himself almost beyond control. He must have as much self-confidence as skill.

Before the race, skiers are allowed a day to practice on the course, which usually drops at least 2,500 feet between start and finish. They work out a precise play beforehand for how they will run the course, but often the course conditions change within minutes and then even a well-prepared skier might find the going treacherous. Racers start one at a time and race against the clock. In most com-

166

Cross-country is the most quiet form of skiing, certainly the least dramatic. Instead of whizzing down a mountain, the cross-country skier treks through snow-covered woods and fields. It's hard work but very satisfying, and if ·you enjoy nature at its most serene, the scenery is tops.

petition the winner is the racer with the lowest total time after two runs. (Recently, professional racers have skied against each other, flashing down the slopes two at a time on side-by-side courses. Racers exchange courses after each heat.) On flat straightaways racers stay in a low crouch, the "egg" position, and carry their poles tucked well up under their arms.

SLALOM

Both slalom and giant slalom require the racer to weave between small flagpoles called gates. He may hit or even knock down the gates without penalty (though he will slow down if he does), but competitors must pass on the correct side of each gate.

An Olympic slalom race drops 617 feet and has more than 60 gates. The competitor must have excellent and precise control. Even though his speed is not great—about fifteen miles per hour—the gates are set so close together that an error in judgment or the loss of rhythm can prove disastrous.

The giant slalom was originally begun to make downhill racing safer. The course, with a drop of 1,600 feet, has from 20 to 50 gates. The skier must choose the route that will permit him to get down the hill in the least time. Because turning at each gate checks his speed, the skier must accelerate hard between gates.

The nonskier and even the recreational skier often don't realize what strenuous conditioning world-class skiers must undergo. The skier slides downhill and gravity does much of his work for him, but the source of top speed is within him—particularly the leg muscles. When well conditioned, they thrust him down the course without tiring over two minutes of intense action.

CROSS-COUNTRY

No one doubts that cross-country skiing requires stamina. Most skiers would rather endure the long weekend lift lines that plague the recreational alpine skier than take up cross-country. But the cross-country skier has rid himself of the crowds and tinsel of the ski resort. Any open snowy terrain will do for his sport.

Most cross-country skiers do it simply for the enjoyment of the trek, but there are cross-country races in the Olympics and elsewhere. The courses range from 10 to 50 kilometers, one-third uphill, one-third downhill, and one-third on more or less flat terrain. Competitors usually start one minute apart and race against the clock. The race is grueling, made only slightly easier by the special light skis. Cross-country skiers have special bindings, too, which leave the skier's heels free, allowing the skier to push better. Top skiers may average 11 miles per hour, even over a 50-kilometer course.

JUMPING

For the spectator some of the most thrilling skiing is ski jumping. It is thrilling for the jumper too. Air-borne, he often has the irrational fear that he will land in the crowd below.

Ski jumping hills are steep, man-made chutes that level off shortly before the takeoff point. The jumper, without poles, skates one step at the top of the in-run, then assumes the tucked "egg" position to whiz down the chute. Just as he reaches the takeoff point, he snaps his legs, springing over his skis as if to "kiss his ski tips." His arms are at his sides, his tips pointed up. In this position, called vorlage, he is leaning far forward to create an airfoil effect, much as the wing of an airplane does. To land, he crouches almost to the point of kneeling, arms wide, his knees and hips absorbing the shock of landing. His hands may not touch the ground as he lands.

Ski jumping is judged both for distance and for form. A panel of five judges rates the jumper's form on a 20-point system. The extreme scores are excluded, leaving a possible 60 points for a perfect jump. Points are added for the jumper's distance. Some say the best form will result in the longest jump and that judging should be eliminated.

STUNT SKIING

As skiers have become better, they have taken to performing wild movements on the slopes. The beginning skier may roll head over heels in a fall; the hot-dogger somersaults on purpose. "Hot-dog," or freestyle, skiers compete in three categories: aerials, moguls, and stunt/ballet. Aerial skiing is acrobatics performed in the air—front flips, back flips, splits, and so on. In mogul competition the skier hot-dogs down a steep hill with lots of bumps, or moguls, and is judged for the imagination and fluidity of his run. In ballet skiing elegance and technique are judged.

ORGANIZATIONS

In 1969, skiing acquired an above-board professional organization. (Until then the best skiers, like other amateur athletes, had been doing well enough financially, though as amateurs they weren't supposed to be profiting from their skills.) In 1974, pro racers of the International Ski Racers Association competed for about a half million dollars in prize money.

The Federation Internationale de Ski (FIS), world governing body of the sport, was founded in 1924. Through its efforts, skiing events were included in the first winter Olympics, held in 1924. Skiing has been an important part of every Olympics since. Of perhaps equal importance to top skiers are the amateur World Cup competition for individuals, and the Nations Cup for teams. The World Cup is the Grand Prix of skiing. It is a series of races on an international circuit, with racers accumulating points as auto racers do in their Grand Prix. The Nations Cup is based on the points won in World Cup competition by the racers of each national team.

Skydiving

HISTORY

The first illustration of a parachute was found in the notebooks of Leonardo da Vinci, who also made drawings of gliders and other flying machines. It is less certain who made the first jump with a parachute; many claimed the honor. However, the first witnessed jump was made in 1797 by a French balloonist, André Jacques Garner. He stood in a basket at the end of the pole of a large umbrella-like contraption. Because the silk canopy over his head had no vents, the parachute swung crazily from side to side, but Garner survived.

During World War I, German and Austrian pilots wore parachutes to save their lives. Few American pilots did so, but after the war, the government began efforts to develop reliable parachutes for pilots who had to bail out of their planes. The parachute had to be a free fall parachute—one that would be opened by the jumper while he was falling, not before. However, no one had ever made such a jump, and most people believed it was impossible. They thought that the air would be sucked from the jumper's lungs or that he would be unable to control his movements in midair.

A woman who didn't believe these myths, Georgia "Tiny" Broadwick, made the first free fall jump, in 1914 near San Diego, California. From a plane 2,000 feet in the air, she dove into the air, waited a few seconds, and then pulled the cord.

Since then, there have been quite a few advances in the sport, including the important development in the early sixties of canopies that allow the skydiver to steer his parachute.

SPORT JUMPING

The sport jumper usually drops from a slow-moving plane at an altitude less than 10,000 feet. He opens his parachute usually between 2,500 and 1,800 feet above the ground. Anyone doing free fall jumps must first learn how to remain stable in the air. By learning certain principles of body control, the jumper can make a number of maneuvers.

Jumpers usually carry an altimeter. This, plus a knowledge of the rate of descent, tells them when to open their parachutes. The rate of descent varies with the jumper's body position—the more spread the body, the slower the descent. Jumpers can even glide and attain speeds of up to 60 miles per hour moving horizontally, called tracking. For this reason maneuvers involving two or more jumpers, called relative work, are not easy. Professionals learn to slow down as they approach each other.

COMPETITION

Skydiving contests today usually include events in style (maneuvers such as a back turn performed in as short a time as possible), accuracy (landing as close as possible to a certain point on the ground), and relative work (team competition of more than one jumper performing maneuvers such as linked circles or other formations).

Below right and left: *Skydivers do most of their work while falling free, descending three-quarters of the way to the ground before opening their chutes.* Opposite: *Not as heart-stopping but just as scenic is soaring —riding in a plane that is powered only by air currents.*

Soaring

Man has always envied the free, soaring flight of the birds, but the only way he has been able to imitate this flight is in a sailplane. The sailplane pilot flies a craft without an engine, using only rising air currents to remain aloft.

Although a sailplane may be called a glider, there is a difference. A glider is a plane without an engine. After launching or release from tow, it will make a controlled descent to a landing. A sailplane is designed and built to descend more slowly than a glider and will gain height when flying in rising air.

The first successful gliders were built and flown in the mid-nineteenth century. A number of people experimented with gliders, including the Wright brothers. They developed a good control system and made more than a thousand glider flights.

The sailplane was first developed in Germany after World War I.

TECHNIQUE

In America nearly all sailplanes are towed aloft by small, powered airplanes at a speed of about sixty mph. Upon reaching the desired altitude, the sailplane pilot releases the tow line by pulling a knob on the instrument panel.

After release, the sailplane pilot searches for a thermal. This is a rising column of warm air that results from the sun heating the air next to the ground. By turning within the thermal, the pilot can climb and stay aloft. Rising air is also generated when surface wind blows against the face of a hill and is pushed upward. A soaring pilot uses this type of lift also.

THE INSTRUMENT PANEL

The instrument panel of a sailplane is quite simple. It contains an airspeed indicator, a bank indicator, a variometer, which measures the rate of climb or descent, and an altimeter, which measures the sailplane's height in the air. Competition sailplanes have more instruments and equipment, including radio and oxygen.

The controls are similar to those of a power plane—a control stick and rudder pedals. The sailplane also has a dive brake or spoiler control handle that opens little doors on the wings when the pilot wants to increase the rate of descent for landing. A sailplane has a single wheel and usually a nose skid. It lands at thirty to forty miles per hour and can stop in a very short distance.

COMPETITION

The first National Soaring Championships in the United States were held at Elmira, New York, in 1930. National contests are held every year and international and world championships every other year. Good soaring conditions with very strong thermals are found in many parts of the world, including Australia, South Africa, and the southwestern part of the United States.

Today, soaring has become a very popular sport in every section of the country. It attracts both men and women. Although it takes training and skill, the Federal Aviation Administration considers soaring safe enough that it permits some fourteen-year-olds to fly solo.

Soccer

More people play it, watch it, bet on it, than any other sport in the world. In 1970, about 800 million people watched its premier event, the World Cup, on television, making that series of games more popular than the astronauts' moon walk. In this country, where football, baseball, and basketball are distraction enough, it's called "soccer," and, until recently, was practically ignored. In the rest of the world, it's called football, and followed intensely.

Passions run high in soccer, both on and off the field. To Americans any mention of the sport frequently conjures up images of great numbers of foreigners running riot in huge stadiums. Riots have occurred often enough for this reputation to be more than a stereotype; the game's history has been marred by many incidents of mass insanity. The worst of these, a 1964 riot in Lima, Peru, resulted in 309 deaths and more than a thousand injuries. In more than one stadium, (the world's largest in Rio de Janeiro is an example), a huge water-filled moat encircling the playing field discourages spectators from attacking players and officials.

The violence associated with soccer is sometimes hard to understand, but the popularity of the game is not. It's a simple game to follow, both fascinating and fluid, that builds its own momentum. Whereas Americans seem to prefer the high scores of basketball, football, and even baseball, dedicated soccer enthusiasts are more than satisfied with the steadily building tension of many scoreless matches. To them, the agility, deceptiveness, and sheer inventiveness of the best players are as exciting as a score. Many of those seated in the stands have played the game themselves (there are about twenty million players in the world), so it is no wonder that soccer has such an enormous following.

HISTORY

Soccer descends from the ancient British football game that also produced rugby and American football. A rather free-form sport at first, it often degenerated into huge street brawls. The pastime was periodically banned by various kings, roundly condemned by scholars and poets, and heartily enjoyed by the masses. Over the centuries, rules were established to civilize the sport. By 1863, soccer had become a sport distinct from rugby football with the formation of the Football Association in a tavern in London. (The word *soccer* is simply an abbreviated form of "Association.") The sport grew rapidly, and in 1885, professional play was legalized.

With almost religious enthusiasm, the British—emigrants, sailors, and other travelers—took their game to foreign countries. The simple, inexpensive sport caught on everywhere, and in 1904 the Federation Internationale de Football Associations (FIFA) was founded. England's attitude toward the Federation was rather snobbish at first, but after World War II, England became a permanent member. Today, more than 140 countries are represented in the organization, and soccer belongs to everyone.

FIELD AND EQUIPMENT

The ball is between 27 and 28 inches around, made of leather or plastic, and weighs 16 ounces. Shoes have small round studs on the bottom and should be soft and well fitting to allow the wearer better control of the ball. Players wear jerseys, shorts, and long socks. Players often wear shin guards under their stockings for protection.

The size of the field may vary but the usual size is 115 yards long and 75 yards wide. At each end of the field stands a goal (8 yards wide, 8 feet high), consisting of two white goalposts and a crossbar. The sides and back of the goal are usually covered with netting that billows dramatically when a goal is scored.

THE GAME

One reason for soccer's popularity is its simplicity. The game requires little equipment other than a ball and a stretch of level ground. Compared to American football, a more static game of elaborate plays and tactics in which the foot rarely touches the ball, soccer is true football. The essence of the game is for one team, using mainly the feet but also heads and chests, to propel the ball downfield into the other team's goal. Only one player on each 11-man team, the goalkeeper, may use his hands.

Soccer games consist of two 45-minute halves, separated by a short intermission. The play is continuous, and substitution, prohibited until recently, is still severely limited. Each team may make only two substitutions per game. If a player is injured after the second substitution, the team plays short-handed. If regulation play ends with the score tied, the game is usually considered a draw. In important contests, such as Olympic and World Cup competition, overtime periods are played, pushing the endurance of the players to the limit.

At the beginning of each half and after each goal, play begins with a kickoff from the center spot at midfield. These are the only times the two teams are arrayed facing each other on opposite sides of the field. Unlike American football, the kickoff is to another member of the same team. The kicker must kick the ball forward, and neither he nor the other team may touch it again until another player on his side has played it.

The kicking team then tries to advance the ball downfield to score, while the defending team tries to frustrate the attack and gain possession of the ball. An offensive player may move the ball from foot to foot as he runs downfield, or he may pass the ball to his teammates. Defenders try to "tackle" the player in possession, but their methods are limited. They may not jump in to take the ball with both feet, or trip the opponent, or make any form of body contact with the hands or arms. Shoulder charging is allowed on players in possession of the ball or those moving to play the ball, but it may not be done in a violent or dangerous fashion.

Soccer is the world's game—it's played practically everywhere—and so it stands to reason that the best player will be known everywhere. Pele, opposite, is. He played for most of his career for Brazil, then was lured to the United States, where soccer has recently begun to grow impressively. But his fans extend around the globe. Above: The one man on a team who may use his hands usually has to—the goalie, charged with keeping the ball out of a 24-foot-wide, 8-foot-high cage.

Probably the most important and most confusing rule is the offside rule. One of the oldest rules in the game, it was first formulated in 1847 by the boys at Eton. They wanted to prohibit "sneaking," that is, gaining an unfair advantage by constantly stationing players near the goal for easy scores. The offside rule stipulates that a play is to be whistled down if, at the moment the ball is passed, the player who intends to receive the ball is ahead of it and if there are less than two defenders between him and the goal. The rule applies only in the offensive half of the field and not when a passed ball touches an opposing player first.

There are nine major fouls in soccer, most of which penalize unnecessary roughness. These include holding, striking, pushing, kicking, tripping, charging, or jumping at an opponent. (*Attempting* to strike or kick an opponent is also a foul, but obviously not one that is interpreted without dispute.) Handling the ball is also a major foul. For any of these fouls, a direct free kick is awarded. The offended team kicks the ball from the point where the foul occurred, and all members of the opposing team must be at least 10 yards from the ball. The defending team may choose to line up a

wall of players, arms linked, between the kicker and the goal if there is a danger of the kicker scoring on such a shot.

If a major foul is committed by the defending team within the rectangular area around its goal, known as the penalty area, a penalty kick is awarded. The penalty kick is taken from the penalty spot, 12 yards from the goal line, and in top competition is an almost certain score because the only player defending against it is the goalie, and he is not allowed to budge until the kicker contacts the ball. A penalty-kick goal, like any goal, scores one point.

Indirect kicks are awarded to penalize technical infractions, such as an offside, a goalkeeper taking more than four steps with the ball, or a minor fault such as blocking. An indirect free kick is also taken from the spot of the infraction, but the ball must be kicked to another player before a goal can be scored.

When one team knocks the ball over the sideline, or touchline, the ball is awarded to the other team, and a throw-in takes place. Standing with both feet on the ground outside the touchline, a player must throw the ball from over his head using

both hands and try to get the ball to a teammate.

When the offensive team propels the ball over the end line, or goal line, (but not into the goal), the defending team is awarded a goal kick. A member of the defending team, usually the goalie, kicks the ball through the penalty area and upfield, while all members of the opposing team remain outside the penalty area.

A corner kick is given to a member of the attacking team whenever the defending team drives the ball over the end line. The ball is placed in the one-yard corner area on the side of the field where the ball was knocked out, and the player takes a free kick. The opposing team members must be at least 10 yards away from the kicker. It's legal to score directly on a corner kick and it is possible with a good, curving drive, but not very likely.

A drop ball is the soccer version of a basketball jump ball or a hockey faceoff. It happens after play has been stopped by an injury or when the linesmen are uncertain of which team touched the ball last before it went out of bounds. Two members of each team, usually the quickest kickers, vie for the ball after the referee drops it between them.

Games are officiated by two linesmen and one referee, probably the most powerful official in all of sport. He makes all the big decisions on fouls and may eject a player from the game after three of four serious offenses. He is the sole timekeeper (no one else knows exactly when the game will end), and in keeping up with the play, he runs six to eight miles a game. For all this work, he is usually paid very little and risks much because an irate crowd may vent its displeasure by more violent means than booing.

STRATEGY AND TECHNIQUES

The forward wall in soccer is made up of five men: from left to right, the outside left (left wing), the inside left (left forward), the center forward, the inside right (right forward), and the outside right (right wing). The leader of the attack and generally the best scorer is the center forward. The ball is passed to him more often than to any other player on the team, and he must be able to control it quickly and attack the goal with split-second timing, usually surrounded by defenders. The most famous center of all time is the Brazilian star of the sixties, Edson Arantes do Nascimento, or more commonly, Pele. He is a player of phenomenal grace and agility, and in 1970 he led Brazil to its third World Cup.

Behind the forwards are the halfbacks—right, left, and center. These men should be playmakers,

Because they can't use their hands, soccer players develop incredible dexterity with other parts of their bodies—not only the legs, opposite, *but even their heads,* right. *A good soccer player can control a ball in the air as well as one on the ground.*

moving the ball upfield to set up a score, and good defenders as well.

The last line of defense before the goalie is made up of the left and right fullbacks. Generally big, forbidding-looking players, they must be strong kickers able to move the ball quickly out of the dangerous scoring area.

The attributes of the goalie are agility, fast reflexes, and courage. He makes many of his saves by catching the ball and hugging it to his chest, the best way to keep the ball from falling accidentally into the net. Often he has no time for such precautions, and he must save the ball any way he can— by jumping and deflecting it over the crossbar, or by punching it away with hands or feet. He must be able to outguess his opponents and, when all else fails, be willing to venture from the goalmouth and dive to smother the ball at the feet of an otherwise sure goal scorer. The goalkeeper must be dressed in a color that distinguishes him from the other

players and the referee. But to the spectators he needs no extra identification: he is either the savior or the last casualty.

A team's strategy, its ways of deploying its players, will depend on a number of variables. Soccer is too fluid a game and too dependent on the individual skills of its players to become completely dominated by elaborate tactics. Before the 1970 World Cup competition, a trend in soccer toward a more defensive, conservative style began to develop. The opening games of the 1974 World Cup finals seemed to confirm this trend. There were several scoreless ties. But then the team from the Netherlands began winning with a completely different style of play. The Dutch unveiled a furious attacking game that at times had the entire team within 50 yards of the opposing goal. Although the Dutch were defeated in the final game by host West Germany, the majority of the coaches who watched the "Flying Dutchmen" in Munich conceded that this was the style of the future, which should make soccer an even more exciting game in years to come.

COMPETITION

The biggest event in soccer is, of course, the World Cup, first offered in 1930 by Jules Rimet, president of the FIFA. Rimet felt that professional soccer should have a championship playoff similar to the amateur event of the Olympics. He set up a competition to take place every four years between Olympic years. World Cup competition consists of a series of international tournaments, culminating in a 16-team final (for which the host country and the previous Cup winner automatically qualify). Each team is an all-star team of the nation's best players, many of whom, in this most international of sports, have to be released from contracts in other countries in order to play for their own.

Promoters, working from the top, have poured millions of dollars and many foreign players into the professional game. The North American Soccer League (NASL), formed in 1968, represents one of their efforts. Most of the players are foreign born, but NASL rules state that each team must have at least six American or Canadian citizens (who may be naturalized citizens) on a roster of sixteen players.

Opposite: All eyes follow the ball as it heads for the corner of the goal. Below: To protect against such close-in shots, the goalie will often come out and jump to bat a high pass away (while a teammate covers for him, just in case).

SOCCER FIELD

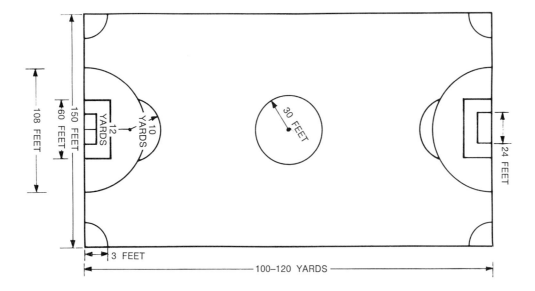

175

Squash

Viewed from the catwalk above the court, squash looks like an exercise in self-torture: two players dashing madly back and forth in a white, boxlike court after a fast-bouncing black ball. The chances are good, though, that these enthusiasts are enjoying themselves enormously. Like handball, squash is good for the body and the soul. It provides a lot of exercise in a short time and is such a fast-moving, intense game that one can't help concentrating. The sport's real name is squash racquets, to distinguish it from another game, squash tennis, but squash racquets players refer to their game as simply squash.

HISTORY

Squash was invented around 1850 by boys at the upper-class British school of Harrow. At first simply a practice game for the larger-court game of racquets, the new game, played with a softer, "squashier" ball, was to prove much more popular than its parent. In Britain players of the sport were invariably well bred, and squash remained an upper-class sport for a long time. Played today by 1.5 million people, the British game has lost its reputation as a rich man's game, but in the United States squash remained a sport of the privileged until the mid-seventies, when the construction of public courts became widespread. With its harder, faster ball (1.75 inches diameter), the American game

requires more durable walls and therefore more expensive courts than the British and Australian versions. Until recently there were only about two thousand courts in this country, mostly at universities and in clubs in the East.

Although a "rich man's" pastime, the origins of the game of racquets could hardly be more disreputable. As described by Charles Dickens in *The Pickwick Papers,* it was first played by debtors in prison, London's Fleet Street Gaol, against a wall in an exercise yard. After release from jail, upper-class insolvents spread the game, and it gained prestige until it was transformed into the four-wall game adopted by the Harrow schoolboys. The game reached the United States around 1800 but did not catch on for about fifty years. The American game was played on courts of many different sizes, and in 1924, the United States Squash Rackets Association was formed to standardize it.

THE GAME

A regulation squash court is stark white, except for the red boundary and service lines. After entering the court through a little door set into the back wall, the players are completely enclosed within the court's four walls. Play resembles four-wall handball very closely, except that in squash the ceiling is out of bounds and, in the American game, every winning shot, not just those of the server, scores a point. Normally, a total of 15 points wins the game, but as in badminton, the strange custom of "setting" is followed. That is, if the score is 13–13, the player who first scored 13 may choose to keep the game at 15 or extend it to 16 or 18 points. If tied at 14, the game may be set at 15 or 17.

Starting from either service court (see diagram), the server gets two chances to serve correctly. Standing with at least one foot within the service box, he must hit the ball against the front wall above the 6-foot service line and below the 16-foot out-of-court line. The ball must then rebound into his opponent's court, either directly or indirectly (by bouncing off another wall). Hitting the ball either on the fly or after one bounce, the receiver must return it to the front wall, again either directly or indirectly. The ball must hit above the "telltale," an aptly named strip of tin whose top is 17 inches above the floor. The telltale is a kind of audible net. Any return that is too low will crash against it with a disappointing clank.

Squash players might be expected to become claustrophobic. Not only do they play surrounded by white walls, opposite, but they seem forever to be bumping into each other, left. The key to squash is controlling the middle of the court, so much jostling for position is inevitable.

Play continues with competitors returning the ball on the volley or after one bounce until the game or match (best three of five games) is finished.

TECHNIQUE

One of the attractions of squash to beginners is that it is almost impossible to hit the ball out of bounds. The novice flails away happily, releasing his aggression, and rarely experiences the frustration of other racquet sports. Past this primitive stage, however, squash is an almost blindingly fast, complex game. Top players, whose reactions are incredibly keen, will often play seemingly endless points.

The squash racquet is about the size of a badminton racquet and light enough to permit the player to use his wrist in making shots. The pace of the game demands that he does. There is no time for full-arm, tennis-type strokes. The racquet, held like a hammer, is flailed at the ball with a motion similar to a baseball sidearm throw.

COMPETITION

Essentially an amateur sport, squash is played on a variety of levels. Players without the stamina for singles may try doubles, a game of real strategy. As players age, they may compete in tournaments for "veterans" (those over 40) and for "seniors" (those over 50).

So far, attempts to create an international game have failed. The British and American games differ radically, so compromise is difficult. Played on a larger court with a slower ball, the British game emphasizes stamina. (One man, Jonah Barrington, a rather mediocre player at first, embarked on a rigorous training regimen and became the British champion for several years running, simply by out-lasting his opponents in matches.) The American game places a premium on agility. Few players have been able to master both the British and American styles.

One who did was Hashim Khan, the most famous member of the Khan family, the ruling dynasty of squash. Now in his sixties, Hashim won the British Open several times (before he was beaten by his brother, Azam), three United States Opens, three Canadian Opens, and one Australian Open. His several sons now win at the game a great deal of the time themselves.

SQUASH COURT

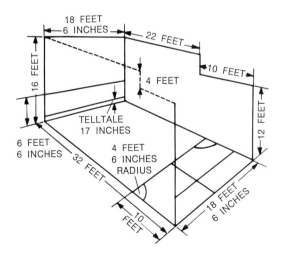

Surfing

HISTORY

> And suddenly, out there where a big smoker lifts skyward, rising like a sea-god from out of the welter of spume and churning white, on the giddy, toppling, overhanging and downfalling precarious crest, appears the dark head of a man. Where but the moment before was only the wide desolation and invincible roar, is now a man, erect, full-statured, not struggling frantically in that wild movement, not buried and crushed and buffeted by those mighty monsters, but standing above them all, calm and superb, poised on the giddy summit . . . and he is flying. . . .

When he wrote this passage in the early twentieth century, Jack London had been badly bitten by the surfing bug. He was far from the first. Polynesians had been riding the waves for centuries. One officer who visited "O why hee" with Captain Cook in 1777, recorded a sight new to European eyes—natives skimming along the water balanced atop long wooden boards. "The boldness and address with which we saw them perform these difficult and dangerous maneuvers was altogether astonishing, and scarcely to be credited," the Englishman wrote. The sight was then, as it is even now, somewhat miraculous.

Surfing held a prominent place in the Hawaiian culture and was treated as a part of religion. Royalty used the best surfboards and the best waves, sometimes banishing commoners from beaches where the waves were breaking particularly nicely. But everyone surfed—men and women, princes and commoners. The Calvinist missionaries who came to the islands from Boston strongly disapproved of this national passion. They saw it as a frivolous diversion, because at the Hawaiian equivalent of "surf's up" the people would abandon all practical tasks and rush down to the sea. Discouraged by the missionaries, the natives had practically given up surfing by the late eighteenth and nineteenth centuries. Surfing wasn't completely extinguished though, and in the early part of this century, the efforts of such Hawaiian surfers as Duke Kahanamoku and George Freath were important in bringing surfing to the attention of Americans and Australians.

EQUIPMENT

Before the 1950s, surfboards were heavy wooden planks between 60 and 120 pounds. Their weight discouraged all but the most muscular from surfing. The advent in the 1950s of a lighter board of fiberglass polyurethane foam revolutionized the sport. Today, boards come in a wide variety of sizes, weights, shapes, and designs. They vary with the size of the waves and the type of surfing to be done. In general bigger waves require bigger boards. Boards used for "hot dogging," or fancy surfing, must be shorter and lighter so as to be maneuvered more easily. Stability is provided by the skeg, a sort of small rudder or fin at the end of the board. Surfers wax the top of their boards with paraffin to keep their feet from slipping.

TECHNIQUE

It takes waves to surf but not just any waves. The best surfing waves rise steeply but break with a regular curl and leave an open shoulder. This shoulder, or wall, is the part of the wave that the surfer rides, moving diagonally along the wave in a race to stay ahead of the breaking water. It was not always so. Surfers once rode directly toward shore, trying to remain upright for as long as possible. The heavy boards of the day left them little choice. Those boards could not have performed the delicate maneuvers that permit today's surfer to move across the unbroken face of a wave.

Surfing is not a sport for the faint of heart or the short of wind. Before he can even ride a wave, a surfer has to paddle out through the surf, struggling against buffeting waves, current, and wind. He needs enough stamina to chase his board when it is lost and to hold his breath under water for long periods—often to avoid the danger of being hit by a flying surfboard. In short he must be an excellent swimmer. Once he has caught a wave at exactly the right moment and he stands up to begin his ride, his balance and control of the board and his power of judgment all come into play.

No one learns to surf overnight, but the thrill of surfing has attracted a more devoted following than that of more humdrum sports. For many people it is a life-style more than a sport.

COMPETITION

To many surfing purists, contests violate the spirit of the sport. Nevertheless, competition has been associated with surfing since its earliest days, when the Hawaiians would wager heavily on contests. Today, it can't be said that the stakes are high—the most lucrative professional event is the Smirnoff Professional Tournament, which paid only $10,000 top money in 1973. Other important events are the Makaha International Championship and the United States Championship held at Huntington Beach, California. So far, no universally recognized rules exist, though events on the West Coast are governed by regulations of the Western Surfing Association (formerly the United States Surfing Association). Many contests include events for senior men (over 35), men (over 16), women, girls, and boys. There is also a tandem event in which a man-woman balancing team surfs on the same board. In all events except the tandem, surfers have to ride a certain number of waves in a given time. Riders are judged on the basis of the difficulty of the wave, the distance it is ridden, skill, style, and sportsmanship. The last quality may seem a strange requirement but in surfing contests surfers compete against five or six others at a time, so the sportsmanship of the surfer who allows another to use the best wave can determine the outcome of an event.

Skimming across a wave, particularly if he has only one foot on his surfboard, a surfer needs extraordinary balance and some courage. He tries to "beat the curl"—stay just ahead of the breaking wave.

Swimming and Diving

Competitive swimming is a sport that belongs primarily to teenagers. Women's records are being set by girls of 14, men's by somewhat older youths. Debbie Meyer, the American swimmer, was 15 years old when she won three gold medals in the 1968 Olympics in Mexico City; four years later she had retired. And when Mark Spitz swept seven gold medals in the 1972 Olympics in Munich (a feat that will probably never be repeated in any sport), he was already considered a veteran at 22. It would be natural to conclude that younger swimmers are stronger or have more endurance. But it is more likely the teenagers' greater acceptance of the painful, time-consuming, and pressure-packed regimen of the top swimmer that accounts for the victories of these "water babies."

More than most other athletes, the swimmer must devote himself completely to his sport. He rises early in the morning to practice for a few hours, goes to school, practices again after school, and then goes home for a good night's sleep. On the average, he swims fourteen thousand yards (about eight miles) a day for six days a week, eleven months a year. His family, particularly his parents, become totally involved in his career. Often the pushiness of a swimmer's parent makes the proverbial stage mother seem like a wallflower.

As in figure skating and equestrian competition, two other sports that attract teenagers, the

long and arduous training in swimming costs money. Most champions are the products of exclusive, private swim clubs. With such carefully trained swimmers (they compete from the age of eight), the United States has dominated swimming at the Olympics and at other competitions, and its swimming program has become the envy of the rest of the world. But success has had its price. The world of the competitive swimmer is such an intense place that many swimmers quit before long—not because they can't win anymore but because they no longer want to. Other athletes— marathon runners, for example—seem to gain endurance as they enter their late twenties. They seem to mature into their sport; swimmers seem to mature out of theirs.

Whatever the faults of this system, one certain result of it is that records are toppling constantly. Like track, swimming has become as much a race against the clock as against the competition. In 1878, the record for 100 meters was 68.5 seconds; in 1972, Mark Spitz swam the distance in 51.22 seconds. The record has since been worked down to 50.59. Johnny Weissmuller, star of two Olympics and many Tarzan films, once held 51 world records. Today, all his records have long been broken, many by women as well as by men.

The grueling training methods of today that produce these record-breaking performances were

180

A swimmer gains most of his power from his arms. The arm breaking from the water creates a pretty pattern of drops behind it; the arm that is underwater does the work.

once considered dangerous. Duke Kahanamoku, the great Hawaiian swimmer, characterized his training regimen with this simple observation: "I swam as far as I felt like swimming and then I would quit." Today, not only discipline but sheer pain is part of every swimmer's routine. There is the grueling "internal training," for example, in which swimmers work lung-searing distances with little rest in between. In his book *Deep Water*, Don Schollander, winner of four gold medals at the 1964 Olympics, describes the battle of the champion swimmer against pain.

> As you approach the limit of your endurance, it begins, coming on gradually, hitting your stomach first. Then your arms grow heavy and your legs tighten—thighs first, then knees. You sink lower in the water because you can't hold yourself up. The sounds of the pool blend together and become a crashing roar in your ears. The water takes on a pinkish tinge. Your stomach feels as though it's going to fall out—every kick hurts like hell—and then suddenly you hear a shrill internal scream. At the threshold of pain, you have a choice. You can back off—or you can force yourself to drive to the finish, knowing that this pain will become agony. It is right there, at the pain barrier, that the great competitors separate from the rest. Most swimmers back away from the pain; a champion pushes himself on into agony.
>
> Taken from *Deep Water* by Don Schollander and Duke Savage © 1971 by Donald A. Schollander and Michael D. Savage.   Used by permission of Crown Publishers, Inc.

Recognizing the fact that the career of the world-class swimmer is a short one, the 103-nation Federation Internationale de Natation Amateur (FINA), the international governing board of swimming, decided to stage world championships every four years in addition to the Olympics. The new competition, staggered for non-Olympics years, catches some swimmers who might not have made the Olympics because they were too young or too old.

HISTORY

The first swim probably wasn't much fun; it may have been the result of an unplanned fall. Certainly, man had to learn to swim to survive, but we can only guess how he learned. Perhaps he observed animals, natural swimmers all, and imitated them. The first stroke may well have been the dog paddle.

Man has been swimming since well before the beginnings of recorded history. Cave drawings depicting swimmers have been found in Libya and date back to 9000 B.C. Swimming lessons were given as early as 2200 B.C., according to the written record of one Egyptian of the time. The Greeks, of course, sailors and island inhabitants, were well aware of the practical values of swimming.

During the Middle Ages, swimming was a lost art because the people were afraid of fresh air and water, but with the passing of superstition, man began to swim again. In the nineteenth century,

competitive swimming was beginning in Great Britain, and by 1837, there were several indoor pools.

In 1845, a group of visiting American Indians overwhelmed the English swimmers with a very peculiar style. An English writer noted with distaste that the Indians "thrashed the water violently with their arms, like sails of a windmill, and beat downward with their feet, blowing with force . . . and forming grotesque antics." This style, so queer to the writer, probably resembled the modern crawl, a stroke that is the mainstay of modern swimming.

Not until the early 1900s did Westerners begin to use the crawl, a stroke that changed the sport radically. An Australian family, the Cavills, visited the South Seas and saw that the natives there used a strong kick and brought their arms *over* the water as they swam. News of the new stroke, called the "splash stroke" and only later dubbed the crawl, spread to the United States. Working only from newspaper descriptions, Americans unwittingly developed a faster kick, four kicks per arm stroke instead of two. Later an even stronger, six-beat kick was used. The American version of the crawl dominated competition for years. Different techniques have come and gone (ironically, many people today believe a two-beat kick is the best), but the basic crawl remains the fastest way of moving through water.

EQUIPMENT

To most people water is water, and the idea that one pool could be "faster" than another seems rather strange. But the design of a pool does affect times, and faster pools are one of the reasons for the modern swimmer's superiority. Several churning swimmers create many waves, which bounce off the sides of the pool and slow down the swimmers. A fast pool has deep gutters on the sides and ropes between the lanes to reduce waves. Faster pools are also deep (seven feet or more is the best depth) because waves are less bothersome in deeper water. Finally, the water is specially treated—"softened"—to remove minerals that might slow a swimmer.

Competitive swimming takes place in indoor and outdoor pools. In high schools and colleges, most pools are 25 yards long, but in such major competitions as the Olympics, the pools must be 50 meters long. FINA recognizes only records set in 50-meter pools. Lanes are marked by painted stripes on the floor of the pool and by buoyed ropes across the surface of the water. Most pools for top competition are now being equipped with electronic timing gear. Many have large-faced training clocks that swimmers can use to pace themselves. Often, a string of flags is stretched across the pool above the water near each end. The flags serve to warn backstrokers that they are approaching the end of the pool. Some pools also have a visual signal about midway across to inform swimmers of a false start.

There was a time when competitive swimmers carried more clothes into the pool with them than

Top: *The crawl is the most efficient and powerful stroke. It has become synonymous with the term freestyle because swimmers always choose the crawl for the freestyle events.* Above: *The butterfly (demonstrated by Olympic champion Mark Spitz) is the most awkward and difficult stroke.* Opposite: *The finish of one leg and the start of another in a relay race.*

the average person wears on the street today. Now, however, swimmers spare no effort to make their bodies as sleek and smooth as possible. They wear light, form-fitting bathing suits and shave their bodies completely. The next step in this never-ending quest for speed may well be nudity. Several zealots have already quite seriously proposed it.

STROKES

The tactics and methods of swimming vary with the distance of the event: sprints, middle-distance races, and long-distance events. Sprints are all-out efforts; longer distances challenge the competitors to pace themselves. The basic racing strokes for all distances are the crawl, the backstroke, the breast stroke, and the butterfly stroke.

The crawl is the basic and fastest stroke in swimming, and because swimmers always use it in freestyle events (in which they are free to choose any stroke), the terms crawl and freestyle have become interchangeable. The swimmer moves face down in the water. The arms move alternately, each entering the water with the elbow and wrist up, the fingers pointed down. As one arm completes a cycle, pushing down through the water past the hip, the other arm enters the water. The swimmer moves his legs up and down vertically, ankles flexing. Scientific studies have shown that most of the propulsion in the crawl comes from the arm, so instead of a strong, hard kick that would tire the swimmer, today's swimmers use a kick that is less vigorous and provides balance rather than speed.

The swimmer inhales through his mouth by turning his head to one side. He needn't raise his head from the water because simply by turning, his head naturally breaks the surface of the water. He exhales under the water.

The backstroke is a sort of inverted crawl, with the swimmer stroking through the water on his back. Body position is very important: the hips should be as near the surface as possible. Breathing is no real problem because the face is out of the water.

Probably the oldest stroke is the breast stroke. It is a stroke so similar to the swimming motion of a frog that it is natural to assume that that animal inspired it. The arms are extended straight in front of the head on the surface of the water, pulled outward and back just below the surface, and then drawn toward the chest before shooting ahead again. The kick is aptly labeled the frog kick: the spread legs are drawn together toward the torso and then kicked apart and back. The arm stroke and kick are done at the same time.

One of the newest strokes in swimming is the butterfly, a variation on the breast stroke but a stroke so tiring that it is seldom used for anything but racing. The arms work together in a sort of windmill motion that lifts the head out of the water. Once the arms reach a position under the water on a line with the thighs, they are brought out of the water and thrown to a point in front of the head, where the next stroke begins. The dolphin, or fish-tail, kick is used. This kick is similar to the flutter kick, but instead of moving individually, the legs move as one. The butterfly is the most exhausting stroke in swimming; it is tougher to swim 200 meters of this stroke than 1500 meters of freestyle.

COMPETITION

Racers are assigned lanes on the "spearhead" principle—that is, the fastest racers get the center lanes. Before the final event, heats are run, and the fastest swimmer in the heats is placed in lane 4, the next fastest at his side in lane 5. The remaining six lanes are assigned the same way. The order is lanes 3, 6, 2, 7, 1, and 8, with lane 3 to the fastest of the remaining swimmers and lane 8 to the slowest. This method allows the faster swimmers to see each other as they race and helps the judges determine places when electronic timing is not used. It also gives the better swimmers a slight edge because the middle lanes are less disturbed by waves than the outer ones.

Starts and turns are always important and in the shorter distances crucial. For most starts each swimmer stands on a starting block outside the pool at the end of the lane. His toes curl over the forward edge of the block and he leans forward as far as possible without falling into the water. At the

starter's gun the racer springs forward, body fully extended over the water. For the start of a backstroke race, the swimmer begins in the pool, holding on to grips affixed to the end of the pool and bracing his feet against the gutter. At the gun he pushes off with his hands and feet and throws his head backward.

In the breast stroke and butterfly races, the racers must touch the pool wall with both hands simultaneously before the turn. Push-off from the wall is with both feet at the same time. Since swimmers can glide underwater faster than they can swim using these strokes, a good strong turn is a decided asset. For the crawl and backstroke, swimmers turn by flipping underwater and driving off the end of the pool with both feet. (Before this faster style of turning was allowed, swimmers had to touch the pool end with one or both hands.)

Most events are for individual competitors, but there are some relays. A medley relay team consists of four swimmers, each using a different stroke. The four legs, usually 100 meters each, are the backstroke, the breast stroke, the butterfly, and freestyle in that order. In an individual medly each swimmer does four legs, one each of butterfly, backstroke, breast stroke, and freestyle, in that order.

DISTANCE SWIMMING

The ultimate in long-distance swimming is the English Channel swim. The first man to swim the Channel was Captain Matthew Webb, an Englishman, on August 24, 1873. Later, Webb pressed his luck, and he died trying to swim the rapids below Niagara Falls.

Since Webb, many swimmers, men and women, have made the crossing. Some have even gone both ways. Channel swimming seems to equalize the sexes. One 15-year-old American, Lynne Cox, holds the women's record of nine hours, 30 minutes, only one minute slower than the top speed for men. She established her record the hard way, swimming from England to France against the tide.

The Channel swim is only the most famous distance swim. Marathon swimming is a big sport in some countries (Egypt, for example) and most competitors are professionals. On this continent Canada holds several distance events each year, usually in rivers. Like Channel swimmers, each contestant is accompanied by a boat, from which he is allowed to take food (hot chocolate and honey are popular). Touching the boat, however, results in disqualification. Most swimmers never finish, dropping out from cramps or exhaustion. In a 28-mile race in 1969, 22 top marathoners entered; none finished.

SYNCHRONIZED SWIMMING

Synchronized swimming looks easy. But its devotees, all female, know that "synchro" is very demanding. Accompanied by music, the swimmers perform intricate, well-rehearsed stunts. In one, the swimmers almost seem to walk on water. By using the "eggbeater" kick, they hold themselves afloat, arms not touching the surface of the water. Any water polo player will agree that is not easy.

Synchronized swimming is now an event in the Pan American games, and adherents of the sport would like to see it included in the Olympics.

Diving

In swimming good form is secondary to finishing the race in the least amount of time. In diving form is everything. No one cares how quickly the diver gets to the water, only how beautifully.

The diver is a gymnast above water. He must have a sure sense of where his body is in space and how it looks, and he must be able to correct his movements in a split second if necessary. He must also be unafraid. At forty miles per hour (the speed at which a diver may hit the water from a 35-foot-high platform) the water seems anything but soft, and a sloppy entry can produce formidable bruises on arms and shoulders.

The first diver must have been an intrepid sort like the cliff divers of Acapulco, Mexico. Diving has always demanded courage and never more so than at the beginning of this century, the early days of competitive diving. In those days divers jumped from platforms or shaky springboards, and some of the dives required the diver to execute his movements with his hands at his sides. This restriction made diving not only unnatural but downright dangerous because many pools were rather shallow (sometimes 5 feet 6 inches of water)—hardly the proper receptacles for bodies hurtling down headfirst. Today, springier, more adjustable boards and special deep areas for diving have removed such hazards.

Diving is done from a platform 5 to 7 ½ meters (intermediate platform) or 10 meters (high platform) above the water, or from a springboard 1 meter (low board) or 3 meters (high board) above the water. There are five basic groups of dives: front, back, reverse, inward, and twisting.

The most natural is the front dive. The diver faces the water on takeoff and enters the water in a forward position. For back dives the diver has his back to the water on takeoff and enters the water with his face away from the board.

For reverse, or gainer, dives the diver faces the water for his takeoff. As he jumps from the board, he thrusts his feet upward and forward until he is upside down and facing the board as he drops past it toward the water.

The diver has his back to the water when he begins an inward, or cutaway, dive. As in the reverse dive, he then moves his feet upward and away from the board until he is upside down, but here he faces away from the board as he drops past it toward the water.

For a twisting dive the diver faces either way on takeoff and twists his body as he is in the air. His body may face toward or away from the board as he enters the water.

Of all these dives, the inward and reverse dives are considered the most dangerous because the body must move back toward the board after take-off. With slight miscalculation, the diver can clip the board on his way down. Even world-class divers have done it.

The three basic midair positions are the tuck, the pike, and the layout. In the tuck position the diver grasps his knees and pulls them to his chest in preparation for a somersault. The tighter the tuck, the faster the spin. In the pike, or jackknife, position, the diver bends at the hips, keeping his legs straight. In the layout, or straight, position, he arches his back slightly but keeps his body straight.

For a forward dive the diver takes three steps along the board, the first two simple, heel-and-toe walking steps. His eyes are focused on his target, the spot at the end of the board where he will land on his third, "hurdle," step. Hopping from one foot and landing on both, he depresses the board and then, with the aid of the recoiling board, springs into the air.

A backward dive has a less spectacular beginning. The diver simply stands at attention, back to the water, at the end of the board and then depresses the board with a "sitting-down" motion.

In competition, blends from the five basic categories and three midair positions produce a great number of dives. Today, more than sixty distinct dives are recognized. Once, a single somersault in the air and a feet-first entry was considered accomplished. Today there are dives of multiple spins and movements, such as the forward 2½-somersault with two twists and a vertical, hands-first entry.

A well-executed dive is one of the most beautiful sights in sport but also one of the most fleeting. The human body seems to soar free but for only one and a half seconds. A new entry technique has been developed, in which the hands are several inches apart, the fingers curved and spread, and the palms flat as the diver enters the water. This entry causes hardly any splash, creating at least the illusion of perfection.

Most diving competition includes both required and optional dives. The six required dives are the forward, back, reverse, inward, twist, and handstand. Each of these can be performed in any of the three midair positions. In the optional diving the competitor can choose from any of the officially recognized variations in deciding what dive to attempt. The judges have the unenviable duty of evaluating the dive in five categories: approach, takeoff, height, execution, and entry. To aid the judges, most dives are rated in degree of difficulty, but it is nevertheless extremely difficult to gain a clear impression of such a short performance. Not surprisingly, the judging is subjective, so the high and low scores of the judging panel are discarded.

In diving good form is everything. The entry is particularly important. The diver tries to knife into the water, leaving hardly any sign as she submerges that she's been there at all.

Table Tennis

In 1937, the United States won the world team table tennis championships for both men and women. But because of poor publicity and organization, table tennis gained the reputation of a fat man's game. Recreational players stood next to the table and batted the ball back and forth to each other in a style of play that made a quilting bee seem exciting by comparison. It was a popular diversion but the public hardly considered it a tournament-level sport.

Then in 1971, the American team visited China, where the game is truly a national sport, and Americans got a glimpse of the real thing—a rapid-fire contest that requires agility, speed, and stamina from the players. Americans were enchanted and rushed to buy equipment. Their enthusiasm may have been the signal of a change in the game's status in this country.

HISTORY

Table tennis has a short but mystery-shrouded history. The British claim to have invented it, but it is certain only that it was first played in the late part of the nineteenth century and attracted a substantial following in Great Britain. A kind of rambunctious parlor game, it was played on dining room tables with small wooden bats and a variety of cork or rubber balls. Manufacturers eager to capitalize on the game sold their versions of equipment and gave the game such names as gossima, flim flam, and whiff whaff. An American firm that marketed the game, Parker Brothers, hit the winning combination: "Ping-Pong," and the name stuck.

Today, table tennis is a truly international sport. The 91 member nations in the International Table Tennis Federation make it the largest sports federation in the world. Unlike many other international sports, this one is peaceful. So far no table tennis match has been the site of a riot.

EQUIPMENT

It is important to have a table of regulation size (9 feet by 5 feet, 2 feet 6 inches high), but players can compensate for a substandard table by lowering the net one inch for each foot the table is short. No compromise should be made with the playing surface: it should yield a bounce of at least eight or nine inches when a standard ball is bounced from twelve inches above it. There should be at least 15 feet of running room at each end of the table.

The ball must be spherical (players used to spin balls on the table to make sure they were), between 1½ and 1¾ inches in diameter. The ball is white and weighs from 37 to 39 grams.

The paddle need not be any particular size, shape, or weight, but it must be wooden, of even

thickness, flat, and rigid. There are basically two types of paddles: the sponge rubber "sandwich" bat and the normal rubber bat. Since the 1952 World Championships, when a relatively unknown Japanese player introduced the sandwich bat, normal rubber paddles are rarely used in tournament play. The sponge paddle gives a little on impact with the ball, thus allowing for more speed and spin on the return. There are actually two different kinds of sponge sandwich bats currently in vogue: the flat-surfaced sponge rubber bat, called an "inverted" bat, with pips lying face downward; and the pips-up sponge bat. Top tournament players are generally divided between these two types, but it is generally conceded that the pips-up sponge is better for speed and the inverted sponge better for spin.

THE GAME

The server begins the game by striking the ball with his paddle from behind the edge of the table. The ball must bounce on his side of the table, over the net, and then on the receiving side of the table. A let serve, one that touches the net before bouncing on the other side, is played over. The server must toss the ball in the air from an uncupped palm and hit it as it descends. (Before 1937, when this flat-palm rule was instituted, players would put "finger spin" on their services.)

The return must pass over the net on the fly and touch the opponent's court. The players then bounce the ball back and forth across the net, always bouncing their returns on their opponent's side but not on their own. Each player must let the ball land on his side before returning it. When one player fails to make a good serve or return, his opponent scores one point.

Service changes after every five points, except at 20–all, when it alternates after each point. The first player to reach 21 is the winner unless his margin is only one point. In that case the game continues until one player gains a two-point advantage. In men's play a match is generally the best of five games and in women's the best of three.

Today, most tournaments are played by the expedite system, under which the rules are changed for any game that lasts longer than 15 minutes. At that point the players begin to alternate service and the server is allowed 12 strokes (excluding service) to win the point. If he has not won the point after 12 strokes, he loses it. This rule put an end to the protracted matches that were once common in table tennis. One famous match, in the 1937 World Championships, lasted seven hours (and one of the points took two hours and twelve minutes).

In doubles competition an important factor is

the center line, which divides the table in half lengthwise. The server must serve from his right court to the receiver's right court. After the serve, the ball may be hit to any area of the table. The partners must take turns returning the ball, and therein lies the excitement and fun of doubles. The partners must understand each other at least well enough to avoid running into each other as they scramble to make returns. In more sophisticated play the server may give a hand signal to his partner, telling him what kind of serve he is delivering.

trol and power is topspin. Applied with a forward and upward motion of the paddle as it contacts the ball, topspin keeps the ball from sailing over the end of the table and causes it to kick up as it bounces. Defensive shots are often "chopped," that is, hit with backspin, produced by moving the bat downward, underneath the ball with a short, chopping motion. With its low, relatively dead bounce, a backspin shot can bedevil a receiver, but an experienced opponent will smash all but the deepest backspin shots for easy "kills."

TECHNIQUE

Most Westerners grip the paddle as they would a tennis racquet—with the "shake-hands" grip. (Until very recently, some of the West's finest players were former tennis players.) Shots are made with either side of the paddle, with the body in the traditional position of most racquet sports—facing the ball.

The elementary shot is the push, played forehand and backhand. With forearm horizontal, the player tilts the bat slightly back at the top and moves steadily through the ball and slightly down. Although not a point maker, this stroke is the basis for every other shot in table tennis. Experts continue to practice it, though they can exchange approximately sixty push shots a minute.

Played on the smallest "court" with the smallest bat and ball of any racquet game, table tennis requires great control. And yet to win one almost always tries to hit balls so hard that one's opponent cannot return them. The trick to gaining both con-

Table tennis became the rage in America in 1971 after the American team went to China. Then the Chinese came here, and Americans saw firsthand the Oriental slam-bang style of play.

THE TABLE

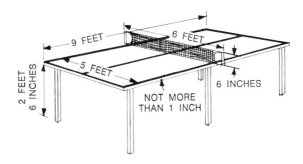

Top players always try to be well balanced, their feet spread wide apart so that they are ready to return all shots and don't have to stretch too far to reach them.

Few sports are played with such different styles. Players from the Far East, using the "penhold" grip, have recently dominated world competition. Gripping the shaft of the paddle in the crook between thumb and forefinger, they stand to the backhand side of the table so that they can hit all their shots with their forehand. Their position leaves the whole forehand court unprotected, but they more than compensate with speed and nimble footwork. The result is an aggressive, forehand attacking game. (In China, where there are more than six million tournament-level players, top players spend the better part of each day in demanding training.)

The main virtue of the penhold grip is the ease with which shots can be disguised. In a game in which deception counts for so much, disguising one's shots is no small advantage. With the penhold grip, the wrist can be turned 270 degrees (as opposed to 90 degrees for the shake-hands grip) and can flick the ball almost anywhere.

In general the player who uses this grip is capable of fewer kinds of shots than the player who uses the shake-hands grip. But Asians willingly sacrifice diversity for the added power of their forehand game. To further overpower their opponents, the Chinese usually stand only two to three feet behind the table and hit the ball just as it bounces—a movement that requires perfect timing. Westerners generally stand four to five feet behind the table and hit the ball at the top of its bounce. The best Western players try to outmaneuver their Eastern opponents by moving them from side to side and keeping the ball in play to force errors.

COMPETITION

The biggest event in table tennis is the World Championships, first played in 1926. Players compete in team events for the Swaythling Cup (for men) and the Corbillon Cup (for women), and in singles, doubles, and mixed doubles. Today, more than 50 countries send a total of some six-hundred players to the event, which has been held every two years since 1956. Until the early fifties, the Hungarians and Czechs dominated competition. In the years since, the Japanese, Chinese, South Koreans, Swedes, and, lately, the Yugoslavs have been dominant.

The governing body of table tennis in this country is the United States Table Tennis Association, formed in 1933.

The greatest difference in styles of play stems from the different ways in which players grip the paddle. The "shake-hands" grip, shown here, is the most versatile, though most Oriental players favor what for them is the more natural penhold grip.

Team Handball

International, or team, handball is a strange combination of basketball and soccer that resembles the wall variety of handball in name only. Started in Europe in the early 1900s, the game was originally a simple counterpart to soccer. The object of soccer is to advance the ball into a goal without using the hands; team handball was designed to accomplish the same objective by allowing players to use their hands. In countries such as Germany and Austria, team handball is still played on a huge soccer field with eleven players, but the majority of play is now indoors with seven men to a side instead of the eleven used in soccer.

THE GAME

An indoor team handball court is 65 feet 8 inches wide by 131 feet 4 inches long. The object of the game is to throw the ball into a netted goal that is 9 feet 9 inches wide and 6 feet 6 inches high. A goalie protects the goal, but he is much less a deterrent to scoring than his counterpart in soccer. The ball was originally identical to the soccer ball, but its size was subsequently reduced to seven inches in diameter to afford the players a better grip.

The rules allow a player to advance the ball with any part of his body above the knees. He may hold the ball in his hands for no longer than three seconds and may dribble indefinitely. Defensive play generally resembles basketball defense. Tackling or pushing is forbidden, and infractions are penalized with free throws and penalty throws that follow the rules of the free kick and penalty kick in soccer. Games are divided into two halves of 30 minutes each.

COMPETITION

Team handball is popular throughout the world, though the United States has mostly overlooked it. The International Handball Federation, founded in 1926, claims 64 member countries and estimates that the game is played by more than five million men and women of all ages. The sport was played in the 1972 Olympics, and world championships are staged every four years.

Recently, team handball has been increasing in popularity in the United States as well. Following the lead of the military academies, many colleges are incorporating the game into their physical education programs.

Above right: The court for team handball looks like an indoor soccer field; team handball began as an indoor version of soccer. Right: In team handball, players may use their hands, making it much easier to score goals than in soccer.

Tennis

A 1973 survey discovered that twenty million Americans were playing tennis. This was double the figure for 1970, an astounding rate of growth. If any sport deserves to be called "the sport of the seventies," tennis is it.

This sudden popularity is not easy to explain. Certainly tennis is great exercise, but so are many sports that are more easily mastered. Some people suspect that part of the sport's popularity stems from snob appeal. Not long ago some of those without the money or social standing to belong to clubs looked on tennis players as somewhat effete, if not downright effeminate, with their spotless whites and scrupulous good manners. Today, showing signs of culture is more acceptable, even demanded, and in certain circles playing tennis is the thing to do. But it is not only aspiring snobs who are discovering tennis. The game itself has changed to accommodate a variety of sports fans—from fitness freaks to bleacher bums. Today, tennis is a game of power and speed as well as grace, and

the fans feast on the slam-bang style. Jimmy Connors bashing an overhead past his opponent may not yet thrill America as much as Joe Greene squashing an all-but-defenseless quarterback, but it is with Connors that an ordinary mortal can identify. Many Americans have experienced, as he has, the exquisite feeling of power that comes with a perfectly dispatched, unreturnable overhead smash. Those who haven't can foresee the day when they will have mastered the skill. How many sports fans have had, or can hope to have, the opportunity of crashing into a quarterback two-thirds their size?

HISTORY

It was an aristocrat, Major Walter Clopton Wingfield, scion of a distinguished English family, who invented the modern game. When the family estates began to deteriorate a bit, Wingfield cast about for a way to upgrade them and decided that a fortune could be made by someone who could

One of the pleasant surprises in tennis is finding out all you can do. Balls that seem hopelessly out of reach have a habit of being returnable, given a big stretch and a last-second lunge.

devise a lively lawn game for men and for women (who were becoming more athletic and a little tired of croquet). So, borrowing a net from badminton, a ball from the game of fives, and some principles from the ancient game of court tennis, Wingfield invented a game he called "sphairistike," a word taken from the Greek for "to play." The name, the shape of the court (which resembled an hourglass), and the rules (which gave several advantages to women), were his ideas.

Wingfield was hoping his game would be original enough to deserve a patent, and after he was awarded one in 1874, he quickly marketed sets of equipment for the game. But he wasn't destined to make a fortune from his invention. People began to fashion their own equipment, and groups such as the Marylebone Cricket Club and the All England Croquet Club changed Wingfield's rules and court dimensions. All were outraged at the major's nerve in patenting a game that was, after all, largely a hodgepodge of other sports.

In 1877, the All England Club staged the first of what has today become the most famous tennis tournament, the English Lawn Tennis Championships at Wimbledon, a tournament known today simply as Wimbledon. A racquets player, Spencer Gore, bested 21 other males for the first title. Gore confounded the opposition by rushing to the net (sometimes even leaning over it) to put away shots. He wasn't able to retain his title the next year, however, because his opponent did what came naturally in facing these charge-to-the-net tactics—he lobbed the ball over Gore's head.

From such innocent beginnings tennis progressed to the modern "power" game—from showmaster Bill Tilden to the rapierlike backhands of Donald Budge, to the all-around power games of Jack Kramer, Pancho Gonzalez, and Rod Laver. Like most major sports, tennis has made the transition from amateur to professional, but the transition was a painful one, marred by unusual hypocrisy. The amateur establishment, represented by the International Lawn Tennis Federation (ILTF), founded in 1913, and the United States Lawn Tennis Association (USLTA), formed in 1881, fought tenaciously against professionalism in the sport. Their opposition didn't stop some players—Bill Tilden was one of the first—from becoming professional, or others from making a living from under-the-table "expense" money. In the fifties, Jack Kramer became the head of a professional circuit and stormed the amateur citadel with lucrative contracts to lure the best players away to the pros. But not until 1968, when Wimbledon became an open event (that is, open to professionals) was the professional player fully accepted. Before 1968, prize money was almost nonexistent; by 1973, tennis players were earning collectively about seven million dollars.

Even with the amateur-professional war over, there is still unrest in the tennis world. A plethora of organizations and interests are constantly bicker-

Left: *Walter Wingfield called his creation "sphairistike," a genteel game for England's upper classes.* Below: *By 1883, the date of this drawing from* Harper's Weekly, *well-off Americans had taken to the English invention.*

ing. One power is the USLTA, which runs tournaments, sanctions others, and still holds amateur tours for certain age groups. Then there is World Championship Tennis (WCT), a professional tour of the top male professionals started by oil millionaire Lamar Hunt. The WCT pros (84 in 1975) are divided into leagues and compete for the richest prize money in tennis at the annual finals in Dallas. The Association of Tennis Professionals (ATP) is another male group, a player's union formed in 1972 with Jack Kramer as its executive director.

If the male pro has had rough going, pity the poor woman player. Until recently, the women made far less money than the men. It was said, mostly by men, that the women's game was dull. That myth faded in 1973 and all tennis was given a boost with the famous match between Billie Jean King and Bobby Riggs. A former Wimbledon champion and hustler extraordinaire, Riggs was far past his tennis prime (but still hustling) at 55. With a

United States Open at Forest Hills. Chris Evert had gained superstar status by 1974, when she won Wimbledon. In 1976, Evonne and Chris, the reigning female stars, would each earn somewhere in the neighborhood of half a million dollars each, counting endorsements and unofficial winnings.

A recent development in tennis is World Team Tennis (WTT), a league of teams composed of three women and three men each. Located in various North American cities, the teams compete against each other in a game of radically changed rules and scoring, designed to appeal to the sports fan who has found the rules and customs of tennis too stuffy. WTT began shakily, attracting only sparse crowds, but it has been steadily growing in popularity. Few are the world stars who don't compete in WTT. Meanwhile, the tennis spectator has probably changed for good. He is no longer the reticent, polite observer who would do nothing more demonstrative than applaud a fine effort and, at his most audacious, whistle to question the call of a linesman. Today, cheers and even boos are the rule and not the exception.

Despite all the new, money-making ventures in tennis, the oldest tennis events are still the most prestigious. The Grand Slam of each tennis year consists of four events: Wimbledon; the French Open, first played in 1891; the Australian Open, first played in 1905; and the U.S. Open (Forest Hills) first played in 1924. Only two men, Donald Budge and Rod Laver, and two women, Maureen Connolly and Margaret Court, have captured the Grand Slam.

The Davis Cup competition, though played only for a trophy (donated in 1900 by Dwight F. Davis), still attracts top professionals. Four- or five-man teams from all over the world compete. Every year a team of amateur women from the United States and one from Great Britain compete for the Wightman Cup.

COURTS AND EQUIPMENT

Tennis is one of the sports in which different playing surfaces strongly affect the style and tactics of the game. The harder surfaces, such as grass and concrete, produce a faster game and give the advantage to the player who has a power game. But grass, long the surface for the most hallowed tournaments, is falling into disfavor. Not only are grass courts expensive to maintain, but they produce erratic bounces. After one final at Forest Hills, Rod Laver said, "They should dig up center court." Forest Hills abandoned grass for the 1975 tournament.

In Europe, approximately ninety percent of the courts are clay. The ball bounces higher and slower on clay, so skillful placement of the ball rather than sheer power is rewarded.

The variety of racquets today is amazing. Originally, racquets were all made of wood, but today they are made of a variety of metals, fiberglass, and wood. The metal racquet craze bloomed in the late sixties, when many pros and quite a few weekend players discarded their wood for the more powerful,

straight set victory over a top woman player, Margaret Court, he had embarrassed not only Court but women's tennis in general before King, America's best woman player, accepted his challenge to a "battle of the sexes." In the Houston Astrodome, an unlikely setting for a tennis match but not for the nationally televised sports spectacle that this match had become, Billie Jean trounced Riggs in probably the most widely watched tennis match in history.

Even before the King-Riggs match, women's tennis had gained respectability and prize money. Led by King, the women pressed their cause for pay and playing conditions equal to the men's. They succeeded suddenly and dramatically. Within a few years they went from one-tenth the pay of men to parity. Then two teenagers, American Chris Evert and Australian Evonne Goolagong, burst to prominence, and suddenly women's tennis was the rage.

An unheralded Aborigine from Australia, Evonne shocked the tennis world with a stunning upset victory at Wimbledon in 1971, and in 1973, she won more than $75,000 (more than Billie Jean King), finishing second to Margaret Court in the

The best tennis players used to have the unhappy choice of remaining famous amateurs or becoming obscure, barnstorming pros. "Open" tennis allowed such superstars as Rod Laver, top left, *the best of both worlds. Billie Jean King,* top right, *led the women's revolution, helped along by the popularity of Evonne Goolagong and Chris Evert,* above left and right.

lighter metal. Older professionals, especially, appreciated the new racquets, which added years to some careers. The problem with metal racquets is that they are more difficult to control than wood ones are. Also, they cost more. In 1975, two totally new racquets were introduced—one featuring an oversized hitting surface, the other strung on both sides of the frame.

The tennis racquet has an oval face, tightly strung with nylon or gut (made from sheep intestines). The tightness with which the racquet is strung, its weight, its grip size, and the weight distribution all vary with the taste of the player.

There are two main types of balls—heavy duty, for hard surfaces, and regular, for clay or grass. Balls are hollow, made from rubber, covered with a fuzz called nap, and have a diameter of 2½ inches. In most competition new balls are brought into play at predetermined intervals.

THE GAME

Many beginners find tennis somewhat mystifying, especially its scoring. The trick is to stop looking for logic in the scoring system and accept its basis in tradition. Then one can tend to the real business of the game—as in all racquet sports, hitting the ball where the other player isn't.

Tennis is played with one player per side (singles) or two per side (doubles). Mixed doubles, the form for which Wingfield invented the game, is played with one woman and one man on each team.

Each point begins with the serve. On the first serve of each game, the server stands behind the baseline, to the right of a hashmark that marks its center, and serves the ball to the service court diagonally opposite him. The service courts are the rectangular boxes that extend from a line through midcourt to the singles sidelines, and from the net to a line 21 feet from it. The ball must clear the net and land on or within the lines of the appropriate service court. If the server misses, or faults, on the first serve, he is allowed a second attempt. If he misses the second, a double fault is called and his opponent scores a point. A serve that touches the net and lands in the service court is called a let (from "let us play another") and is played over; one that hits the net but lands outside the service court is a fault.

TENNIS COURT

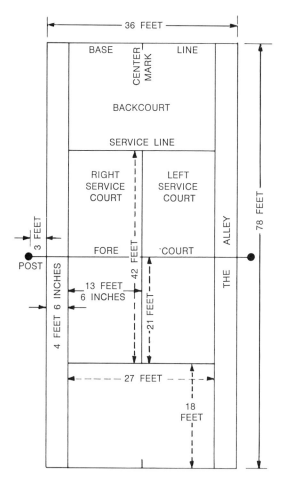

Top: *Receiving service in doubles. In both singles and doubles, the server serves the ball from behind the baseline into the service court diagonally opposite him.* Bottom: *Serving in singles.*

Once a legal serve has been made, the ball may be hit to any part of the court. A point is awarded whenever one side fails to make a legal return. Whenever a ball lands outside the boundary lines, fails to clear the net, or bounces more than once, the point is lost. A ball that hits the net and continues over is good as long as it lands in bounds.

The evidence of tennis's descent from the royal French game of court tennis is its scoring. A game consists of four points, which for some ancient and unknown reason are called not 1, 2, 3, and 4, but 15 (sometimes shortened to 5), 30, 40, and game. The server's score is always given first, and no score (0) is called "love" (perhaps deriving from the French l'oeuf, meaning egg). Thus, after the first point has been played, the score is either love–15 (if the server loses the point) or 15–love (if he wins it).

After the first point, the server moves to the left of the center line and again hits to the service court diagonal to him. The server continues to alternate courts for each point.

A score tied at 40–all is called deuce because at this point a player must win two points in a row to win the game. The player who wins the first point after deuce is said to have the advantage, often abbreviated "ad." When the server has the advantage, the score is called "ad-in"; when the receiver has it, it's called "ad-out." If the player with the advantage wins the next point, the game is his. If not, the score returns to deuce.

Serve alternates between opponents after each game, and players exchange sides on every odd-numbered game so that court conditions are equalized.

Usually the first side to win 6 games wins the set. In traditional scoring a player has to win the set by at least 2 games. So at 5–all, play continues until one side establishes a 2-game margin (7–5, 8–6, or 9–7 for example). In the modern game, especially in professional play, a "tie-breaker" is often used to prevent dreary, long sets and matches. There are various systems of tie-breakers. All consist of a limited series of points, and the player who wins the majority of the points wins the set. Tie-breakers usually go into effect when a set is tied at 6 games all. Serve always alternates during a tie-breaker, though not always after each point. Many professionals (usually after they have just lost a set on a tie-breaker) complain about the system because to win the tie-breaker a player need not break service, that is, win a point on the opponent's serve. Spectators like the tie-breaker because it gives the match a dramatic finish. Television executives like it because it allows them to schedule programs around a televised tennis match without the fear of having to pre-empt them for a five-hour marathon.

Men's matches usually consist of the best of five sets, women's the best of three. Doubles play is for the best of three sets.

TOURNAMENT PLAY

Most tournaments are conducted on a single elimination basis: players or teams are excluded from further competition after losing one match. Thus, after each round, the field is cut in half. The players that the tournament officials consider most talented are usually seeded—that is, their matches are arranged so that they won't face (and eliminate) each other until the later rounds.

194

Opposite left: *On the overhead especially, the player watches racquet meet ball.* Opposite middle: *Forehand volley at net.* Opposite right: *Evonne Goolagong slices a backhand.* Above: *Bjorn Borg needs only to block the ball on this backhand volley.*

Above: *Marty Reissen is carried into the court by his momentum on the serve.* Opposite left: *Cliff Drysdale's forehand.* Opposite middle: *Arthur Ashe's backhand.* Opposite right: *Jimmy Connors shows the power of a two-handed backhand.*

TECHNIQUE

The basic strokes in tennis are the serve, the forehand, the backhand, the lob, the overhead smash, the volley, and the half-volley. To all these strokes, a variety of spins can be added.

The serve was once delivered with an underhand motion, when its purpose was simply to put the ball in play. Today, all serves are overhand. The ball is thrown into the air and, with the server's arm fully extended, hit with so much force that sometimes the point is won on that stroke alone.

For a right-hander, the forehand is simply any stroke hit on his right side and the backhand any stroke hit on his left side. The forehand is the first and the easiest stroke most players learn. The backhand is a more graceful-looking and natural shot and, once mastered, more satisfying.

The lob is hit high in the air over the opponent's head. It's a shot more popular among amateurs than professionals, who can easily dispatch a less-than-perfect lob with a devastating overhead smash, a stroke similar to a serve. Offensively, the lob is used against someone playing too close to the net; defensively, it's often the only way a player can gain the time to reposition himself after a particularly good shot by his opponent.

A volley is a ball hit before it has bounced, usually by a player at the net. A half-volley is a ball hit immediately after the bounce, as the ball is rising, and requires precise timing and coordination.

All shots can be hit flat, without spin, but most competitive players use several kinds of spin: topspin, underspin, or sidespin. Topspin allows play-ers to hit the ball hard and still keep it in bounds. The racquet rolls over the ball, causing it to take a looping trajectory over the net and to bounce briskly forward on the other side.

Underspin, or slice, is produced by moving the racquet down and under the ball. The trajectory of the shot is flatter than one hit with topspin, and the ball takes a more sluggish bounce, sometimes straight into the air or even backward. The dropshot is a shot hit with a lot of underspin, usually to a player who is playing far from the net. A well-executed dropshot leaves the ball so close to the net that a player behind the baseline can't reach it. But poorly placed, the dropshot can be reached and is easily put away.

An individualistic game, tennis is a sport in which confidence is often the most important element in victory. Most of the competitive players today are superbly conditioned and able. There is often little difference in their levels of play, so the winner of a match is often the player who is mentally tougher.

OFFICIALS

The chief official of a match is the umpire, who sits in an elevated chair at the side of the net. He keeps score and regulates the match. Linesmen are assigned to areas of the court to call balls that go out of bounds. The number of linesmen varies with the match. Ten is a full complement.

Strangely, enough, for a sport that offers more lucrative prize money than ever before, virtually all tennis officials remain volunteers. It is the last vestige of amateurism for a sport in which that spirit died hard.

Platform Tennis

Platform tennis, often (and erroneously) called paddle tennis, was invented in 1928 by James Cogswell and Fessenden Blanchard in Scarsdale, New York. It combines elements of tennis and walled-court games.

The game is played on a platform 60 feet long and 30 feet wide made of planks of wood, laminated wood, aluminum, or steel. A 12-foot-high wall of tightly strung wire mesh surrounds the platform.

The court measures 44 feet by 20 feet. It is centered on the platform. A net 2 feet 10 inches high at center court divides the court in half.

The paddle is made from laminated wood, steel, or plastic. It has a short handle of wood or metal and an oval face. The wood face is rimmed with metal. All racquets are perforated. The ball, usually bright yellow, is made of firm sponge rubber and is about the size of a tennis ball.

The rules are similar to those of lawn tennis. The major differences are that the server is allowed only one serve per point, and the ball may be played on the rebound from the side or back walls, provided that it has first bounced in the appropriate court.

Only doubles are played. It is considered a winter game. Most courts are built outdoors with no roofing. In cold weather gloves and sometimes headwear are necessary, but the game is so fast that players need to wear only light sweaters.

A national championship is sponsored each year by the American Platform Tennis Association. In 1976, a tournament for prize money was held at Forest Hills.

Platform tennis is played with paddles and is therefore often mistakenly called paddle tennis. The unique feature of platform tennis is the 12-foot-high wire-mesh screen enclosing the court. Balls that hit the screen are in play provided that they first bounce in the court.

Track and Field

The athletic events that are perhaps the purest and most natural to man can be found in track and field. Running, jumping, and throwing, activities prehistoric man pursued in deadly earnest as a matter of survival, are now done for sport. The contests are almost always simple, a matter of who can run the fastest, jump the highest, throw the farthest. But more than competing against each other, men and women compete against the record book. Years are spent in training to gain fractions of seconds or inches, to set new standards that will very soon be old ones.

HISTORY

Although they had no split-second timing devices, the ancient Greeks had a near-fanatic sense of the glory of winning in athletics. What we call track and field events were the backbone of the ancient Greek Olympics. Indeed, the first recorded Olympics, in 776 B.C., consisted of one event only, the *dromos,* or running. As the years went by, contests in other events were added, and the Olympics, taken over by the Romans, continued until 393 A.D.

Olympic champions were considered by their countrymen even greater heroes than victors in battle. Indeed, it was this adulation of the winners that led to the downfall of the games. The Greeks accused the Roman champions of accepting material rewards, in violation of the spirit of the Olympics. The argument grew so heated that eventually the Roman emperor settled it by abolishing the games.

In 1896, the Olympics were reborn. The man most responsible for the rebirth was Baron Pierre de Coubertin, a Frenchman and a true internationalist. Although the Olympics have often been the occasion for displays of political rivalry among nations—quite contrary to de Coubertin's intention—there is no question that the games have showcased magnificent athletics. The most exciting and enduring Olympic events, in a history that has included contests in bowling on the green, croquet, and fishing, have been those of track and field.

Although the Olympic games are the stage for the most important track and field meets, these are not the only meets, nor even the oldest. The modern sport was getting its bearings in the latter part of the nineteenth century. The first intercollegiate meet was held in England in 1868, between Oxford and Cambridge. Four years later, competition had begun in the United States.

TRACKS

Track meets are held year-round indoors and outdoors, though the events differ from indoor to out-door meets. The tracks used for outdoor meets in the United States have usually been made of crushed cinder and brick, mixed with loam, but these cinder tracks may soon be outmoded. A more recently developed surface is a rubber-asphalt composition that provides greater spring and significantly faster times. Official indoor tracks are made of wood and sometimes covered with a composition similar to that of the outdoor, all-weather tracks. Most indoor tracks are 11 laps to the mile, or 160 yards. The outdoor track is a quarter-mile around. Field events for both outdoor and indoor meets usually take place in the track's oval infield.

TRACK EVENTS

The training, technique, and strategy for each of the running events differ so much that each event is almost a sport in itself. Most runners are specialists, concentrating on sprints, hurdles, middle-distance races, or endurance races.

SPRINTS

Certainly the most famous sprint is the 100-yard dash (100 meters in international competition). The record holder in this event is traditionally dubbed "the world's fastest human." Today, the record holder is Ivory Crockett, who in 1974 ran the 100 in 9 seconds flat, breaking the long-standing record of 9.1 seconds first achieved in 1963 by Bob Hayes. New records come hard over so short a distance (in 1890, the race was run in 9.8 seconds), but some coaches believe a sub-9-second dash is within reach of the world's top sprinters, provided that the track surface and competition are right.

A 100-yard dash in 1929 was the first race in which blocks were set behind the starting line to help the runners in their starts. The excavated stadium at Olympia shows that the ancient Greeks used hollowed stones that the feet could grip for the push-off, so the idea of starting blocks was certainly not new. However, the Amateur Athletic Union (AAU) resolutely ignored the precedent and refused to recognize the record set in 1929 (9.4 seconds) because of these "artificial aids."

Today, every runner uses the blocks. Using them to fullest advantage is not only one element of a good start but sometimes the key to victory, for in sprint races the margin of victory is usually minute. At the signal "On your mark," the runner assumes a position with his feet against the blocks (right foot usually in the rear block) and his rear knee on the ground. Both hands are set on the ground with the thumb and forefinger directly behind the starting line. At the command "Set," the runner leans his shoulders over his hands and raises his hips until

they are slightly higher than the shoulders. At the crack of the gun, he must react instantly, with the leg from the back block moving to take the first step. If the runner moves between "Set" and the pistol's "Go" signal, the race is started over. Two false starts disqualify the runner. Armin Hary, the 1960 Olympic 100-meter champion from West Germany, had perfected his start so completely that many officials thought he was jumping the gun. He wasn't; he simply reacted to it with startling quickness.

The sprint running style is all-out. The 100-yard-dash runner tries constantly to accelerate. There is no conserving of energy for a final kick, as there is in middle- and long-distance running. The sprinter runs high on the balls of his feet, his knees driving and arms pumping. Jesse Owens, the fine American runner of the 1930s, said he ran as if his feet were on a "hot plate," getting them on and off the ground before they got "burned." Generally, the longer the stride, the better, but each stride should be so coordinated that it appears to be effortless. The truly great runners, even in the middle of intense competition, appear almost relaxed.

The winner of the race is the runner whose body first crosses the finish line. A tape is stretched across the finish line, and most runners lean into the tape for that extra edge. However, the recent development of the "photo-timer," a device similar to those used in photo finishes in horseracing, has made the "breasting of the tape" more of a prop for photographers than a guide to race officials in determining winners.

The 220-yard run (200 meters in international meets) is also a sprint event. It is usually run around a turn, but world records are listed for both the turn and straightaway distances. (Tommie Smith of the United States holds both.) Many consider the 220 an even more exciting event than the 100 since there is more time for a good race to develop.

QUARTER MILE

The 440, a tour once around the track, is not a favorite of runners. It was once considered a middle-distance race. The strategy was to run the first 220 yards at close to full speed, then slow down for the next 100 yards or so to conserve energy for the run down the stretch. But the competition has improved so much and times have dropped so low over the years that any runner who decides to conserve energy in the 440 will find himself pulling up the rear. The 440 has become a race in which the distance is just short enough to require furious speed and just long enough to torture the runner for maintaining that speed. The greatest 440 runners today are those who can maintain top speed with a "floating" style of running that requires a tremendous stride and unusual speed and stamina.

Until the 1950s, lanes weren't used for the 440, and so there was quite a lot of jockeying for position. Today, racers run in lanes in a staggered start; the runners in the outside lanes start farther along the track to make up for the greater length of the outside lanes.

HURDLES

Hurdle races demand speed, timing, and coordination from the athlete. Races are generally run at 50 and 60 yards indoors, and 120 yards (or 110 meters) and 440 yards (or 400 meters) outdoors, so speed is important. In fact only runners who are highly competitive in flat sprints can hope to win at the hurdles. But even the fastest sprinter may not have what it takes to be a good hurdler.

The 440-yard hurdle event consists of ten sets, or flights, of intermediate hurdles (3 feet high), one per hurdler at each flight. The 110-, 60-, and 50-yard events use high hurdles (3 feet 6 inches high)—ten flights for the 110, five flights for the 60, and four flights for the 50. It is crucial for the runner to maintain a good running stride, so that he reaches each hurdle at the precise moment required for a smooth pass. A top-flight hurdler seems to glide over the hurdles, his head leg extended straight ahead and the trail leg whipping over the barrier quickly to take the first stride as he lands. There is no penalty for knocking over hurdles, though knocking one over can easily throw the runner off stride and cost him the race.

MIDDLE-DISTANCE RACES

The 880 (880 meters), or half mile, is a run, not a sprint. The half-miler and all middle-distance runners run more upright than the sprinters and don't pump their knees quite as high. It is crucial for the middle-distance runner to plan his strategy before a race and then, if possible, to stick to it, remaining undistracted by the actions of the runners around him. Dave Wottle, the 1972 Olympic 800-meter champion, ran practically every race the same way. With 200 meters to go, Wottle would almost invariably be dead last, but his amazing ability to explode down the last straightaway was usually enough to put him first at the finish.

The mile (or its metric equivalent, the 1500 meters) has always awed track fans and runners as well. For a long time no one expected that anyone would ever run the mile in less than four minutes. This view persisted even though runners flirted for years with that magical time. In 1945, the great Gunder Hagg of Sweden had run 4:01.4. But it wasn't until nine years later that Roger Bannister, an Oxford medical student, broke the magic barrier. On May 6, 1954, Bannister ran the distance in 3:59.4, capping a personal crusade that had con-

sumed him night and day. Seven weeks later, Australian John Landy broke Bannister's record with a 3:58.0 mile in Turku, Finland.

The stage was set for a showdown and it came shortly afterward, in the British Empire Games held in Vancouver, British Columbia. Landy led for most of the race, but Bannister, a student of the great Paavo Nurmi's pacing method, had enough left at the finish to nip Landy with a time of 3:58.8. Landy's time of 3:59.6 made it the first race in which more than one runner had cracked the four-minute barrier. Although the barrier had been hurdled, it wasn't until 1958 that it truly fell. On August 6, 1958, in Dublin, one of the most dramatic races in history took place. It was a confrontation between Herb Elliot, perhaps the greatest middle-distance runner of all time, his countryman Merv Lincoln, and the Irish Olympic champion miler, Ron Delaney. After a grueling three-quarters of a mile, Elliot took over and won in a record-smashing time of 3:54.5. Lincoln was second (3:55.9), Delaney tied with Murray Halberg of New Zealand for third (3:57.5), and yet another runner, Al Thomas of Australia, also finished under four minutes (3:58.6). The four-minute jinx was gone for good.

Elliot's record stood until 1962, when a 22-year-old New Zealander, Peter Snell ran 3:54.4—

Opposite: *In sprinting there is no such thing as pacing. The runners explode from the starting blocks and try to accelerate to the finish.* Above: *Good hurdlers must be fast sprinters, but the reverse is not always true, for hurdling requires a kind of timing and coordination different from flat-out running.*

remarkably, on a slower, grass track. Snell then took the Olympic gold medal in both the 1500 meters and 800 meters in 1964, and broke his mile record in November of that year with a 3:54.1 clocking. The record dropped again in June 1965, when France's Michel Jazy ran 3:53.6, but Jim Ryun, the American who had achieved the incredible with a sub-four-minute mile in high school, shocked the world again with a 3:51.1 mile in 1967 in Bakersfield, California. John Walker of New Zealand reduced the record to 3:49.4 in 1975.

RELAY RACES

The relay race, long a favorite of physical education teachers across the country, is an American staple. But in competition the passing of the baton from racer to racer is more than the gimmick it is in gym classes to involve a lot of people in a race. It *is* the race. The more skillful the baton passing, the better the team's chances of winning. A team of slow runners with perfectly synchronized passing technique will often beat a faster team of sloppy passers, especially in a shorter, sprint relay.

Each relay team has four members, each of whom runs one leg of the race. Each runner carries the baton, a short cylinder that he must pass as he completes his leg to his teammate running the next leg. Runners are allowed a 22-yard or 20-meter exchange zone in which they must complete the exchange or be disqualified. The fastest runner on the team is usually the anchor man, and the second fastest is usually the leadoff man.

Relays range in length from 440 yards (110 yards a leg) through the 880 (220 yards a leg), the mile (440 yards a leg), the 2-mile (880 yards a leg), and the 4-mile relay (1 mile a leg). On the shorter relays especially, passing is so important that a "blind pass" is used. The runner receiving the baton listens for a signal from the incoming runner. When he hears it, he extends his hand backward and starts running. The incoming runner, if he has timed his signal right, will be ready to pass just as his teammate is hitting full stride. With an upward motion of the arm, the passer will slap the baton in his teammate's hand. In the longer relays (2 miles and more) the burden is on the outgoing runner to watch the incoming runner and time his start to ensure that the baton is passed properly. Because speed is not as crucial in the long relays, the outgoing runner usually will turn toward the passer, with his arm extended to make sure that the baton isn't dropped.

LONG-DISTANCE RACES

It was once thought that runners who trained too much would "burn themselves out." Emil Zatopek, the famous Czech runner, put such theories to rest with his twice-a-day workouts. "Running and more running" was his self-proclaimed secret of success, and in the 1952 Olympics he astonished the world by winning the 5,000 meters, the 10,000 meters,

In 1954, many people were convinced that a sub-four-minute mile was impossible. Then Roger Bannister, above, broke the barrier (psychological as well as physical), and in the decades afterward milers such as Jim Ryun, below, lowered the mark much further.

and the marathon. Today, a distance runner may run as much as one hundred miles a week. The ability to outlast pain, to keep going while the body is screaming to stop, is the hallmark of the long-distance runner.

THE MARATHON

The first marathon ended with the words, "Rejoice, we conquer," and a fatal collapse. Pheidippides, an Athenian, had just run from the Greek town of Marathon to Athens, some twenty-five miles, to inform the Athenians of the Greek victory over the Persians. More than 2,000 years later, a marathon race was included in the first modern Olympics.

In the Olympics at least, the marathon is as dramatic as it is unpredictable. The runners leave the stadium in a flock and then string out over the course in the countryside like a bedraggled army. Hours later, after other events have diverted the crowd, the lead runner can be sighted running to the stadium for the final leg of the race. By this time he has acquired an entourage of guards, race offi-

cials, television technicians, and assorted glory hounds, and when he enters the stadium, he provokes a roar of triumphal greeting that Caesar would have had difficulty matching. It is a glorious reception for a man who looks anything but glorious, his face drawn with exhaustion, his clothes hanging limply from his body. Usually the outcome of the race is no longer in doubt, so the leader circles the track toward the finish line with the stage to himself while television commentators extol his bravery and stamina and the crowd roars even louder. Finally he crosses the finish line, and a man who was very much alone for hours is engulfed by people.

Marathon runners are often almost superhuman athletes. Their normal pulse rates are sometimes as low as the mid-thirties, thanks to the tremendous strength of their hearts. Perhaps the greatest marathon runner was Abebe Bikila of Ethiopia. In the 1960 Olympic marathon over the cobblestones of Rome's Appian Way, Bikila won running barefoot. He decided to wear shoes when

Left: *In short relay races there is no time for a runner receiving a pass to look back at the baton as it is handed to him. He has to know where it will be, and the passer has to get it there. Neither man should break stride.* Above: *Marathon running can be a very lonely trial, but winners, such as Frank Shorter in the 1972 Olympics, attract the attention and the encouragement of bystanders.*

he set the Olympic record four years later in Tokyo. After finishing the grueling marathon, Bikila seemed no more tired than he had been when he had started. He proceeded to unlimber with a series of vigorous calisthenic exercises. There were few disbelievers when it was announced that Bikila had trained in his home country by chasing pheasants until they dropped from exhaustion.

THE STEEPLECHASE

The steeplechase is an extremely grueling race, more than 3,000 meters in length, in which the runner negotiates seven times a course with four hurdles and one water jump. The hurdles, each of which is three feet high and solid, are placed around the track at equidistant intervals, and another is set just to the inside of the track, 76 yards from the finish line. This hurdle is also three feet high, but it has a two-foot pool of water on the other side. Steeplechasers do not negotiate their hurdles the way 60-yard hurdlers do. Jumps have two distinct stages—one step to reach the top of the barrier, where the runner rests for an instant, and then the next step down to the ground. On the water jumps the runner jumps atop the hurdle and then down into the water. The steeplechaser always tries to land in the water with the same foot—one dry shoe is better than none. The combination of two miles of hard distance running and strength-draining jumps makes the steeplechase one of the most difficult events in track. The fans love it; the runners hate it. The bronze medal winner in the 1968 Olympics said bitterly, "That is the last steeplechase anyone will see me run."

CROSS COUNTRY

Cross-country races are generally run in the fall by high school and college teams in the United States. This unique event is run over natural terrain courses of a mile and a half for high school freshmen, two and a half to three miles for high school varsity, and five to seven miles for college runners. A cross-country race requires great endurance and stamina, not only because of the many hills that the runner must traverse but also because each race may have well more than a hundred participants, all pushing and jockeying for position. The basic rules for scoring are that each team enters seven runners and the finishing position of the first five are totaled for the team score. The team with the lowest score is the winner.

The two biggest cross-country races in the United States are the National Amateur Athletic Union and the annual National Collegiate Athletic Association championships.

WALKING EVENTS

In the United States the ungainly spectacle of walking races is usually met with indifference and sometimes with derision. Once fans jammed New York City's Gilmore Garden to see six-day walking races, but today the Europeans take walking races more seriously than Americans do. Nonetheless, ours is a nation increasingly concerned with its cardiovascular condition, for which walking is almost every doctor's tonic, so the dog days of walking may be past. Walking races are held at distances of from one mile to 75,000 meters. In the

Opposite: *A walking race may be the strangest-looking track event.* Right: *The latest style of high jumping is flopping over the bar.* Below: *Pole-vaulting heights have soared since the introduction of the fiberglass pole.*

Olympic Games, there currently is a 20,000-meter walk. The rules stipulate that the racer must be touching the ground at all times with one foot and that the leg be straightened for an instant while the foot touches the ground. It is often difficult for a judge to determine whether a contestant is complying with these rules.

FIELD EVENTS

HIGH JUMP

In 1834, one expert wrote that a "first-rate high leaper" should be able to clear five and a half feet. Today a first-rate jumper must manage seven feet just to qualify for major competition. A lot of changes, in style and in the opinions of the rules-makers, who grudgingly accepted the different styles of jumps, made way for this progress.

The basic object of the high jump is for the competitor to jump over a horizontal bar that is suspended between two upright poles. The jumper may touch the crossbar but may not knock it off the poles.

Today, most jumpers use the classic "belly roll" style, approaching from one side, springing from the inside foot (the one closer to the bar) with the body inclined slightly back, kicking the front leg over the bar, and rolling over. For a long time officials considered this sort of jump a "dive" and refused to accept records set with anything but the awkward scissors style. Today, however, the high jumper's style is limited only in that he must take off from one foot. In the 1968 Olympics the United States's Dick Fosbury set a new Olympic record with a style of jumping that came to be known as the "Fosbury flop." Fosbury would take off with his back to the bar, clear the bar looking straight up, and land on the back of his neck. Dangerous as it was, many jumpers soon copied the style when they saw Fosbury's results. Dwight Stones, the man who holds the world record of 7 feet 6½ inches, is the most successful practitioner of the flop.

Each jumper is allowed three jumps to clear each height. Any jumper may abstain from jumping or pass at any time. His final standing in the competition is based on the last height he cleared or, in case of ties, on fewer misses.

POLE VAULT

Probably the most complex and dangerous event in all of track and field is the pole vault. It demands speed, power, strength, and acrobatics. The vaulter speeds down a narrow runway, slams his pole into a small box located under the bar, and uses the pole to hoist himself over the bar.

The springier, fiberglass "sky poles" have revolutionized the sport with their great flexibility. Purists scoff that modern vaulters merely have to hang on for the ride because the spring of the pole now

does all the work, but this criticism is an oversimplification. The vaulter still must be technically perfect to complete a successful vault, and strength is still very much a factor. Not long ago, a 15-foot jump was considered spectacular. The world record now stands at more than 18 and a half feet, with no indication that pole vaulters are nearing their limits.

LONG JUMP

Starting about fifty yards from the takeoff board, the long jumper sprints down the path and hits the jumping board at top speed. His jumping foot slams hard on the board, and he springs upward and outward, feet well in front, body leaning forward from the hips. He lands in a pit filled with sawdust or sand. His distance is measured from the front edge of the takeoff board to the nearest impression made by any part of his body in the landing pit. Hitting the takeoff board in exactly the right place and at exactly the right time is crucial. If any part of the foot goes over the takeoff board, a foul is called. If the jumper doesn't hit the takeoff in full stride, the jump will surely be a poor one.

TRIPLE JUMP

Known as the hop, step, and jump until 1963, the triple jump is more popular in other parts of the world than in the United States. It is similar to the long jump in the approach, but different in the jump itself. The jumper plants one foot on the takeoff board and lands on the same foot he used to take off. He then takes one step, landing on the other foot, from which he executes a long-jump-style jump. The three maneuvers must be done in a continuous motion. Top-level competitors can cover 50 feet or better in a triple jump.

DISCUS THROW

Throwing the discus is unlike any other motion in sport. With his fingers hooked over the edge of the discus, the athlete whirls about to work up centrifugal force and hurls the plate into an area formed by two lines that radiate at a 90-degree angle from the thrower's circle. To the ancient Greeks, who invented the sport and prized it so much that they included it in the Olympic pentathlon, the beauty of form was almost as important as the distance of the throw. Today, any man or woman who can throw a discus more than two hundred feet need not worry about aesthetics.

The typical discus thrower is big and has long arms. For men the wooden and metal plate weighs 4 pounds 6½ ounces. The women's discus weighs 2 pounds 3¼ ounces. Competitors must throw from a circle with a diameter of 8 feet 2½ inches. A thrower who steps outside this circle on his turn commits a foul, nullifying the throw. One of the greatest discus throwers of all time was an American, Al Oerter, who won four straight Olympic gold medals between 1956 and 1968.

Top: *The long jumper soars through the air, intent on landing so that no part of his body touches down in the pit behind his feet.* Above: *Unleashing the discus, the discus thrower taps the power from a whirling approach.*

SHOT PUT

Bigger even than discus throwers are shot putters. The shot is a metal ball that weighs 16 pounds. In high school competition a 12-pound shot is used, and in women's competition the shot weighs 8 pounds 13 ounces.

The shot putter must throw from within a seven-foot circle, and as in the discus throw, distance is measured from the front of the circle to the spot at which the projectile first hits the ground. In one Olympics in which the United States and Russian shot putters were heavily favored to fight it out for the gold medal, the American shot putters completely unnerved the Russians by sneaking to the practice field early one morning and simply dropping the shot at distances well over the existing world record. When the Russians noticed the indentations at so great a distance, their throwers were demoralized and the Americans won.

For many years shot putters heaved the shot by simply standing at the front of the circle, rearing back, and throwing. But in the mid-fifties, Parry O'Brien introduced a style that revolutionized the event. Standing at the rear of the circle with his back to the throwing area, O'Brien would spring forcefully from his rear leg and hop backward until he approached the front of the circle. At the last moment he would twist his torso around and deliver the shot with all his weight behind it. This new style put a new emphasis on speed and quickness in the shot put and earned O'Brien two Olympic gold medals.

In the 1970s, Brian Oldfield pioneered a technique whereby he whirled like a discus thrower before releasing the shot.

JAVELIN THROW

The javelin is a wooden spear with a metal point, 8 feet 6 inches long, weighing 1¾ pounds. There is a hand grip at its balance point, slightly forward of the center of the shaft. The thrower takes a long run up to the foul, or scratch, line and hurls the javelin with an overhand, elbow-straining motion. If any part of the javelin strikes the ground before the point does, the throw is invalid. Javelin throwers undergo training schedules as severe as any field event competitor, and top throwers can heave the javelin more than 280 feet.

HAMMER THROW

The original hammers in this event were sledgehammers, but today's hammer isn't really a hammer at all. It consists of a steel ball connected to a loop by a heavy wire about four feet long. The entire hammer weighs 16 pounds, and the throwing circle is identical to that used for the shot put. The thrower grasps the handle grip with both hands, spins it over his head, and then spins his entire body in a whiplike fashion before hurling the hammer into an area formed by two lines radiating from the thrower's circle at a 90-degree angle. Top competitors throw about two hundred fifty feet. The event is confined to men.

Above: *The javelin thrower throws with his arms, but in his approach to the scratch line, his legs provide momentum that will help his throw.*
Left: *The strain is intense in shot putting.*

THE DECATHLON

The decathlon is probably the best test of all-around athletic ability, and therefore it is one of the most coveted prizes in the Olympics. The name of the event comes from the Greek word for "ten contests" because there are ten parts to this test of strength and swiftness. Traditionally, Olympic decathlon champions—men such as Jim Thorpe, Bob Mathias, Rafer Johnson, and Bill Toomey—have been men whose imitative ability and inborn talents allowed them to pick up the diverse skills of the decathlon quickly. In short they were natural athletes, but they had to perfect their skills over many grueling years of practice.

The decathlon is a two-day ordeal of five events per day: the 100-meter dash, long jump, shot put, high jump, and 400-meter race on the first day; the 100-meter hurdles, discus, pole vault, javelin, and 1500-meter race on the second. To score the events, a standard based on time, height, or distance, depending on the event, is set. A performer who equals this standard scores the full total of points allotted to that event. If he falls short of the standard, he loses a proportionate amount of points. If he does better than the standard, he receives bonus points. Naturally, no competitor is equally good in all ten events, so each athlete tries to hold his own in his weaker events and then pile up points in his specialties.

ORGANIZATIONS

Between 1830 and 1870, professional runners were common. Since then, track and field has been mostly amateur, governed in the United States by the Amateur Athletic Union and the National Collegiate Athletic Association, organizations whose feuding has often inhibited American track and field. The world governing body is the International Amateur Athletic Federation.

In 1973, a professional track circuit was organized, the International Track Association. The athletes who participate are ineligible for the Olympics because the pro tour allows runners to earn a living at their trade. Some of the top track stars who joined were milers Ben Jipcho, Jim Ryun, and Kipchoge Keino, pole vaulters Bob Seagren and Steve Smith, and quartermilers Lee Evans and Vince Matthews.

Opposite: *In the hammer throw the contestant flings a 16-pound contraption consisting of a heavy steel ball and connecting wire.* Above: *The decathlon is a two-day, ten-event track-and-field medley. Those who master it, such as Bill Toomey, are some of the world's most gifted and dedicated athletes.*

TRACK WITH MARKINGS FOR FIELD EVENTS IN THE INFIELD

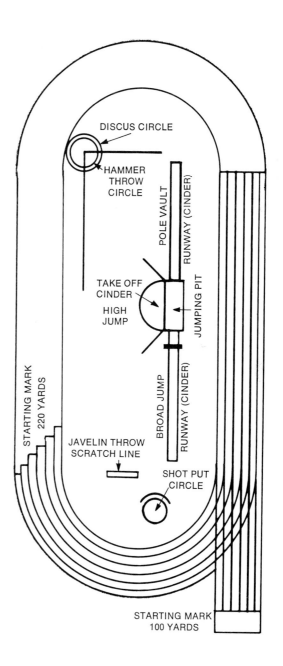

DISCUS CIRCLE

HAMMER THROW CIRCLE

POLE VAULT

RUNWAY (CINDER)

TAKE OFF CINDER

HIGH JUMP

JUMPING PIT

STARTING MARK 220 YARDS

BROAD JUMP

RUNWAY (CINDER)

JAVELIN THROW SCRATCH LINE

SHOT PUT CIRCLE

STARTING MARK 100 YARDS

Volleyball

Like basketball, volleyball was invented to provide moderate exercise, but it has now become a sport that, on the highest levels at least, is played in a frenetic, blood-and-guts manner that would have baffled its creator.

The man who invented the game (in 1895), William G. Morgan, was the director of the YMCA in Holyoke, Massachusetts. Seeking a relatively mild, noncontact sport that his classes of businessmen could play, Morgan devised a kind of handball with a high net. Any number could participate, and the teams were allowed an unlimited number of hits to volley the ball over the net.

The object of Morgan's game was to keep the rally going, to keep the ball in the air, but today the object is just the opposite—to smash the ball to the floor so that the opposition cannot return it. "Power volleyball," the game as it is played in top competition, is a sport of complex strategy and quick, well-conditioned athletes. Its ultimate weapon is the spike, a downward smash of the ball into the other court by a player who has leaped high and reached well above the net.

An Olympic sport since 1964, volleyball is played in more than one hundred countries today. Although an American invention, it has been dominated by teams from the Soviet Union, Japan, East Germany, Italy, and the Netherlands. Probably the most famous team was the Japanese women's team from the Dai Nippon mill. After working all day, the players endured relentless drills under their single-minded coach, Hirofumi Diamatsu. One of his favorite exercises for his charges was to send them diving after balls that were literally impossible to return. Sadistic as it may have seemed, such coaching apparently contributed to the Japanese team's easy victory in the 1964 Olympics.

COURT AND EQUIPMENT

A volleyball court is 60 feet long by 30 feet wide and is divided in half by a net that is suspended from poles at either sideline. For the men's game the 3-foot-high net is hung so that the top is 8 feet from the ground and for the women's game so that the top is 7 feet 4½ inches from the ground.

Morgan's first volleyball was the bladder of a basketball, but that was too light and slow. The basketball itself proved too large and heavy. Finally Morgan developed a ball much like today's, which is leather covered, weighs a maximum of 10 ounces, is about 26 to 29 inches around, and is inflated to a pressure of about seven pounds.

THE GAME

In many American schools—from elementary schools to colleges—volleyball is a major sport in physical education classes. One reason is its simplicity: the rules and the basic skills are quickly and easily learned.

The server, standing behind the right side of the service line, begins play by hitting the ball over the net. The receiving team may hit it no more than three times and must never allow it to bounce before returning it over the net. The two teams volley the ball back and forth across the net until one team fails to make a legal return: one that is hit, not "carried," with any part of the body above the waist over the net into the opposite court. Points are scored only on service. If the serving team wins the exchange of volleys, it scores one point. If the receiving team wins, no points are awarded but it serves for the next point. The winning team is the one that first scores fifteen points unless its margin is only one point when it reaches that total. Then play continues until one team gains a two-point advantage.

The referee sits or stands on a platform overlooking the net. His job is quite difficult because no one fully agrees on what constitutes a carry. The rules state that the ball may not be held but must be "cleanly hit"—obviously a definition open to a variety of interpretations.

Each side has six players, arranged on the court in two lines of three: the right, center, and left back; the right, center, and left forward. Whenever a team gains the service, its players rotate one position clockwise. The right forward becomes the right back (or server) and the left back becomes the left forward. Once the ball is served, however, all the players may leave these positions and move freely about the court.

TECHNIQUE AND STRATEGY

The ball may be served either underhand or overhand, but in highly competitive volleyball, almost all service is overhand. Most top players use the overhand "floater" serve, which, because it does not spin, drifts unpredictably to the receiver. To produce this effect, the server contacts the ball very briefly just below its center with his fist or the heel of his hand.

Servers try to direct their serves to weaknesses in the receiving team. Usually they serve deep, forcing the receiver to move backward to play the ball. In 1965, servers were forced to perfect their skills when their teammates were prohibited from waving their arms during the service in an attempt to screen the receiving team.

With the exception of a player blocking a smash, no one may contact the ball twice in succession. Most teams use all three hits to return the ball. The classic pattern is pass, set, and

In volleyball the action is at the net—one team trying to bash the ball down into the opposing court, the other team trying to block it. This time the offense wins.

smash. The pass is the reception of service, usually by a back-line player. Most passes in top competition are made underhand, the passer bending at the knees and contacting the ball with both forearms. The old overhand pass was discarded because officials often ruled that the ball rested on the receiver's fingertips, a carry. Overhand passes are still used in recreational volleyball, but today, most teams learn the forearm pass.

The passer directs the ball to the setter, who uses an overhand or forearm pass to position the ball so that a teammate can spike it. Most teams use the man in the middle of the front line as the setter, and he usually sets up one of the other forwards for the spike, but there are many formations and plays for spiking and for other volleyball maneuvers as well. Setting is the least spectacular part of volleyball, but it requires coordination and intelligence. The setter is the tactician.

The payoff in volleyball is the spike, a flashy play in which the spiker leaps high for the set and slams the ball down into the opposing court. A good spiker is tricky as well as strong, fooling the opposition by appearing to hit one way then suddenly changing direction. Sometimes he doesn't spike at all but instead lightly taps the ball over the net, and the receivers are sent scrambling to recover.

When a team from the Philippines introduced the spike to volleyball, it was almost indefensible. But defenses soon evolved, and today, blockers jump with the spiker and often "stuff" the ball back into his face. If a spike eludes the blocker, there is still a second line of defensive players to return it. Only ten years ago few defensive players dove to the floor after spikes; today most top players do.

Important rules changes in recent years have tried to maintain the balance between offense and defense. Two rules adopted in 1968 helped the defense to combat spiking. One permitted blockers to reach across the net to contact the ball after the spiker had. The second allowed a blocker to contact the ball twice in a row, eliminating the frustration of a blocker who, having blocked a spike, had to watch helplessly as the ball fell to the ground at his feet before a teammate could reach it. By 1969, the defense against the spike had become so effective that a rule was passed to allow only the three front-line players to block.

ORGANIZATIONS

Volleyball is strictly an amateur sport. The international governing body is the Federation Internationale de Volleyball. In the United States, the United States Volleyball Association, the Amateur Athletic Union, the National Collegiate Athletic Association, and the National Association of International Athletics all sanction tournaments. But the mainstream of volleyball is still the recreational game. On beaches and in parks across the country, volleyball is a popular sport for socializing. Played in a leisurely fashion, Morgan's game still flourishes in almost its original form.

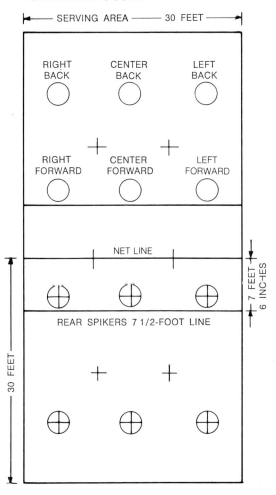

VOLLEYBALL COURT

Water Polo

Although the sport of water polo may suggest a frolicking afternoon of leisurely entertainment in a backyard swimming pool, it is in fact one of the most grueling and demanding of all competitive sports. Serious water polo players may well be the best conditioned athletes in all of sports, combining the stamina and endurance of the long-distance swimmer with the agility, coordination, and gamesmanship of the basketball guard.

HISTORY

Invented in London around 1870 to "liven up" swimming pool activity, and introduced to the United States about ten years later, water polo in its original form was even more brutal than the modern version. Kicking, choking, dunking, and strangling were just some of the features of the early games. They were played using a soft, semi-inflated, leather ball that made scoring difficult enough even under the mildest conditions. In one near-fatal game in 1910, four players were carried unconscious from the pool.

In the 1940s, a number of rules changes were finally instituted to produce the fast-paced yet safer game of today.

COURT AND EQUIPMENT

Although usually played in a pool, water polo may also be played in an open body of water. The minimum standard is 20 meters by 8 meters, but in the Olympics the pool size is 30 meters from goal face to goal face and 20 meters from side to side. The water should be at least 1.8 meters deep. Each team has seven players—six field players and a goalie. Players wear numbered caps, blue and white. At each end of the pool there is a goal, 3 meters wide and 1 meter high, that is backed with netting. Two meters in front of the goal line is an offside line (marked on the side of the pool) over which the attacking team may not cross ahead of the ball. Four meters in front of the goal line is a line that marks the end of the goalkeeper's area and an extreme penalty area. There is also a line that marks the center of the playing area.

The soggy leather ball of old times has been replaced by a 14- to 16-ounce, waterproof rubber ball.

THE GAME

A game lasts twenty minutes and is divided into four five-minute stop-time quarters. The teams exchange goals after each quarter. At the beginning of each quarter, the two teams line up along their goal line. The referee tosses the ball into the pool at the center line and both teams sprint for posses-

sion. Once in possession, players may move the ball only by passing to teammates, carrying the ball in one hand, or dribbling—rolling the ball between the arms while swimming. Only the goalie may touch the ball with both hands. A rules change that has been proposed would prohibit the goalie from throwing the ball farther than the center line after a save.

The object of the game is quite simple: to score goals, each worth one point. Offensive strategy resembles the "open man" patterns of basketball. The defense uses zone and man-to-man formations, another basketball concept. But unlike basketball, in water polo offensive drives succeed only about thirty percent of the time.

A free throw is awarded when the referee calls an ordinary foul against a team. Ordinary fouls include standing while handling the ball, taking the ball underwater, splashing, using both hands on the

Water polo seems innocent enough—a ball game in the water. In reality it's more like combat in the water. Although reforms have made it much less brutal than it used to be, water polo remains a very rough game.

ball, putting the ball out of play, and being over the offside line without the ball. Free throws are taken from the point at which the infraction occurred. Before 1948, players were required to remain stationary during free throws. Now players are allowed to improve their positions while the free throw is being taken.

Players may be ejected from the pool for penalty time in the case of more serious infractions, and in extreme cases the referee may decide to eject a player for the rest of the game. Despite the close supervision of the referees, however, water polo remains a tough, aggressive sport. There is much underwater maneuvering that the referee cannot see.

Water polo in its different variations has been an Olympic sport since 1896. Although it has been dominated almost since its inception by Hungary, Yugoslavia, and the Soviet Union, the United States has been steadily improving in international competition and took a bronze medal in the 1972 Olympics.

Goals are scored by firing the ball past the goalkeeper into the cage. More often than not the shots are too fast and from too close a range for the goalie to catch them, so he tries to block them with his arms and/or his body.

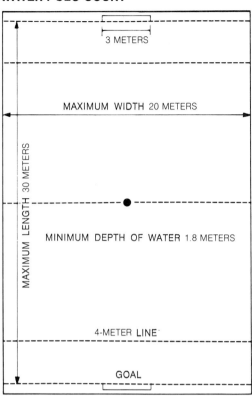

WATER POLO COURT

3 METERS

MAXIMUM WIDTH 20 METERS

MAXIMUM LENGTH 30 METERS

MINIMUM DEPTH OF WATER 1.8 METERS

4-METER LINE

GOAL

Water Skiing

The beauty of water skiing is its simplicity. After only a few trials the beginner is usually up and away. The boat does most of the work, pulling the happy skier along in its wake. Since the end of World War II and the boom in power boats, millions of Americans have taken up the sport. An estimated twelve million skiers in the United States (far more than in all the rest of the world) make water skiing one of this country's most popular recreational sports.

Some forms of water skiing—slalom and jumping—resemble those of snow skiing, but others—trick riding, tandem riding, and barefoot skiing—are unique to the water sport.

HISTORY

There are many arguments about who was the first to water ski. Various Frenchmen and Americans have claimed credit. Whoever he was, he began by aquaplaning—being towed along behind a boat on a rectangular or square plank about five or six feet long. The plank itself, not the rider, was attached by a line to the boat. It was this concept that Fred Waller, an American inventor, used for his "Dolphin Akwa Skees," patented in 1925. Waller soon devised more practical skis, much like the ones used today. The new skis fit on the skier's feet and the skier himself held the line to the boat.

The first American contests were held in 1936 in Massapequa, Long Island. Three years later the American Water Ski Association was formed. This association still oversees competition today. The World Water Ski Union, founded in 1949, sanctions world speed records and governs international competition, which American teenagers have almost completely dominated. The men's speed record is 125.69 miles per hour, set by Danny Churchill of Malibu, California, in 1971. The women's record of 105.14 miles per hour was set by Sally Younger of Hacienda, California, in 1970.

EQUIPMENT

Most skis are made of wood or fiberglass. They vary in length according to the skier's size and ability—from four to six feet—and are usually six to seven inches wide and one-half to three-quarters of an inch thick. The tips of the skis are curved upward slightly to keep the skis from spiking the water and toppling the skier. Most skis have stabilizing fins on the bottom. The skier's foot fits tightly into rubber cups, or bindings, mounted on the ski.

Slalom skis, used for one-foot skiing, are sturdier and longer than those used for regular skiing. Jump skis are quite sturdy, naturally, and rectangular. Trick skis are wider and much shorter than the others, and because trick skiers perform many free-wheeling movements, their skis have no fins.

TECHNIQUE

The skier starts in deep or shallow water, more or less squatting on the skis, ski tips up. He holds the tow bar between his legs, then signals to the boat pilot, who moves the boat slowly until the 75-foot line is taut and the skier is pulled to his feet. (Beginners often make the mistake of trying to pull themselves up.) More advanced skiers may begin from a sitting position on a low dock. Once they have reached their feet, beginners should try to keep their arms and back straight, their knees slightly bent, and their skis shoulder-width apart.

The tricks in trick water skiing include holding the tow rope with a toe. A trick skier has only 20 seconds to go through his routine as he whizzes past the judges.

215

COMPETITION

Water skiers compete in three basic types of events: slalom, jumping, and trick skiing.

SLALOM

The single slalom ski is more maneuverable and less tiring for the skier than two skis. Many skiers, whether competitive or not, never go back to two skis once they have graduated to the single ski.

Slalom competition is run on a course of six buoys, three on each side of the boat's path. As the boat goes down the center of the course, the skier swings around the buoys, cutting from side to side. In men's competition the boat's speed increases in successive runs until it reaches 36 miles per hour, the top speed. After that, the line is shortened by 12 feet and then in increments of 6 feet, making it much more difficult to negotiate the course until finally it becomes impossible. The winner is the skier who lasts longest without missing a buoy. The sharp, closely spaced turns in the slalom make it the most graceful form of water skiing.

JUMPING

The first water ski jump was made in 1928 by Dick Pope, founder of Florida's Cypress Gardens, where today the most colorful water ski shows are staged. His 25-foot jump was spectacular then but nothing compared to today's records (169 feet for men, 110 feet for women). The skier jumps off a slick, inclined wooden ramp 21 feet long and 5 feet high. Although the boat may go no faster than 35 miles per hour, skiers who swing wide of it and then cut hard toward the ramp gain a whiplike effect and can hit their takeoff at between 50 and 55 miles per hour. They travel up the ramp in a crouch, and at the top of the ramp, they spring into the jump. A good spring may increase the length of the jump significantly.

TRICK SKIING

Trick skiers are permitted two passes of 20 seconds each on a 200-yard course. In that brief time they must perform as many difficult maneuvers as possible. They are judged for form and the difficulty of their tricks.

Barefoot skiing is possibly the most difficult stunt in water skiing, one that calls for a lot of agility. The stunt was first performed by Dick Pope, Jr. in 1947 at his father's Cypress Gardens.

For the speed demons, there is slalom skiing, in which the object is to negotiate a slalom course at ever higher speeds. The side effects are spectacular.

Weightlifting

In Russia and Eastern Europe, where their numbers are great, weightlifters are national heroes. Some of the Russians are pinup idols in their country, and in Europe the world championships attract live crowds of more than ten thousand and countless more followers through radio, television, and newspapers. Weightlifting has never been a glamour sport in this country, but for American athletes as well as others, training with weights has become almost mandatory. There are few sports in which muscular strength is not important and few better ways to develop it than through weightlifting. Today, most male athletes train with weights, and there is a good chance that the women will follow, once they dispel the feat and myth that such training is unladylike.

HISTORY

The sport of competitive weightlifting is relatively new, though for centuries men have been practicing forms of it to test their strength against each other. Boulder-throwing contests, for example, were and still are popular in parts of Germany and Switzerland.

One of the first weight training programs was that of the famous Greek wrestling champion, Milo of Croton, six-time victor at the ancient Olympic games. According to legend, Milo used to carry a live calf on his shoulders wherever he went. As the calf grew larger and heavier, Milo grew stronger.

Circus and vaudeville strongmen gave birth to modern weightlifting in the early nineteenth century. In those days the strongmen used dumbbells, long shafts with two fixed weights attached to each end. Today's weightlifters use barbells, steel bars or rods to which a number of cast-iron discs can be attached. The discs range in weight from 1.1 pounds (½ kilo) to 55 pounds (25 kilos).

The first world championships were held in 1891 in London. When the Olympic Games were revived in 1896, there were two weightlifting events: a one-hand and a two-hand clean and jerk. The lifts at that time were 156½ pounds in the one-hand event and 244½ in the two-hand. Today, even the flyweights (who weigh between 114 and 123½ pounds) can do better. One-arm lifts are no longer

Weightlifting in the clean and jerk event is a two-part movement. First the lifter brings the barbell up to his shoulders, as he has here. Then, on a signal from the referee, he jerks it overhead.

done, but the flyweight record for the two-hand clean and jerk is 308½ pounds.

As a glance at the record book shows, weightlifters are constantly setting new records, but some authorities think there is a limit to the weight a man can lift. They cite the increasing number of wrist injuries in the sport as evidence that lifters are nearing the limit.

COMPETITION

Lifters compete in classes according to body weight (see chart). Ideally, weightlifters should be stocky. Most lifters hit their peak between 25 and 35 years of age.

The major weightlifting competitions in the United States are sponsored by the Amateur Athletic Union.

At one time Olympic competition consisted of five events, but in 1928 it was pared to three and after the 1972 games to two. The three traditional events were the press, the clean and jerk, and the snatch, but today only the last two remain. In each event each lifter is allowed three attempts to lift a given weight. If he succeeds, he progresses to heavier weights. His best lifts in each category are added, and the lifter with the highest total wins.

The clean and jerk is a two-part movement. The barbell is first brought from the ground to shoulder height while the lifter splits or bends his legs. On the way up the bar may only brush the thighs; it may not rest on them. At a signal from the referee that this part of the movement (the clean) has been satisfactorily completed, the lifter jerks the bar above his head, again splitting or squatting, and finishes with legs braced and arms extended. Demanding speed as well as strength, the clean and jerk is the method that allows the heaviest weights to be lifted. Vasily Alexov, the undisputed world champion, jerked 529 pounds in the 1972 Olympics.

The snatch is a showier style. It requires a violent, explosive lift. The lifter must bring the bar from the floor to an overhead position in one movement. Usually he squats or splits his legs in the process. To prepare himself for this sudden strain, the lifter sometimes paces around in deep concentration before abruptly running to the bar and snatching it. The Olympic record for the snatch is 402½ pounds, set by Serge Reding of Belgium in 1972.

HEAVIEST WEIGHT FOR EACH CLASS

114 pounds—flyweight
123 pounds—bantamweight
132 pounds—featherweight
148 pounds—lightweight
165 pounds—middleweight
181 pounds—light heavyweight
198 pounds—middle heavyweight
242 pounds—heavyweight
More than 242 pounds—super heavyweight

POWERLIFTING

In 1972, a new form of weightlifting was legitimized with the formation of the International Powerlifting Association. Powerlifting consists of three basic events: the bench press, in which the competitor lifts from a prone position; the squat or deep knee bend while lifting as much weight as possible; and the two-hand dead lift, in which the lifter raises the weight from the ground to hip level in one movement.

In the overhead position the weightlifter splits his legs to brace himself. It's astonishing how much a man can lift. Men weighing little more than 100 pounds have lifted more than 300.

Wrestling

An ancient and honorable sport is wrestling, one of the most basic sports known to man. For thousands of years men have grappled with each other in contest. Today, wrestling is a universal sport, practiced in various styles in almost every part of the world.

HISTORY

Practiced in some primitive form at least twenty thousand years ago, wrestling was greatly developed by the Egyptians. In tombs near the Nile, paintings some five thousand years old show wrestlers using a variety of holds. In Greece wrestling was an institution and it was an Olympic sport as early as 708 B.C. Almost everyone wrestled. Young Greeks trained for the sport in special buildings, *palestra.* The Romans modified the Greek style of wrestling, and today, this style of wrestling, known as Greco-Roman, is one of the most popular forms, especially in Europe.

There are some fifty to sixty different styles of wrestling. The most popular forms in the United States and Europe are freestyle (often called catch-as-catch-can), Greco-Roman, and professional. Americans have always preferred freestyle, and in the late nineteenth and early twentieth centuries,

they flocked to watch such wrestling matches. But the rise of a more spectacular sport, boxing, and a more melodramatic spectacle, professional, entertainment wrestling, put an end to the widespread popularity of traditional wrestling. Freestyle is practiced in schools and colleges throughout the country, and its popularity is again on the upswing, especially in the Midwest.

Sumo wrestling is the most popular form in Japan, where it has existed for about twenty-five hundred years.

COMPETITION

Wrestling matches take place on padded canvas or rubber mats. In intercollegiate competition the wrestling area is either a circle 28 feet in diameter or a square 24 feet on each side. There must be at least 5 feet of excess mat outside the boundaries, and there is a circle 10 feet in diameter in the center of the wrestling area. When supporting parts of both wrestlers cross the boundary, the referee

Greco-Roman wrestling, below, limits the combat zone to above the waist, whereas in freestyle wrestling the legs are a prime target. In both forms the wrestler tries first to take down, then to pin his opponent.

blows his whistle to stop the action, whereupon the wrestlers return to the center of the ring.

Much of the action in freestyle wrestling takes place with the wrestlers in a prone position. Wrestlers are allowed to use holds on any part of the opponent's body and may use their legs to trip and hold opponents. They may also use their hands to tackle an opponent around the legs. Greco-Roman wrestling prohibits leg holds and trips, thus placing a greater premium on upper body strength. Wrestlers may use their legs only to support themselves, and they may not attack an opponent below his waist. In both forms of wrestling, it is illegal to use any hold that chokes, causes injury, or causes excessive pain.

In freestyle, whether international or collegiate rules are used, a pin, or fall—scored when both shoulders of one's opponent are put to the mat— wins the match. The main difference between international and collegiate rules is that collegiate rules emphasize control wrestling. Once wrestlers are on the mat in high school and college matches, points are awarded for the amount of time each wrestler is in control of the other. For each wrestler there is a separate clock that records the amount of time he is in control. At the end of the match, the lesser total is subtracted from the greater and the wrestler with the time advantage is awarded one point per minute up to a maximum of two minutes and two points.

In addition one point is awarded for an escape (breaking from an opponent's hold) and two points for a reversal (escaping and gaining control). In both international and collegiate freestyle, stalling or obvious lack of aggressiveness is penalized.

Other methods of scoring include the takedown (simply getting an opponent off his feet), and the near falls (coming close to pinning an opponent). A takedown is worth two points. The near falls is worth two points if the opponent is held for less than five seconds, three points if more than five seconds.

In high school wrestling meets, matches consist of three two-minute periods. College matches consist of three periods, lasting two, three, and three minutes. At the beginning of the second and third periods and whenever either wrestler goes over the boundary, the wrestlers resume action from the center of the circle in a stance called the referee's position. One wrestler assumes the defensive position on his hands and knees. The other assumes the offensive position by kneeling beside his opponent, placing one hand on his opponent's elbow and placing one arm around his opponent's waist. Positions at the beginning of the first period and the second and third if the score is tied are decided by a coin toss. If one competitor has more points when the second period begins, he chooses positions. The competitor with the least points chooses positions when the third period begins. When the wrestlers go out of bounds and the action is stopped, the one who was in control is awarded the offensive position.

In international competition matches consist of three 3-minute periods. Points are awarded for a takedown and for a near falls, but there is no time advantage awarded for being in control of an opponent. If the wrestlers are in prone positions and the referee feels that no progress is being made, he may stop the action and return the wrestlers to a standing position in the center circle.

Sumo wrestling bears only some resemblance to freestyle. It is highly stylized, ritualistic, and closely connected to the Shinto religion. Sumo wrestlers usually weigh well over three hundred pounds and they wrestle wearing only a ceremonial sash and loin cloth. They are greatly respected and hold a high place in Japanese society.

Matches take place in a circle 15 feet in diameter. The basic object is to try either to get the opponent out of the circle or to throw him to the ground within the circle.

HEAVIEST WEIGHT FOR EACH CLASS

High School

91 pounds
98 pounds
105 pounds
112 pounds
119 pounds
126 pounds
132 pounds
138 pounds
145 pounds
155 pounds
167 pounds
175 pounds
215 pounds
unlimited weight

College

118 pounds
126 pounds
134 pounds
142 pounds
150 pounds
158 pounds
167 pounds
177 pounds
190 pounds
More than 190 pounds—heavyweight

International and AAU

105.5 pounds
114.5 pounds
125.5 pounds
136.5 pounds
149.5 pounds
163 pounds
180.5 pounds
198 pounds
220 pounds
More than 220 pounds—heavyweight

Yachting

A man interested in sailing once asked J. P. Morgan how much it would cost to own a yacht. Morgan, one of America's richest men, told him, "If you have to ask, you can't afford it."

Yachting has certainly changed in the years since Morgan's prominence in the late 1800s. Then yachts were owned only by the very wealthy, who treated their yachts like oversized toys, hiring professional crews and watching them race. Most often, the owners' only concession to the racing spirit was to bet on the outcome—from ashore.

HISTORY

Yachting came to the United States from England, where King Charles II introduced it. Charles learned it during his European exile. When he was restored to the throne in 1660, he brought with him a sailing craft, a gift from the citizens of Holland. The term *yachting* is derived from a Dutch word, *jaghtschip,* meaning "pursuit ship," though yachting can also be used to describe other types of boating.

The sport of yacht racing caught on in England, and by 1720, the first yacht club, the Cork Harbor Water Club, had been founded.

Sailing captures two exhilarating elements in nature—the wind and the sea. Sometimes a sailor enjoys them almost independently of his sailing.

The oldest existing yacht club in the United States is the New York Yacht Club, founded in 1841. Ten years later America stepped into the forefront of the yachting world when John Cox Stevens sailed his yacht, *America,* to victory over several British boats in a race around the Isle of Wight. A cup was donated to the New York Yacht Club to acknowledge his victory, and thus the America's Cup was born. A competition for the Cup is held whenever another country challenges for it, but in the 22 challenge competitions since Stevens's victory, the United States has never relinquished the cup. In September 1974, the Cup was again successfully defended against the winner of a French and Australian elimination competition.

"The Mariner," one of the entries to defend the America's Cup in 1974, cost her backers $1.2 million before she was eliminated. Although America's Cup racing is still the province of the wealthy, boat racing is also done on a more inexpensive level today and in all types of crafts, from small catboats to large schooners. Yachting is an Olympic sport, and it has become popular in North America, South America, Europe, Australia, and New Zealand.

BOATS AND COMPETITION

There are six basic types of sailboats: catboats, sloops, cutters, yawls, ketches, and schooners. A boat's type is determined by its size, its number of masts, and its sail arrangement. Catboats have one mast, located near the front, or bow, and one sail. Sloops and cutters have one mast, usually located about one-third of the boat's length from the bow, and they have between two and five sails. Yawls and ketches have two masts, the taller of which is for-

ward, near the bow. The shorter is near the stern or back. They have between three and eight sails. Schooners have two or more masts, the tallest of which is near the stern, and they have three or more sails.

For racing purposes boats are further divided into hundreds of different classes, such as Atlantic, Star, Snipe, Lightning, Tempest, and Penguin, to name just a few.

For the most part these many classes of boats compete in what is called "one-design" competition. That is, all competing boats must conform to exact design specifications. The America's Cup race is a one-design competition between 12-meter sloops (about 35 feet long), but different variations in hull design are permitted.

There is also handicap competition (used primarily in offshore racing), in which boats of different sizes and designs race against one another using a time handicap formula. All boats start the race together, but at the end of the race, each boat's handicap is subtracted from its total race time. The boat with the lowest total time wins, regardless of order of finish. The handicap system is used in most long-distance ocean races. Some of the more famous are the Newport (Rhode Island) to Bermuda Race, the Trans-Pacific Race, and the Chicago Yacht Club to Mackinac Island Race. Some of these races last for weeks and just finishing is an accomplishment.

The rules for most racing competition are set and governed by the International Yacht Racing Union. The governing body for North America is the North American Yacht Racing Union, a member of the international body.

ACKNOWLEDGMENTS

The editors wish to thank the following persons, who served as consultants and fact-checkers on one or more chapters in *The Sports Encyclopedia:*

Caylor Adkins, World Union of Karatedo Organizations; Bill Amick, American Motorcycle Association; Nancy Archie; J. W. Bailey, International Cricket Conference; Irwin Bernstein; Nouveau Black, Field Hockey Association of America; Barbara R. Boucher, *Skating;* Clayton Chapman, Eastern College Athletic Conference; Frank Kumisky, U.S. Gymnastics Federation; Don Davidson, U.S. Auto Club; Maroun Doher, Amateur Athletic Union; John Fell; Stan Gallup, Golden Gloves; Dale T. Gaskill, National Rifle Association; Robert Grossberg, U.S. Amateur Jai Alai Player Association; Harry Hainsworth, Amateur Athletic Union; Jim Keane; Bill Lambart, Jr., U.S. Cycling Federation, Inc.; Ruthe Larson, U.S. Polo Association; William Lauder, New York Racing Association; Susan Lurie; Patsy Martin, *SKATE;* John McGinley; Ursula Melendi, U.S. Soccer Federation; Dick Padgett; Stan Platkin, Biscayne Kennel Club, Inc.; John T. Sammis; Stan Saplin; Sol Schiff, U.S. Table Tennis Association; Burt Shaw Amateur Athletic Union; C. D. Strang, American Power Boat Association; Michael Truffer, U.S. Parachute Association; George Wilson; Randy Witte, Association of Professional Rodeo Cowboys.

Photo Credits: Allen's Studio 96; Atlanta Braves 31 top left; Ely Attar 81, 83 top, 112 all, 113 all, 143, 204, 205 left, 218; John E. Biever 90 top; Vernon J. Biever 86, 92, 93 all, 94 all, 96–97, 98, 99 bottom, 100, 101; Buffalo Bills 95; Pat Capone 126; Chicago Black Hawks 127; Melchior DiGiacomo 2–3, 4–5, 6–7, 11, 19, 43 right, 48 top, 61, 117, 131, 133 all, 136 all, 137, 141, 142, 190, 207 right; Malcolm W. Emmons 42, 44 all, 90 bottom left; Richard E. Farkas/ Pegasus Photographics 147 all; Marion Geisinger 20, 191 all; Steve Goldstein/Spectra-Action 30 right, 32; William H. Gordon 36; Fred Kaplan 192 bottom left, 193 bottom, 194 middle and right, 196, 197 left; Jack Mecca 16 all, 46 bottom right, 132, 192 bottom right; Peter S. Mecca 1, 38, 40, 46 left, 47 all, 123, 124, 129, 135, 145, 150, 176, 177, 192 top right, 193 top, 194 left, 195, 197 middle and right; Richard Pilling 45, 128, 170; Ken Regan 43 left, 46 top right, 78–79; Joseph Reichler 22, 29; Les Rosner 125 bottom; Manny Rubio 97; David Russell 48 bottom; Rutledge Books 28 top, 35, 198 all; John Sammis 192 top left; Schweizer Aircraft Corporation 169; United Press International 9, 10, 12–13 all, 13 all, 14, 15, 17, 21, 23 bottom, 24, 25 all, 26 all, 27, 28 bottom, 30 left, 31 top right and bottom, 38–39, 39, 41 all, 50 all, 52, 53, 54, 55, 56, 57, 59, 62, 63, 64 all, 65 all, 66, 67 all, 68 all, 69 all, 70, 73, 76, 77, 83 bottom, 84, 84–85, 88 all, 89 all, 90 bottom right, 99 top, 102, 103, 104, 105 all, 106 all, 107, 108 all, 109 all, 111, 114, 118 bottom, 119, 120, 122, 125 top and middle, 134, 139, 140, 144, 148, 149, 151 all, 152, 155, 159 all, 160, 161, 162, 163, 164, 165, 166, 168 all, 171, 172, 173, 174, 175, 179, 180, 182 all, 183, 185, 187, 188, 189 all, 200, 201, 202 all, 203 all, 205 right, 206 all, 207 left, 208, 209, 211, 213, 214, 215, 216, 217, 219, 221, 222, 223; United States Handball Association 115; Wide World Photos 23 top, 118 top.